THE GOLDEN AGE OF CONDUCTORS

JOHN W. KNIGHT

Published by
Meredith Music Publications
a division of G.W. Music, Inc.
4899 Lerch Creek Ct., Galesville, MD 20765
http://www.meredithmusic.com

MEREDITH MUSIC PUBLICATIONS and its stylized double M logo are trademarks of
MEREDITH MUSIC PUBLICATIONS, a division of G.W. Music, Inc.

Copyright © 2010 MEREDITH MUSIC PUBLICATIONS
International Copyright Secured • All Rights Reserved
First Edition
December 2010

International Standard Book Number: 978 1–57463-118-0
Cataloging-in-Publication data is on file with the Library of Congress.
Library of Congress Control Number: 2010929884
Printed and bound in U.S.A.

Dedication

To the immortal memory of Arturo Toscanini—whose never-ending

quest for musical truth exemplified through his masterful interpretations

reflect the highest standards of uncompromising musicianship.

His legacy can inspire us all to become better conductors.

Arturo Toscanini has been of the paramount importance in my own

musical journey. Through him my love and dreams for music soared.

"Go my thoughts on Golden Wings."

Contents

Preface

In Search of Maestros

My interest in conductors started as a teenager when the world seemed full of music, wonder, and mystery. The magical interpretations of Arturo Toscanini were my first encounter with greatness. There was such excitement and intensity in his RCA recordings that I was in awe. As I began to know Toscanini through many biographies, I found myself imitating his volatile temperament and mannerisms. I would practice his famous scowl in front of a mirror as I stood on a chair for a podium. I used sticks for batons and conducted to a recording of Beethoven's Ninth Symphony. Occasionally I shouted in a hoarse Italian voice to my imaginary orchestra, "*Bah, stupido, ignorante, con spirito, andiamo.*"

Later when I stopped trying to imitate Toscanini's personality and really listened to his superb interpretations I learned the essential qualities that make a conductor great. From Toscanini I learned that music can be truthful, moving, and intensely alive. After a lifetime of listening to his recordings I still find the music eloquent, sincere, and filled with passion.

For me, the greatest baton technician was Fritz Reiner. His baton artistry reminds me of a quote by Japanese mime Masumi Kuni: "Creativity without discipline is ugly. Discipline without creativity is brutal, but disciplined creativity is beautiful." The recording of Reiner conducting Bartók's Concerto for Orchestra makes it apparent why Reiner is known as a conductors' conductor. This remarkable and fantastic performance captures Reiner at the height of his power and displays the wonderful virtuosity of the Chicago Symphony Orchestra. Reiner taught me that there is no need to use superfluous gestures to call attention to the conductor, only those that are essential to the music.

Sometimes the art of conducting seems like a great mystery, especially with the unconventional and mystical personality of Wilhelm Furtwängler. It was hard at first to appreciate the flexible musicality of Furtwängler because I was brought up on the Toscanini-Reiner approach of strict adherence to the score. Furtwängler had a deeply personal approach to music, one characterized by elastic tempos and intense romanticism. The visionary Furtwängler taught me that exploring a musical score can be an aesthetic experience if it remains true to the composer's message.

Bruno Walter was never in doubt about the function of a conductor. For him truth in music comes from God. The purpose of a conductor is simply to reveal the spirituality within the music. When St. Augustine said, "Beauty is the glory of truth," his words seem to have become Walter's credo. The extent to which a conductor understands this spirituality will determine the depth of his interpretation. Walter believed that a great performance can be a spiritual transformation only if the conductor understands and communicates the spirit of great music.

Walter's legendary interpretation of Mahler's *Das Lied von der Erde* with Kathleen Ferrier is eloquent, noble, and spiritual. Ferrier had cancer at the time of this Vienna Philharmonic recording, which was her deeply emotional farewell to the world and its beauty.

Other essential qualities in great conductors are honesty and humility. I found these qualities in Kurt Masur during an interview one summer before a New York Philharmonic concert in Chicago. I first became acquainted with Masur's conducting in a videotape of an all-Wagner concert with the Gewandhaus Orchestra in Leipzig. During the interview he spoke passionately about conductors, composers, and the value of music. When I asked which accomplishments he was most proud of, he paused for a moment, then answered that his piano teacher had firmly declared that talent is a gift we are born with, not something to be proud of.

Over time I have come to realize the qualities of a great conductor are the musical integrity of Toscanini, the disciplined creativity of Reiner, the vision of Furtwängler, the spirituality of Walter, and the honesty and humility of Masur. Very few conductors possess all these qualities, and perhaps this is why the world has many conductors but only a few Maestros.

Acknowledgements

Most importantly, I wish to thank the following outstanding musicians who took their valuable time from rehearsals and classes to grant me interviews regarding the art of conducting: Pierre Boulez, Christoph von Dohnányi, Kurt Masur, Herbert Blomstedt, Richard Hickox, Michael Debost, and James DeSano.

I am deeply appreciative to James T. Rohner, Publisher, *The Instrumentalist Magazine*, for 25 years of professionalism and friendship. James T. Rohner generously allowed the reproduction of articles previously published and the use of extraordinary photos from The Instrumentalist Archives for the book.

I am grateful to Dr. Garwood Whaley, president and founder of Meredith Music Publications, who accepted this work for publication, and who went through the manuscript word by word offering many valuable suggestions.

Lastly, I acknowledge my conducting students at the Oberlin Conservatory who have made it possible for me to teach the subject I love.

CHAPTER 1

The History of Conducting

P rior to 1800 orchestras relied on a musician at the harpsichord, usually the composer, for the beat, while other groups employed someone to strike the floor with a stick or stamp his foot to set the tempo. As music became more complex it became increasingly difficult for ensembles to play without direction or for the composer to conduct from the keyboard. Thus, a figure eventually stepped to the front of the orchestra and waved a rolled-up paper or violin bow to keep the tempo, and on April 10, 1820 Ludwig Spohr initiated an historic change by using a baton with the London Philharmonic. Spohr later recreated the event, which is documented in *The Romantic Period of Music*.

> I then took my position with the score at a separate music desk in front of the orchestra, drew from my pocket my directing baton, and gave the signal to begin. Quite alarmed at such a novel procedure, some of the directors [other conductors of the day] would have protested against it; but when I pleaded with them to grant me at least one trial, they became pacified…. Surprised and inspired by the result, the orchestra immediately after the first movement of the symphony expressed aloud its unanimous assent to the new mode of conducting. The triumph of the baton as a time giver was decisive. (Klaus 263)

Despite Spohr's breakthrough, performers still shared conducting duties, and occasionally confusion resulted when three or more musicians directed at the same time. The unfortunate players had to choose between the gestures of the pianist at the keyboard, the bow waving of the first violinist, and even the composer giving signals.

From his first experience with the baton, Mendelssohn realized the importance of a single conductor. Nonetheless, divided authority persisted and at a London performance in 1847 as Mendelssohn conducted his *Elijah*, the concertmaster frequently beat time with his bow and blocked Mendelssohn's view of the orchestra.

Through Mendelssohn's tenacious efforts, he made the public aware of new conducting methods and approaches; today we recognize him as one of conducting's first practitioners and the originator of the classical style that continues to the present. While Mendelssohn based his style on precision clarified through the baton, Franz Liszt brought a creative impulse and subjective interpretation to conducting. In the mid-19th century conductors no longer looked upon themselves as mere timekeepers, but saw themselves as interpreters.

Mendelssohn believed that conductors should provide an objective interpretation of the score and emphasize rhythmic control. Liszt had no interest in a

---

© *The Instrumentalist*, March 1991. Reprinted with Permission.

literal or strict interpretation and promoted freedom of beat patterns, flexibility
of rhythm, and exaggeration of nuance for dramatic effect.

Based on the observations made by contemporaries of the two men, we can
now detect the formation of two schools of conducting. In 1820 Eduard Devrient,
the German baritone, outlined his opinion of the duties of a conductor as
follows:

> The continued beating throughout a movement, which must necessarily
> become mechanical, vexed me and does so still. It always appeared to me
> that the conductor ought to beat time only when the difficulty of certain pas-
> sages, or unsteadiness of the performers, rendered it necessary. Surely the
> aim of every conductor should be to influence without obtruding himself.
> (Schonberg 89)

Mendelssohn, a friend of Devrient, met those qualifications, and Devrient
obviously was pleased. "Many whole sections were often beaten through, but
Felix, as soon as large sections were running smoothly, dropped his baton and
listened with seraphic transport, occasionally beckoning with eye or hand."
(Schonberg 118)

Such serenity was absent from Liszt's conducting, as Ferdinand Hiller
described a Liszt performance in 1853. "He does nothing but keep changing the
baton from one hand to the other—sometimes, indeed, laying it down altogether
—giving signals in the air with this or that hand, or on occasion with both, having previously told the orchestra not to keep too strictly to the beat." (Schonberg
162)

Liszt did not maintain strict tempos and said that mere time beating was
enough to beat down the life-nerve of a beautiful symphonic performance. He
played the piano in phrases, and he conducted the same way, because he felt
regular accents with a heavy beat at each bar line were obtrusive to the music.
Liszt emphasized thematic elements of each piece and discarded standard beat
patterns, outlining instead the rise and fall of the musical line. Liszt felt standard
baton techniques produced a mechanical orchestral sound that emphasized
rhythm instead of the complete musical line. George Smart, an English conductor who introduced the works of Beethoven and Schumann to London audiences, commented that the expressive beat of Liszt caused "plenty of twisting of
the person." (Schonberg 161)

Such movement contrasted with Mendelssohn's style, which was refined and
never theatrical. His austerity on the podium reflected his classical training.
Schumann noted his approval of Mendelssohn's style:

> It was a joy to watch, and note how with his eye he anticipated and com-
> municated every meaningful turn and nuance, from the most delicate to the
> most robust, an inspired leader plunging ahead, in contrast to those conduc-
> tors who threaten with their scepters to thrash the score, the orchestra, and
> even the audience. (Schonberg 120)

Violin virtuoso Joseph Joachim described Mendelssohn as conducting "almost without motion, but [using] extremely lively gestures through which it was possible to transmit the spirit of his personality to chorus and orchestra, to correct little errors with a flick of his finger." (Kupferberg 138)

Mendelssohn relied on precise baton technique, which gave him the appearance of calmness and clarity. His refinement extended to his baton, a whalebone stick covered with white leather to match his white gloves. Mendelssohn was the first conductor to fully use a baton to emphasize rhythm and control.

Liszt's podium style reflected his temperament; he used the baton for effect with care, suppleness, and knowledge of coloring, rhythm, and expression. Unfortunately his actions on the podium were often misunderstood. Joseph Joachim observed:

> At the conductor's desk Liszt makes a parade of moods of despair and the stirrings of contrition…and mingles them with the most sickly sentimentality and such a martyr-like air that one can hear the lies in every note and see them in every movement…I have suddenly realized that he is a cunning contriver of effects who had miscalculated. (Schonberg 161)

Liszt's advanced techniques were not appreciated by those who favored the classical conducting style. He believed that the conductor should be the servant of the public, while Mendelssohn maintained that conductors should be the servants of the score, using technique that was free of subjective emotions. Such strictness of performance stemmed from rigorous rehearsals with the conductor firmly in control. In 1841 Mendelssohn described his experience as guest conductor of the Berlin orchestra, which was noted for being unruly when its regular leader was away.

> At the first rehearsal the orchestra was disposed to behave badly. Disorder and arrogance prevailed, and I could not believe my eyes and ears. At the second rehearsal, however, I turned the tables. It was my turn to be rude. I punished half a dozen of them, and now they regard me as another Spontini. Since then there has been no sulking. As soon as they see me, they are attentive and they do their best. Instead of being haughty they are now obsequious; they bow and scrape. (Schonberg 161)

With his own orchestra at the Gewandhaus in Leipzig, Mendelssohn raised the performance level by playing only the finest music and approaching each score with classic integrity. Composer Julius Benedict recounted an occasion when Mendelssohn requested this respect for the score.

> Once, while conducting a rehearsal of Beethoven's Eighth Symphony, the admirable allegretto in B♭ not going at first to his liking, he remarked smilingly that he knew everyone of the gentlemen engaged was capable of performing, and even composing, a scherzo of his own but that just now he wanted to hear Beethoven's, which he thought had some merits. (Kupferberg 138)

This literal recreation of the composer's intent included a fastidious interpretation of every musical notation. No longer were players allowed a mediocre reading of their parts; and the conductor demanded meticulous attention to tempo, balance, and nuances of expression. Through such rehearsals the Gewandhaus became an orchestra unequaled in Germany.

Liszt also had rigorous rehearsals, but they followed a different pattern. He used preliminary sectional rehearsals to work on tone color, rhythm, and expression. Liszt gives an interesting picture of his ideas on rehearsal techniques in his directions of the score of his *Symphonic Poems*.

> At the moment I would like to remark that the usual mechanical, cut and dried performance customary in many cities be avoided and in its place the new period style which stresses proper accentuation, the rounding off of melodic and rhythmical nuances be substituted. The life-nerve of a symphonic production rests in the conductor's spiritual and intellectual conception of the composition, it being assumed of course, that the orchestra possesses the necessary power to realize this conception. Should the latter condition be absent, I recommend that my works be left unperformed. (Stoessel 5)

Liszt believed that the concept of a musical work was more important than what was printed on paper and that the composer cannot "put down in black and white everything that gives a performance character and beauty." (Schonberg 160) His interpretation and intuition resulted in a performance of Wagner's *Tannhauser* that was a union of two minds. Wagner described the experience:

> Though mainly concerned with the musical rather than the dramatic side, [the performance] filled me for the first time with the flattering warmth of emotion roused by the consciousness of being understood by another mind in full sympathy with my own. I saw Liszt conduct a rehearsal of *Tannhauser* and was astonished at finding my second self in his achievement. What I had felt in composing music, he felt in performing it; what I wanted to express in writing it down, he produced in making it sound. (Sitwell 214)

Mendelssohn and Liszt initiated two divergent approaches to interpretation, the elegant and the passionate. Mendelssohn was like a mirror, reflecting the composer's image; Liszt, a prism, producing a personal synthesis of the musical parts. The art of conducting had developed into the classical and romantic schools, respectively.

Nowhere were the ideas of these two men more opposed than in their concepts of tempo, with Mendelssohn emphasizing strict rhythms and metronomic exactness, and the antithetical Liszt stressing subtle nuance, flexible rubato, and the expressive qualities of romanticism.

Liszt could not be chained to the formality of classicism in conducting. Long before he ever picked up a baton, his virtuosity at the keyboard instilled abandonment in him. At the piano he had played in phrases, ignoring the bar line, modifying tempos to the benefit of expression and drama. Once applied to the art, these characteristics became the pioneering step that turned conducting away from classicism and into romantic expression. Always seeking an expressive interpretation, Liszt could not hold to a basic tempo and was critical of the shortcomings he saw in the printed work:

> Although I have tried through exact markings of the dynamics, the accelerations and slowing up of the tempo, to clearly indicate my wishes, I must confess that much, even that which is of the greatest importance, cannot be expressed on paper. Only a complete artistic equipment on the part of the conductor and players, as well as a sympathetic and spiritually enlivened performance can bring my works to their proper effort. (Stoessel 5)

According to Schonberg, Liszt used a concept that was more than simple rubato. It was a rise and fall, slowing and speeding, variation of tempo, with the use of ritards to link contrasting passages. (Schonberg 160) Liszt tried to define the indefinable and to draw universal rules from what basically were his own intuitions.

Wagner, who built on the ideas of Liszt and became a giant in the history of conducting, recognized the importance of tempo. He believed the proper tempo depended upon a correct understanding of the *melos*: "It is unnecessary to give the exact tempo since a gifted conductor will find the right one and the untalented will never grasp it regardless of what the score says." (Schonberg 136)

True tempo to Liszt varied according to the rise and fall of the expressive content, but Mendelssohn was completely against rubato tempo because it was sentimental and distracting. Mendelssohn preferred to emphasize rhythm and control, and demanded a sense of rhythm from his players. With such clarity and precision, he naturally enjoyed fast tempos.

After watching Mendelssohn direct a rehearsal of Beethoven's Eighth Symphony, Wagner made this comment about tempo:

> As to conducting, he personally informed me once or twice that too slow a tempo was the devil, and he would rather choose to take things too fast, that a really good performance was a rarity at any time, but that it was possible to delude the audience so that a bad one would not be too much noticed, and that this was best done by not lingering too long on the piece, but passing rapidly over it. (Schonberg 122)

However, it is not possible to make a true estimation of Mendelssohn's tempo from the previous statement, because Wagner's voice "is the only major dissenting viewpoint about Mendelssohn's ability as a conductor, and that alone makes it suspect." (Schonberg 124)

The creative forces of Mendelssohn and Liszt ignited a revolution in the art of conducting, and through their efforts the status of conductors rose from that of crude time beaters to polished interpreters. The conflicting styles are the foundations of conducting techniques today, and the classical and romantic characteristics are the elements from which conductors now choose. Some modern conductors faithfully represent the composer's intention, while others reflect themselves in the works they conduct. Mendelssohn dominated the period of conducting from 1830 to 1850, but as the passion and freedom of Liszt's performances came to public attention, the younger generation abandoned convention.

Liszt succeeded in freeing the spirit of the composition from the limitations of bar line rhythm by a new style of conducting gestures. He used both hands for cues, conducting in phrases instead of in strict beats, showing new shadings of expression. By giving the art these techniques, musicians recognize Liszt as the founder of modern conducting, but the spirit of Mendelssohn's classical style was never completely extinguished. The most recent philosophy in conducting does not follow any one school of thought; contemporary conductors balance classical and romantic attitudes. This eclecticism, though, is only the temporary top of the pyramid that continues to rest on the foundation started by Mendelssohn and Liszt over a century ago. ≈

CHAPTER 2

The Conductors Who Developed Six Fine American Orchestras

The art of conducting in America evolved in tandem with the development of major American orchestras. European conductors have dominated the American scene throughout the 20th century and shaped much of our cultural heritage.

New York Philharmonic

The oldest symphony orchestra in the United States is the New York Philharmonic, founded in 1842 by Ureli Corelli Hill (1802–1875), whose middle name reflected his father's hope that the son would become a violinist like the virtuoso Arcangelo Corelli. Hill played violin in theater orchestras in New York as a boy. He studied in Germany from 1835 to 1837 with Ludwig Spohr, who is remembered today as the first conductor to use a baton when he directed the Royal Philharmonic in London in 1820.

After returning to New York in 1842, Hill became founder, conductor, and first president of the New York Philharmonic. With an ensemble of 53 members, the New York Philharmonic performed Beethoven's Fifth Symphony at its first concert in 1842.

The eccentric Hill had dreams of obtaining instant wealth and joined the 1849 Gold Rush without success. Eventually he returned to the Philharmonic, not as conductor, but as a member of the violin section. His musical career came full circle when he returned to playing in the theater orchestras.

Hill's many efforts at business ventures all failed, leading to exhaustion, depression, and eventually suicide. Hill never realized that his legacy was having established one of America's great orchestras.

After Hill, four German-born conductors shared the New York Philharmonic during the next 27 years: Henry Christian Timm (1811–1892), Theodor Eisfeld (1816–1882) William Scharfenberg (1819–1895) and Carl Bergmann (1821–1876). A cellist by training, Bergmann came to America in 1850, and made an impressive conducting debut with the New York Philharmonic on April 21, 1855. He was associated with that orchestra until his death in 1876, and struggled to introduce the music of Berlioz, Liszt, and Wagner to a largely uneducated and apathetic American audience. His efforts to thrust great music upon a uniformed audience eventually cost him his job in 1876.

Theodore Thomas (1835–1905) took over from Bergmann and was the first conductor to make enormous progress in raising the standards of orchestral playing and repertoire. He was the first conductor to introduce unified orchestral

---

© *The Instrumentalist*, January 2000. Reprinted with Permission.

bowings and to employ musicians year-round. According to Harold Schonberg, "he had daring, imagination, and above all, determination: a will that could not be bent, much less broken. It was he who brought the sound of symphonic music for the first time to a large part of the United States." (Schonberg 197) Touring the United States, Thomas gave the American public music at a high level of performance. As a conductor of the New York Philharmonic between 1877–1891, he became known for memorable interpretations of Wagner, Liszt and Brahms, and introduced America to the music of Tchaikovsky, Dvořák, and Richard Strauss.

After Thomas, Hungarian Anton Seidl (1850–1898) conducted the New York Philharmonic from 1891 until his death from ptomaine poisoning in 1898. Seidl conducted the world premiere of Dvořák's Symphony *From the New World* with the Philharmonic in 1893.

From 1906–1909 Russian Vasili Safonov (1852–1918) conducted the New York Philharmonic and was a specialist in the interpretation of Russian music.

Austrian composer and conductor Gustav Mahler (1860–1911) began conducting the New York Philharmonic in 1909. His tenure was marked with controversy in a period when he was weakened by overwork and ill health. Mahler retired to Vienna and died of pneumonia in 1911.

Bohemian conductor Josef Stransky (1872–1936) succeeded Mahler with the Philharmonic from 1911–1923. He instituted daily rehearsals during the 23-week season.

The Romantic conductor Willem Mengelberg (1871–1951) conducted the Philharmonic from 1923–1930, alternating with Arturo Toscanini during some of these years. Mengelberg championed the works of Gustav Mahler, Richard Strauss, Max Reger, and Claude Debussy; Strauss dedicated the score of *Ein Heldenleben* to him.

Arturo Toscanini (1867–1957) often led the Philharmonic between the years 1928 and 1936, which are considered to be the finest in the history of the Philharmonic. His performances of Beethoven, Verdi, Wagner, Puccini, and Debussy set the standards for other conductors.

John Barbirolli (1899–1970) was the unfortunate conductor to succeed Toscanini. During the years 1937 through 1943 New York critics were merciless in comparing Barbirolli with Toscanini. Barbirolli returned to England in 1943 to conduct the Hallé Orchestra in Manchester. With this orchestra Barbirolli established himself as one of the world's great conductors, noted for his interpretations of Elgar, Delius, Vaughan Williams, and Mahler.

Eminent Polish conductor Artur Rodzinski (1892–1958) replaced Barbirolli and conducted the Philharmonic from 1943–1947. Rodzinski also led the Philadelphia, Cleveland, Chicago, and NBC orchestras, but his career was always burdened by controversies with orchestral managements. Rodzinski's conducting genius and artistic temperament kept getting in the way, and his tenures with major orchestras were always brief with the exception of the Cleveland Orchestra where he was tenured from 1933 to 1943.

Greek conductor Dimitri Mitropoulos (1896–1960) led the New York Philharmonic from 1949 to 1956, frequently performing works of the avant-garde and atonal schools. He was a conductor of great emotional power, but New York audiences were firmly opposed to his doses of new repertoire.

The eminent German conductor Bruno Walter (1876–1962) was noted for magnificent performances of Mozart, Haydn, and Beethoven and also for his beautiful interpretations of Schubert, Schumann, and Brahms. Walter was most famous for his interpretations of music by Gustav Mahler, who taught Walter in Vienna from 1901–1907. It was from Mahler that Walter discovered that the essence of musical interpretation comes from the spiritual depths of the music. Walter's American debut was with the New York Symphony in 1923, but he did not lead the New York Philharmonic until 1932. In 1936 Walter returned to Europe and became conductor of the Vienna Opera until the start of World War II, when he moved to America, made his home in California, and became an American citizen. He was conductor and musical advisor of the New York Philharmonic from 1947 to 1949 and its principal guest conductor until 1960.

As a professional conductor for more than 70 years, Walter achieved international fame as the last great representative of the Romantic tradition with the world's most famous orchestras, including the New York Philharmonic, Vienna Philharmonic, Columbia Symphony Orchestra, Berlin Philharmonic, Salzburg Music Festival, and the Metropolitan Opera.

Chicago Symphony Orchestra

Because of Theodore Thomas's success in New York, wealthy businessman Charles Norman Fay asked the conductor to come to Chicago with the promise of a permanent orchestra to conduct. The Chicago Symphony was formed with Thomas leading its first concert in 1891, which featured Beethoven's Fifth Symphony. In the next 14 years Thomas built an orchestra of such quality that when Richard Strauss came to Chicago in 1902 to conduct *Also Sprach Zarathustra*, he did not need more than one rehearsal with them. Orchestra Hall was built in recognition of Thomas's distinguished service to the musical culture of Chicago and formally opened in December 1904. Unfortunately, Thomas caught cold in the unheated building and fell ill with pneumonia after conducting a few programs. He died within a month.

The associate conductor, Frederick Stock (1872–1942) took over the baton. At first he lived in the shadow of Thomas, but Stock was a fine interpreter and developed the artistry of the ensemble to become one of the finest American orchestras. In 1916 the Chicago Symphony Orchestra was the first American orchestra to record commercially with its regular conductor. Stock also founded the Chicago Civic Orchestra in 1919 as the training ensemble for the Chicago Symphony Orchestra. According to Gordon Peters, "There were plenty of American born musicians, but they couldn't play Wagner and Beethoven and Ravel and all the things of the symphonic repertoire." (Furlong 348) Through the Chicago Civic Orchestra Stock taught American musicians how to interpret the basic symphonic repertoire. Stock's tenure with the Chicago Symphony Orchestra lasted for thirty years from 1905–1935.

After Stock, the Chicago Symphony Orchestra had a series of new conductors every few years: Belgium-born Désiré Defauw (1885–1960) from 1943–1947; Artur Rodzinski (1892–1958) from 1947–1948, and the distinguished Czech conductor, Rafael Kubelik (1914–1996) from 1950–1953.

Not until Fritz Reiner (1888–1963) took over in 1953 did the Chicago Symphony Orchestra reach its peak. Reiner's early engagements in America—the Cincinnati Symphony (1922–1931), professor of conducting at the Curtis Institute of Music (1931–1941), guest conductor of the San Francisco Opera (1935–1938), and the Pittsburgh Symphony (1938–1948)—prepared him to lead the Chicago Symphony Orchestra to an era of uncompromising perfection and lasting beauty. Through his studies with Arthur Nikisch and Richard Strauss, Reiner was a master of baton techniques that communicated musical wishes with economy of motion.

As a teacher of conducting at the Curtis Institute of Music, Reiner demanded the highest standards from students. According to conducting lore, the only student to receive an A in Reiner's conducting course was Leonard Bernstein.

The Boston Symphony

Henry Lee Higginson (1834–1919), one of Boston's most prominent patrons of the arts, founded the Boston Symphony in 1881 and hired George Henschel (1850–1934) as conductor. Three years later Wilhelm Gericke (1845–1925) took over. Gericke was a firm disciplinarian who produced an orchestra of technical and artistic brilliance during two terms as conductor, one from 1884–1889, and again from 1898–1906.

The most noted conductor to lead the Boston Symphony was the Hungarian Arthur Nikisch (1855–1922). Conductor of this ensemble from 1889–1893, Nikisch was regarded by his peers as one of the greatest masters of orchestral conducting. According to Schonberg, even Toscanini admitted that Nikisch was the leading maestro of his day. Schonberg wrote, "Nikisch was…the idol of his day, the conductor who was to his generation what Toscanini and Furtwängler were to the period after World War II." (Schonberg 206).

During his four seasons with the Boston Symphony Orchestra, Nikisch became a very influential conductor. His interpretations, which changed with each performance, were replete with Romantic passion and imagination. His advice to fellow conductors reflected his approach to music: "Make all your performances a grand improvisation. If the critics don't like it, they can get a metronome to conduct." (Lebrecht 31) Nikisch was the first conductor to use the anticipatory beat, believing that beating ahead of each note gives the music a sense of forward motion. As a great teacher of conducting in Europe, his pupils included Ernest Ansermet, Adrian Boult, Wilhelm Furtwängler, Serge Koussevitzky, Pierre Monteux, and Fritz Reiner.

German Karl Muck (1859–1940) led the Boston Symphony from 1906–1908 and 1912–1918. Unlike Nikisch, his interpretations were characterized as logical, methodical, and analytical. According to Schonberg, "Along with Weingartner, Strauss, and Toscanini, he (Muck) was one of the founders of the modern style in which the printed note is the ultimate authority." (Schonberg 216). As a strict disciplinarian and faithful interpreter, Muck turned the Boston Symphony Orchestra into one of the best in the world. When the United States entered World War I, anti-German hysteria fed rumors that Muck was a personal friend of the Kaiser Wilhelm and a German spy. At the time Muck's programs were mostly German; he gave the American premiere of Arnold Schönberg's *Five Pieces for Orchestra* in 1914. Another dispute arose when Muck refused to conduct the *Star Spangled Banner* at the beginning of a concert, reportedly stating, "a symphony orchestra is not a military band." (Schonberg 217). However, he did open all later concerts with his arrangement of the national anthem, which used the Wagnerian chromatic accompaniment of the *Tannhauser* Overture as a counterpoint to the main melody. (Schonberg 217). Because of continued bad press Muck left America in 1919. With his departure the Boston Symphony quickly declined in quality; Henry Lee Higginson resigned in protest to Muck's treatment by the press; some German musicians in the orchestra returned to Germany; other musicians in the orchestra went to New York for higher salaries. When the remaining musicians failed to establish a union after a general strike, more than 30 musicians, including the concertmaster, resigned.

The Boston Symphony was only a skeleton of its former self when Pierre Monteux (1875–1964) was appointed in 1919. His first tenure, from 1919–1924 was a period of rebuilding and the orchestra grew from almost nothing to 80 musicians. When he left in 1924 music critic Philip Hale wrote, "He formed and molded the orchestra in the face of obstacles that would have daunted a man of less patience, courage, and artistic enthusiasm. To that well equipped body he gave life and beauty by his skill and taste as an interpreter of ancient, modern, and ultra modern music." (Stoddard 269).

Perhaps the most celebrated person to ever lead the Boston Symphony Orchestra was Russian conductor Serge Koussevitzky (1874–1951). For 25 years Koussevitzky gave highly emotional, untraditional interpretations. He commissioned and encouraged American composers Copland, Harris, Barber, Piston, Hanson, Schuman, Bernstein, and others to write works for the Boston Symphony Orchestra. Not only was Koussevitzky a great conductor, he was also a great teacher. He worked to establish the Berkshire Music Center at Tanglewood, Massachusetts in 1940, and it became a musical mecca for many young musicians at the start of their careers. Koussevitzky, Copland, Hindemith, and others taught there and shaped the future of American music. His years with the Boston Symphony Orchestra from 1924–1949 were filled with creative, imaginative interpretations.

After Koussevitzky, Charles Munch (1891–1968) led the Boston Symphony from 1949–1962 and won critical acclaim for the European tours in 1952 and

1956. Munch began his career at the late age of 41. Noted for his fine interpretations of French music, such as Berlioz's *Romeo and Juliet*, he often told conducting students to find their own way. "If you interpret music as you feel it, with ardor and faith, with all your heart and with complete conviction, I am certain that even if the critics attack you, God will forgive you." (Stoddard 146).

Philadelphia Orchestra

The Philadelphia Orchestra Association, a group of influential music lovers, established the Philadelphia Orchestra in the fall of 1900 and selected the German conductor Fritz Scheel (1852–1907) as its conductor. Scheel led the orchestra until his death in 1907 and was followed by German Karl Pohlig (1858–1928) from 1907–1912. Pohlig emphasized the German repertoire, particularly music by Richard Wagner, which resulted in even smaller audiences.

Leopold Stokowski (1882–1977) took over in 1912 and had 23 brilliant and creative years there. Stokowski was a combination of conductor, showman, and musical genius. This unforgettable personality radiated magic from the podium. Like Nikisch he became the public idol of his day. He conducted without a score and without a baton but magically communicated with any orchestra he directed. He created the famous Philadelphia sound that emphasized the singing quality of the strings. Musicologists often disagreed with Stokowski, but Rachmaninoff and many others considered the Philadelphia Orchestra to be the finest in the world. Stokowski conducted the American premiere of Mahler's Eighth Symphony and the first American performance of Stravinsky's *Le Sacre du Printemps*. He was an innovative conductor who experimented with seating arrangements, lighting effects, made records, and retouched scores.

Hungarian Eugene Ormandy (1899–1985) was associate conductor under Stokowski in 1934 and became the permanent conductor in 1938. A violinist, Ormandy continued to develop the singing quality of the strings during his 42 seasons with the Philadelphia Orchestra, the longest tenure any music director of a major orchestra in America. Ormandy was known for Romantic interpretations of Tchaikovsky and Rachmaninoff and premiered such pieces as Rachmaninoff's Symphonic Dances and Bartók's Third Piano Concerto. He retired in 1980 and was named conductor laureate. Schonberg said of Ormandy:

> Of all the conductors he has one of the most infallible ears and memories, and is one of the fastest studies…He inherited a great orchestra, and at the very least, maintained its aural standards. Many claimed he has improved them…he has carved out an area for himself, and within it he is secure, a perfect workman and a sensitive interpreter. (Schonberg 341).

Cleveland Orchestra

Established in 1918 the Cleveland Orchestra had Nicolai Sokoloff (1886–1965) as its first conductor. Born in Kiev, Russia, Sokoloff came to America at age 12 and played violin in the Boston Symphony from 1904–1907. He held the position of music director of the Cleveland Orchestra from 1918–1933 and went on to be director of the Federal Music Project (1935–1938) under the WPA which sponsored orchestras across the nation during the Depression.

The second conductor of the Cleveland Orchestra, Artur Rodzinski (1892–1958), came from Poland to America as an assistant to Stokowski in 1926. He held conducting posts in Philadelphia and Los Angeles before taking charge of the Cleveland Orchestra in 1933. He obtained excellent results with the orchestra before moving on to conduct the New York Philharmonic in 1943 and the Chicago Symphony in 1947.

The next Cleveland conductor was Austrian-American Erich Leinsdorf (1912–1993). Leinsdorf developed an impressive background as assistant conductor to Bruno Walter and Arturo Toscanini in 1934 at the Salzburg Festivals. In 1937 he became conductor of the Metropolitan Opera in New York, and in 1943 was appointed to the Cleveland post, which he held until being inducted into the U.S. Army. From the army Leinsdorf returned to conduct the Metropolitan Opera, the Rochester Philharmonic, and the Boston Symphony (1962–1969). Leinsdorf wrote three books, *Cadenza: A Musical Career* (1976), *The Composer's Advocate* (1981), and *Erich Leinsdorf on Music* (1997), which offer insights to musical interpretations and life as a conductor.

The Cleveland Orchestra reached a high level of artistry under music director George Szell (1897–1970). From 1946 to 1970 Szell was determined to make the Cleveland Orchestra second to none. With his harsh leadership, insights, and imagination the orchestra gave masterful interpretations of Beethoven, Mozart, and Richard Strauss. Szell had enormous talent as a conductor–absolute pitch, a great sense of rhythm, and a wonderful sense of balance–with which he led the Cleveland Orchestra to play with the clarity and razor-sharp precision of a virtuoso orchestra. His was an era of uncompromised beauty.

NBC Symphony

In addition to the big five, one other orchestra had historical significance among early American orchestras and conductors. The NBC Symphony and its incomparable maestro, Arturo Toscanini, were quintessential examples of artistic integrity. It was one of the greatest orchestras America has ever produced. The NBC Symphony was formed in 1937 just for Arturo Toscanini and profoundly affected the musical heritage of America through its recordings, radio broadcasts from 1937 to 1954, and ten televised concerts. This orchestra gave the nation seventeen years of superb orchestral performances.

Arturo Toscanini made his American debut in 1908 with the Metropolitan Opera in New York, conducting Verdi's *Aida* with Caruso. He brought the La Scala Orchestra to America in 1920–1921 and became the permanent conductor of the New York Philharmonic from 1928 to 1936. He shared the podium with Furtwängler and Mengelberg. In 1936 he resigned from the Philharmonic and returned to Italy.

Toscanini gave up retirement when NBC offered to create a symphony orchestra especially for him. Toscanini accepted the offer with the condition that Artur Rodzinski, then the conductor of the Cleveland Orchestra, audition and train the new ensemble because he had a reputation as a builder of orchestras and for being a strict disciplinarian. When Toscanini returned to America in 1937, Rodzinski had a virtuoso orchestra waiting for him.

Under the baton of Toscanini the NBC Symphony performed at the highest level, with interpretations that are still critically acclaimed today. The time was the golden age of radio and television, when broadcasts reached their full artistic potential. According to Schonberg, "Toscanini was the pivotal conductor of his period: the strongest influence, the one who marks the final transition from the Wagner style to twentieth-century objectivity. He became the greatest single force on contemporary conducting." (Schonberg 52).

CHAPTER 3

Learning from a Legend

For the better part of the 20th century conductors have modeled their techniques after Arturo Toscanini, whose style comprised preparation, precision, and objective interpretation. Beat preparation, however, was Toscanini's most effective tool; it was preparation, not the beat's sharpness or accuracy, that influenced his orchestral sound.

Max Rudolf agreed with the primary importance of gesture: "The more the conductor can express in these gestures, the more response he will get from the players in the way of shading, articulation, and expression." (Rudolf 251) Conductor Wilhelm Furtwängler also found essential the exactness of that "brief, often tiny movement of the downbeat, before the point of unified sound is reached in the orchestra." (Schonberg 272)

NBC Symphony members believed Toscanini's art of preparation was one of his great conducting secrets. When Toscanini conducted the Vienna Philharmonic in 1936, bassoonist Hugo Burghauser observed:

> Toscanini was able to project whatever was in the score and in his mind. The conception of great interpretation, of what it should be, can quite often be found in fine artistic minds, but to project such ideas into the orchestra unmistakably, by technical means that are absolutely convincing–which Toscanini did–this is a sort of miracle which I can explain in part only as a result of a real capability of telepathic communication; and in fact he rarely used words to communicate what he wanted. About half a bar before the occurrence of a detail in the music you saw already on his face and in his gesture what he was coming to and would want. This was extraordinary: the parallel conducting of what was going on now and what was coming the next moment. It was an entirely unheard-of ability, almost like the clairvoyance of a seer. (Haggin 156)

A Toscanini interpretation is marked secondly by precision or line clarity, and many of his contemporaries were critical of this. According to Schonberg, Guido Ricordi attacked Toscanini in the *Gazzetta Musicale*, claiming his execution was rigid, that he lacked poetry. "Ricordi said that Toscanini's conducting of *Falstaff* resembled that of a 'mastadonic mechanical piano.' Later on, Ricordi changed his mind, as did virtually everybody else." (Schonberg 255) Toscanini's technique was precise, winning from an ensemble unanimous, split-second, accurate responses.

The paradox is that Toscanini's baton technique was far from technically exceptional. According to David Walter of the NBC Symphony:

> Toscanini's conducting movements didn't beat time in accordance with the traditional skeletal configurations....They delineated the musical flow,... breaking the prison of these configurations. And so while they were the most expressive movements and gestures of any conductor, they didn't always answer the orchestral players' well-known question: 'Where's the beat?' (Haggin 20)

Violinist Joseph Gingold related that "It wasn't the beat of a specialist in virtuoso conducting; it was the beat of a musician who had a stick and could show whatever he wished with it." (Haggin 136)

Samuel Antek wrote:

> We usually think of virtuoso baton technique in a more spectacular sense, such as beating complicated rhythms, giving very sure, positive entrances, and managing sudden changes of tempo. These are, in a sense, the more obvious conductorial appurtenances. What Toscanini sought was something much rarer, something beyond the rules and textbook formulas. Toscanini never sought, nor did he ever seem aware of, the easy, practical, safe approach to conducting and music making. The secret of Toscanini's conducting is that he never concerned himself with the mere mechanics of stick waving. He was primarily interested in the musical problem and its solution. He was not too concerned with helping the orchestra mechanically, and I always felt that he himself did not know quite what he was doing with the baton. He often spoke contemptuously of those who studied or taught conducting per se. I felt he would rather die than conduct mechanically for ensemble reasons, in order to obtain what he felt should be achieved by the men. (Antek 146)

In light of this how could Toscanini achieve such precision and clarity? Leopold Stokowski offered an answer:

> His beat breaks every academic rule – yet it is always clear and eloquent. But it is between the beats that something magical happens: one can always tell when he has reached the half-beat or the three-quarter beat, even when he does not divide his beats; and it is this certainty and clarity of beats which creates such a perfect ensemble when he conducts. (Ewen 175)

Toscanini discarded standard beat patterns, substituting one that outlined the musical line's rise and fall. He realized standard baton technique produces an orchestral sound equal to it, where concentration is on rhythm, not musical line. Toscanini conducted subtle nuances between the beats.

Toscanini's arrival marked the end of the subjective conducting exemplified by Hans von Bülow and Gustav Mahler. "Toscanini was the pivotal conductor of his period: the strongest influence, the one who marks the transition from the Wagner style to 20th-century objectivity. He ended up the greatest single force on today's conducting." (Schonberg 252)

According to George Szell, "Whatever you think about his [Toscanini's] interpretation of a specific work, [the idea] that he changed the whole concept of conducting and…rectified many, many arbitrary procedures of a generation…before him is now authentic history." Szell claimed Toscanini served as a "not too useful model" for generations of conductors, so fascinated they were unable to see him critically or follow with discrimination. "However, he did wipe out the meretricious tricks and the thick encrustation of the interpretive nuances that had been piling up for decades."(Schonberg 242) Spike Hughes substantiated this: "To clear the romantic grime off the classics was one of Toscanini's greatest achievements. To clean up a romantic work like the Tchaikovsky *Pathetique*, and to know when to stop the operation before the music is stripped of its character and genuine emotional quality is little short of a miracle." (Hughes 383)

Toscanini sought the composer's intentions. He had read about many stylistic, interpretive dilemmas, and came to the conclusion there was no conclusion. He believed it was futile for a conductor to attempt an authentic performance style. Instruments, pitch, and concepts had changed, and Beethoven would not recognize a 20th-century performance of his music. To Toscanini, truth was in the notes, and to interpret a composer's intentions a conductor must rely on musicianship, taste, and instinct.

Rehearsing Beethoven's *Eroica* Symphony Toscanini said, "The tradition is to be found only in one place – in the music! Some say this is Napoleon, some Hitler, some Mussolini. For me, it is simply *allegro con brio.*" (Hughes 39)

> Alan Schulman, cellist with the NBC Symphony, said, What struck all of us, and what we talked about was Toscanini's total honesty, his total dedication, his subordination of himself to the composer's demands. This honesty and sincerity continued through the years. He tried to get as close as one could to the truth in a piece of music. (Haggins 25)

Whether Toscanini discovered composers' intentions is irrelevant; in his quest he enhanced music with a purpose and integrity that remain standards of conducting excellence today. ☙

CHAPTER 4

Lessons in Interpretation from Arturo Toscanini

The oddest thing about conductors, even the best of them, is the way they hold the score up to the light or turn it back to front. They are always looking for something that isn't there and never see what is.
—Arturo Toscanini

Samuel Barber (1910–1981) was one of the last 20th-century composers to write in the Romantic style. Rejecting the modern dissonances of his time, Barber wrote lyrical, expressive, and tonal music. His *Adagio for Strings* is probably his most frequently performed work and has hauntingly beautiful phrases. With its elegiac and nostalgic qualities, the *Adagio* is frequently performed at state funerals.

When Toscanini heard Barber's *Symphony in One Movement* at the Salzburg music festival in 1937, he was so impressed that he asked the young composer to write a work for the NBC Orchestra, which had been formed especially for Toscanini. The work Barber presented to Toscanini was the *Adagio for Strings*, which Barber adopted from the slow movement of his String Quartet in B Minor. Toscanini gave a stunning premiere performance of the work on November 5, 1938 and recorded it with the NBC Symphony in Carnegie Hall in 1942, making Barber's music the first by an American composer that Toscanini had recorded.

RCA Victor reissued this historical performance on compact disc (RCA GD 60307), and it is the definitive interpretation of the *Adagio*. Tender, poignant, intense, Toscanini conducted with impeccable taste. The recording demonstrates the interpretive skills of a musical genius, one many consider to be the outstanding conductor of the 20th century. The interpretation still sounds fresh, intensely alive, and convincing. Toscanini probes the depths of the score and produces an overwhelming and lasting experience for listeners.

The first page of the Schirmer score has no tempo markings, only the Italian directive *espressivo cantando* and *molto adagio* plus Barber's instructions that the playing time should be between seven and eight minutes. Toscanini's recording is just over seven minutes in length and reflects Barber's idea that the tempo should not be too slow to maintain the continuity of the musical line. Some recent performances approach a duration of ten minutes, which was clearly not Barber's stated intention.

© *The Instrumentalist*, December 1993. Reprinted with Permission.

Conductor Felix Weingartner suggests a good rule for selecting tempos: "no tempo must be so slow that the melody of the piece is not recognizable, and no fast tempo so fast that the melody is no longer recognizable." (Weingartner 24) This is good advice for all conductors.

Samuel Antek, a violinist with the NBC Symphony, recalls Toscanini's insistence on precise tempos:

> [Toscanini] held up his hand and in the palm he traced a diagram to illustrate what he had been talking about. He drew a vertical line. 'This,' he said, 'is the tempo,' and then across, weaving in and out sinuously, he traced a wavy line, like a snake wrapped around a stick. 'That,' he said, 'is the way the tempo must change – weaving in and out, but always close and always returning, never like this,' he said, drawing a line away from the original line, at a tangent. 'Yes,' he said, 'in music, just to have the correct tempo without all that goes with it means nothing.' (Antek 129)

Toscanini's choice of tempo for the beginning of the *Adagio* is approximately $\quarternote = 44$–48 and allows the music to breathe with only subtle fluctuations. To enhance the broad $\frac{4}{2}$ meter, Toscanini used a legato four-beat conducting pattern instead of the subdivided four-beats that many conductors use today. According to Antek,

> This insistence in slow movements of beating the broadest possible notes without subdivision is one of the most difficult feats and achievements of a truly virtuoso conductor; the very subtle, musical blending of mood and beat is something few conductors are capable of, and, most, unfortunately, never even seek. What he wanted was not only that each note of a melody come on its appointed beat, but that the note be evenly spread and sustained over the full value of the beat. The effect would be almost like moving in slow motion from one note to the other rather than hopping quickly from note to note. It meant holding on to each note as long as possible before moving to the next. This gives an unusual, broad, flowing, gliding quality to a succession of notes. I cannot recall his ever making a gesture that was purely mechanical, impersonal, and not clearly identified in mood or movement with the expression of the musical phrase as he felt it. He conducted the music, not the orchestra. (Antek 146)

What impresses me most about Toscanini's interpretation of the *Adagio* is its simplicity. His choice not to subdivide beats is a case in point. Many talented conductors have the technique to beat every hemidemisemiquaver of a complex score, but few match Toscanini's masterful interpretations. Other renditions of the *Adagio* seem distorted and exaggerated. With Toscanini's recording I think of Samuel Barber, not of Toscanini; that is as it should be.

Toscanini's control over dynamics reflects his belief that "in a *pianissimo* every player should play so that he can no longer hear his own instrument; in a *fortissimo* every player should play so that he can hear his own instrument above everything." (Hughes 310)

The opening phrase of the *Adagio* is marked *pianissimo*, but Toscanini gives it a sense of drama about to begin, almost like the curtain slowly going up on a great play. He enhances the sustained B♭ in the first violins, certainly not the anemic beginning of many performances. Other strings enter on the crescendo; Toscanini quickly establishes a sense of forward motion with a subtle separation before the second measure. The clarity and balance between the first violins and the inner voices sounds like a string quartet rather than the full string section of a symphony orchestra.

Toscanini produces long arcs of cohesive melody instead of the series of melodic fragments that usually result from subdividing the beat. Nicolas Moldavan, violist in the NBC Symphony recalls the maestro's comments:

> What Toscanini taught me was that a piece of music has a frame, and you
> phrase and build within this frame....Most musicians distort; if you listen to
> a recording you hear this bar a little longer and this one a little shorter; and
> Toscanini said it wasn't necessary to take such liberties to make a piece of
> music beautiful. (Haggin 74)

Toscanini sets the standard for the entire piece with the first phrase; one may call it a conductor's seminar on the art of phrasing. The phrase flows with a forward motion that transcends the bar line and comes to repose at the end, like perfectly balanced architecture. In the third measure Toscanini holds back on the last four quarter notes but gently lifts the final quarter before the $\frac{5}{2}$ measure.

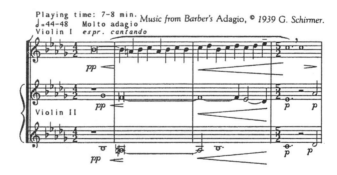

Playing time: 7–8 min. *Music from Barber's Adagio,* © *1939 G. Schirmer.*

Another Toscanini characteristic is to hold the accompaniment back. At ⬚1⬚ the violins, violas, and cellos usually cover the C♭ in the second violins. Toscanini brings out the C♭ to clarify the harmonic change, then balances the first violin octave with the second violins. By clarifying this harmonic change Toscanini followed his admonitions to orchestra members: "I want everything so clear that I can touch it." (Antek 84)

Toscanini had a remarkable ear for instrumental balance and matching dynamics. In measure 22 the violas skip from F to C♭ before the cellos pick up the melody and pass it to the first violins. The Toscanini recording matches these lines so they sound as if one instrument is playing. This is also true in measure 23 where the low A♭ in the cellos is balanced with the F in the violas and D♮ in the first violins. Instead of melodic fragments there is a continuous line, perfectly matched in style and volume.

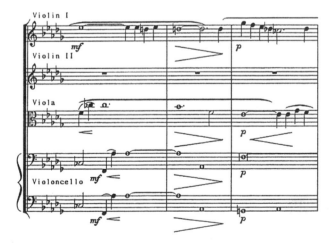

Through many years of conducting operas Toscanini learned the nuances of dramatic structure. He brought this to his symphonic interpretations and always thought of himself as a man of the theater (*un uomo di teatro*). This training is evident as he draws a melodic line from the orchestra that is always singing and sustained. Toscanini intuitively thought of music as song. His favorite words in rehearsal were "*Cantare! Sostenere!*" (Sing! Sustain!)

Spike Hughes says of Toscanini, "the nearer to the human voice he could get the orchestra to sound, the nearer he felt he was to the attainment of his ideal; the interpretation of the composer's melody as the composer himself conceived it." (Hughes 23)

Toscanini's sense of the overall form of a composition also reflects his operatic work. Rudolf Serkin called it "architecture with passion." To Toscanini, musical form was continuous drama with the timing and pacing of a great play. Violist Nicolas Moldavan comments on the Maestro's sense of dramatic continuity:

> Nobody could build up a crescendo as he did, holding you back, holding you back....Other conductors don't know how to do that. They run away with you, and when it comes to the forte they haven't anything left. (Haggin 75)

Nowhere did Toscanini demonstrate his remarkable understanding of musical drama better than in the way he builds intensity in the *Adagio* from measure 44 to the central climax in measure 52. The climax occurs exactly at measurer 52, not before. These are measures that separate maestros from podium posturers. Some conductors reach the climax in measure 50 and the first violins cover up the chord progressions in the inner parts. Others accelerate the tempo too rapidly, then compensate for the anti-climax by adding a crescendo to the fermata in measure 54; this, of course, is not written.

Starting with the theme in the second violins in measure 44, Toscanini creates a sense of forward motion by giving each note full value and never letting up on the intensity. He reaches the climax with a perfectly-timed accelerando and crescendo in measure 52. Toscanini achieves the significant differences between *ff* and *sff* in measures 52–54. He restrains the first violins so the inner parts bring out the chord progressions from measures 50–52. On the *sff* climax all instruments hold the fermata with the same intensity; Toscanini then holds the fermata on the rest to exactly the same length as the previous fermata. The next three measures after the fermata are slower; Toscanini thought of them as one complete phrase.

He returns to the first tempo with the theme at *mf* instead of *pp* as audiences often hear, and the first violins and violas sound as one instrument.

Five measures from the end Toscanini creates a moment of tenderness that almost sounds like a false ending because of the subtle ritard and decrescendo of the theme.

The last four measures offer a perfect example of Toscanini's exceptional timing. Again he emphasizes the *mf* dynamics in the first violins with a slight emphasis on the B♭ and contrasts this with a *pp* entrance in other strings. The last three half notes are *molto espressivo* and *con amore*, which Toscanini broadens and lifts with a slight separation and decrescendo.

As the first violins hold the A♮ the other strings break perfectly at the caesura. The last note is held until it is inaudible and seems like the curtain coming down at the end of a play. The ending is a mirror image of the beginning, a perfectly symmetrical coda.

Those who have always loved Barber's *Adagio* will enjoy it more with Toscanini's remarkable revelation of the score. Not only does his interpretation have lyrical and balanced phrases, but there is also a spiritual quality that cannot be analyzed. When listening to Toscanini's performance I am reminded of George Crumb's comment that music is "a system of proportions in the service of a spiritual impulse." After working for perfect balance, phrasing, and intonation, most conductors still fail to achieve the spiritual level of communication that is inherent in great interpretations. Toscanini reminds us that there is no interpretation without the spiritual essence of a score. By comparing the written notations of Samuel Barber's score for the *Adagio* with Toscanini's great recording of this work, conductors can learn interpretive details of how this conductor brings out the spiritual essence in music.

CHAPTER 5

Lessons in Conducting from Wilhelm Furtwängler

In my opinion the true interpreter must identify himself with the work, and indeed create it afresh. —Wilhelm Furtwängler

As undergraduate music majors in the 1960s, my roommate and I spent many evenings debating the interpretive skills of various conductors. My hero was Arturo Toscanini, who I thought had no equal. Many nights my roommate brought in recordings of different conductors, but I dismissed each with a condescending wave of my hand, "Bah! It's okay, but no Toscanini!" One night he brought in a recording, and with a gleeful look in his eye said, "Now, listen to this and tell me what you think—Wilhelm Furtwängler conducting the Vienna Philharmonic in Beethoven's *Pastoral Symphony!*"

I knew this symphony note for note after wearing the grooves off Toscanini and Bruno Walter recordings. After listening for a few minutes, I remained silent; Furtwängler recorded the quintessential romantic interpretation with plenty of rhythmic flexibility and improvisatory freedom. His performance directly contradicted Toscanini's classical style. This unorthodox, subjective, and personal interpretation produced a performance of incomparable beauty. Although Furtwängler's perspective differed from those of my conducting heroes, I had to admit that this interpretation had both honesty and artistic conviction. After this stunning revelation I collected and studied Furtwängler's recordings to learn how he developed so much emotion with each extraordinary interpretation.

Furtwängler was born in Berlin in 1886 and grew up in an upper-class family; his father was a noted archaeology professor, and his mother was an artist. Furtwängler had an early interest in composition and aspired to write music in the grand tradition of Beethoven, Brahms, and Bruckner. Furtwängler composed throughout his life and at the time of his death in 1954 left behind three symphonies, a Te Deum, a piano quintet, two violin sonatas, and several shorter pieces. As with Berlioz and Wagner, Furtwängler's interest in conducting grew from a strong desire to interpret his own works.

This motivation to conduct soon overshadowed his interest in composition, and his talents on the podium led to several key conducting positions. His most important conducting job came at age 36 when he succeeded Arthur Nikisch as conductor of the Berlin Philharmonic in 1922. Furtwängler once explained, "I had a successful career because I was awkward and shy. When they (other

---

© *The Instrumentalist*, April 1995. Reprinted with Permission.

conductors) finally realized that I was indeed a danger, it was too late," (Schonberg 277)

To many listeners Furtwängler was an interpretive genius who inspired orchestras by force of personality to play better than they thought possible. Emotionally and artistically, Furtwängler employed a conducting style deeply rooted in the romantic traditions of the 19th century, an essential element of his interpretations. His Wagnerian operas with Kirsten Flagstad, and the symphonies of Beethoven, Bruckner, and Schubert are legendary performances that mark him as one of the great conductors of the 20th century. His recordings provide an incomparable documentary of how he sustained the romantic traditions of Wagner, Mahler, and Nikisch into the mid-20th century.

Many musicians also contend that Furtwängler had the most unorthodox baton technique in the history of conducting. According to Harold Schonberg,

> Furtwängler's beat was a phenomenon unduplicated before or since: a horror, a nightmare, to musicians. On the podium he lost himself. He would gesticulate, shout, sing, make faces, spit, stamp. Or he would close his eyes and make vague motions. Until orchestras worked with him and got used to that curious, quivering, trembling baton they could be in a complete mess.... In the Berlin Philharmonic there was a standard joke: Question: 'How do you know when to come in on the opening bars of the Beethoven ninth?' Answer: 'We walk twice around our chairs, count to ten, and then start playing.' Or, question: 'How do you know when to come in with such a mysterious downbeat?' Answer: 'When we lose patience.' (Schonberg 272)

Everything the critics said about Furtwängler's baton technique was true: it was unorthodox, vague, confusing, and gave nightmares to musicians. The critics missed the point because Furtwängler cared little for precision or becoming a "bloody time-beater." He once stated:

> The art of conducting has been terribly mechanical through seeking perfection much more than vision. When technique becomes an end in itself it is a sure sign that you are losing consciousness of form. Therefore, as soon as the rubato is willed and calculated scientifically, it ceases to be true. Seeing a piece of music in its spiritual unity, that is, making the motions of the soul and the architectural balance agree, is something of which the musician of today seldom shows himself capable or even desirous. (Turnabout 4408)

Furtwängler recognized his unorthodox baton technique created difficulties for some musicians but disregarded these concerns because to him great conducting was not in the beat itself but in its preparation. Uninterested in the beating of time, he tried to convey the spirit of the music. Despite mixed feelings about his technique, musicians praised his extraordinary ability to give inspired performances.

Many conductors learn techniques by observing other conductors and the response from an ensemble. The second video of the four-video series, *The Art of Conducting*, focuses on Furtwängler conducting Meistersinger Overture, Brahms' Fourth Symphony, and rehearsals from Schubert's Ninth Symphony.

Watching Furtwängler give the downbeat to *Meistersinger* Overture may come as a shock to those accustomed to elegant and precise conducting. The film captures how his arms seem like a puppet on a string as he gives an unclear downbeat that elicits dead silence from the orchestra. He gives another downbeat, again answered with silence. Finally, Furtwängler gives an anticipatory beat, and the orchestra responds with a glorious sound on the rebound. The video confirms how difficult it was to follow Furtwängler but it also illustrates much more about the art of conducting. His inspiring performance sounds spontaneous with a remarkable fluidity and freedom in the phrasing that taps the emotional content of the music.

A supreme romanticist, Furtwängler traced his individualized interpretations back to the musical roots of Wagner, Bülow, Nikisch, and Mengelberg when evaluations of conductors centered on the degree of emotion and originality put into the music, not a strict adherence to the score. Most 20th-century conductors turn away from subjective interpretations and follow the literal instructions of the composer.

Furtwängler's 1944 Vienna Philharmonic recording of Beethoven's Pastoral Symphony exemplifies his romantic traits. This demonstrates his link to the Wagnerian school of conducting: variations in tempo, dynamics, and the improvisatory freedom to enhance the expressiveness of music.

Although Beethoven calculated metronome markings for all of his symphonies, most conductors disregard some of the published tempos. Historians believe Beethoven used an inaccurate metronome, as the composer himself sometimes described his metronome as"sick". Because Beethoven was not a practicing conductor, he never verified his markings on the podium or selected tempos with conducting patterns in mind. Conductors who want to learn more about the tempos of Beethoven should read Max Rudolf's informative article in *The Journal of the Conductor's Guild*, vol. 1, no. 1, 1980.

Most conductors agree that Beethoven's metronome marking of $\downarrow$ = 66 for the opening of his sixth symphony is too fast; it erroneously suggests that the movement be conducted one beat to a bar. For better control the movement should be conducted with two beats per bar at a tempo of $\downarrow$ = 108–120. The first movement is marked *allegro ma non troppo* with the additional description "cheerful impressions on arriving in the country." Furtwängler follows this direction and slowly recreates the countryside scene at a tempo of $\downarrow$ = 72. He interprets the first phrase in a romantic style by inserting a ritard in the third measure and prolonging the fermata with a decrescendo. Furtwängler enhances the phrase, marked piano, by making it rubato and inserting $<\,>$.

Without pausing after the fermata, Furtwängler starts a new tempo of ♩ = 84 to express the gentle and relaxed mood of a casual stroll through the country-side. Furtwängler never hesitated to modify tempos and dynamics for expressive reasons, and this gave the exposition a certain improvisational quality. He quick-ens the tempo in measure 37 from ♩ = 84 to ♩ = 104–108 as the complete theme appears for the first time in the woodwinds and strings. This becomes the basic tempo for the first movement, although with many rubato modifications.

Measures 53 and 54 have bothered conductors for years because Beethoven's intent is unclear. The clarinet and bassoon triplets in the exposition end on an eighth note.

When the figure recurs in the recapitulation at measures 328–330, with the horns and violins added for color, the composer used a quarter note. Furtwängler resolves this dilemma by ending both examples with a tenuto eighth note.

In the measures 65–66 Furtwängler inserts a perfectly timed ritard to set up the entrance of the subordinate theme which he conducts a *tempo*. The subtle, yet musical, ritard makes the new theme sparkle and radiate with energy.

Bars 93–100 offer a good example of Furtwängler's intuitive tempo modifications. He accelerates the forte passage in the strings to measure 96 and then slackens the pace considerably with the dolce woodwind entry for greater expression.

In measure 106 Furtwängler retouches the orchestration slightly, changing the second horn to a D^4 to avoid the awkward skip from D^5 to G^4. Felix Weingartner, author of *On the Performance of Beethoven Symphonies*, suggests the same adjustment.

In bars 187–190 Furtwängler retards the bassoon and violin duet from ♩ = 116 to a slow ♩ = 84, returning to the original tempo at measure 191.

Another digression from printed dynamics and tempo occurs in measures 472–473 when the strings start *pp* but play an added *subito crescendo* over two measures. This leads to the *f* in the next measure where the strings make the next two eighth-note chords *molto tenuto* ♪ ♪ ♪ ♪ with a slight ritard to enhance the V-I cadence.

The final measures demonstrate how Furtwängler added romantic drama to the piece. He omits the staccato eighth, and adds accents and a crescendo to the *sf* chords, so they ring with full sonority. He inserts a dramatic space between chords and includes a ritard and accents on the two quarter-note chords, performed tenuto at *ff*. He ends the movement in a reflective mood with two F major chords at *p* and a prolonged fermata.

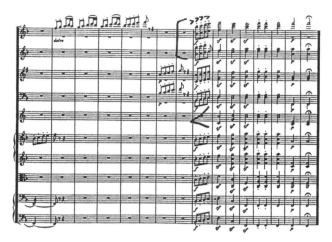

Critics who claim that Furtwängler had poor baton technique should study the recordings of his performance of Beethoven's Sixth Symphony, which documents his remarkable control of the orchestra. Together they achieve a rubato without any breaks in the beautiful and flowing lines. Although Furtwängler delivers a highly subjective and emotional interpretation, his performances are reflections of his solid musical convictions. Wilhelm Furtwängler was a genius on the podium, one who had the courage to challenge the orthodox conducting style of his time.

CHAPTER 6

The Passion and Finesse of Serge Koussevitzky

Serge Koussevitzky was an excellent conductor and a great artist who performed my works with a supreme mastery. I shall ever be deeply grateful to him for all that he has done for my art. His memory is unforgettable. —Jean Sibelius (RCA 1510)

In the first half of the 20th century American orchestras flourished under the leadership of the great conductors of the era with Arturo Toscanini (1867–1957) in New York, Leopold Stokowski (1882–1977) in Philadelphia, and Serge Koussevitzky (1874–1951) in Boston. Each of the three men left a legacy of musical interpretations that still inspires musicians. Koussevitzky will also be remembered as a champion of contemporary American composers. According to Olin Downes, "Of all the conductors who have come here, he will leave the deepest imprint upon the musical evolution of America." (RCA 1510)

Koussevitzky was born July 26, 1874 in Vishny-Volochok in central Russia. His father taught him to play the violin, and his mother gave him piano lessons. Even as a child he dreamed of becoming a conductor and arranged an imaginary orchestra using empty chairs and conducted his favorite scores with them. Koussevitzky left home at the age of 14 to study at the Moscow Conservatory. He became so proficient on the double bass that he passed his final examination with distinction in 1894 and gave solo concerts throughout Russia and eventually the rest of Europe for the following 10 years. His repertoire included his adaptations of Haydn's Cello Concerto, Mozart's Bassoon Concerto, Bruch's *Kol Nidrei*, and the first Cello Concerto of Saint-Saëns.

At the age of 30 Koussevitzky married the daughter of a millionaire tea merchant, and with her money he could afford to study conducting in Berlin with the great Arthur Nikisch (1855–1922). Nikisch conducted the Leipzig Gewandhaus Orchestra, the Berlin Philharmonic, and the Boston Symphony

---

© *The Instrumentalist*, November 1995. Reprinted with Permission.

(from 1889–1893), and was one of the greatest conducting teachers of all time. Nikisch's pupils included Ernest Ansermet, Adrian Boult, Fritz Busch, Wilhelm Furtwängler, Pierre Monteux, and Fritz Reiner. Nikisch passed on to Koussevitzky an approach to conducting that was both passionate and improvisatory. In 1909 Koussevitzky formed an orchestra of the best 75 musicians his father-in-law's money could buy, and he soon earned the reputation as one of Russia's foremost conductors.

He received offers to come to America to guest conduct in 1916, but with the war and the Russian Revolution, he remained in Russia four more years, conducting the State Symphony in Petrograd. After the Bolsheviks confiscated his property, Koussevitzky fled to Paris in 1920 and organized the brilliant Concerts Koussevitzky. In 1922 he commissioned Maurice Ravel to orchestrate Mussorgsky's colorful piano suite *Pictures at an Exhibition.*

In 1924 Koussevitzky became the permanent conductor of the Boston Symphony Orchestra. His early years in Boston were anything but smooth because orchestra members were accustomed to the impeccable baton technique of Pierre Monteux. They adjusted to Koussevitzky's technical shortcomings with difficulty.

Like Furtwängler, Koussevitzky's greatness came from his interpretations, not his baton technique. He was a perfectionist and approached rehearsals with tenacity and never let up until he got exactly what he wanted. He gradually won the orchestra's respect for his penetrating and emotional interpretations. Howard Hanson once described a typical Koussevitzky rehearsal:

> I have heard him rehearsing the opening of the Overture to *The Flying Dutchman* dozens of times, not because the horns could not play the notes, but because the notes as played did not yet convey their emotional and dramatic portent. I have heard him rehearse passages in Elgar's familiar *Pomp and Circumstance* repeatedly until the low trumpets sounded brilliant. Every student of orchestration knows that low trumpet tones cannot sound brilliant, but at the end of the rehearsal they did sound brilliant. (Schonberg 306)

Koussevitzky worked on his technical shortcoming and later mastered the complex meters of works by Bartók and Stravinsky.

One measure of the enormous influence of Serge Koussevitzky and the Boston Symphony on the American musical scene is the list of American composers whose works they commissioned and performed: Samuel Barber, Leonard Bernstein, Aaron Copland, Lukas Foss, Howard Hanson, Roy Harris, Walter Piston, Randall Thompson, and William Schuman. Along with the encouragement he gave to young American composers, Koussevitzky also premiered major works by Bartók, Prokofiev, Ravel, Schönberg, and Stravinsky. With the opening of the Berkshire Music Center on July 8, 1940 in Lenox, Massachusetts, Koussevitzky realized his dream to establish a major American music center where "the greatest living composers will teach the art of composition; the greatest virtuosi the art of perfect performance; the greatest conductors the mystery of conducting orchestras and choruses. The most eminent thinkers and scholars will lecture there." (Galkin 733) Under the visionary leadership of Koussevitzky and his assistant director, Aaron Copland, Tanglewood became a musical mecca for promising young composers and conductors.

Koussevitzky also left a legacy of passionate interpretations of the late Romantics. His musical performances of Rachmaninoff, Tchaikovsky, and Sibelius are unparalleled. Koussevitzky's interpretations remind us that it is acceptable to feel deeply about music and to trust those inner feelings. Koussevitzky wrote about his subjective approach to a score in the August 1948 *Atlantic Monthly*:

> A talented artist, no matter how accurately he follows the markings in the score, renders the composition through his own prism, his own perception of the score, his own temperament and emotion. And the degree the emotion of the interpreter, the greater and more vivid the performance. (RCA 09026)

Nowhere are Koussevitzky's emotions more deeply felt than with Jean Sibelius' Symphony #2, which Koussevitzky recorded on November 29, 1950, seven months before his death on June 5, 1951. This spine-tingling interpretation is one of the great reverberations of the past. At the age of 76 Koussevitzky brought a power and passion that make this the most elegant and romantic reading of the score that I have ever heard.

Sibelius composed the four-movement second symphony in 1901. Along with *Finlandia* the second symphony is perhaps his most popular composition with its uninhibited outpouring of intense emotions. Indeed, some critics have judged the symphony as overly emotional, to which Sibelius replied, "No statues are made of critics after they die."

When Sibelius died at age 92 (1865–1957) he was considered the greatest symphonic composer since Brahms and one of the last of the great Romanticists. As a lover of nature, Sibelius once wrote: "I love the mysterious sounds of the fields and forests, water and mountains. It pleases me greatly to be called an artist of nature, for nature has truly been the book of books for me." (Kaufmann 124) The second symphony evokes powerful images of Finland with its stark, bleak landscapes, and snowcapped mountains.

Sibelius indicated no metronome markings and uses only standard Italian tempo indications. There are 15 tempo changes in the first movement plus the intrinsic fluctuations necessary for a convincing performance. The challenge to conductors is to alter the tempo without losing continuity. According to Howard Hanson, "In the hands of a lesser man such a sense of freedom would be dangerous, but it serves Serge Koussevitzky as a powerful lens revealing the mind of the composer with amazing fidelity." (RCA 09026)

Koussevitzky demonstrates that the intelligent use of rubato is one of the most expressive musical tools in the conductor's arsenal. By shortening one beat and lengthening another, he lifts the music out of its metronomic straitjacket, but rubato depends upon having a definite sense of pulse. A good analogy is the one given by Chopin: "Rubato is gently blowing against the flame of a candle without putting it out." Rubato is an emotional bending of the tempo without breaking it.

Composers sometimes hesitate to indicate rubato because most conductors fail to understand that tempo fluctuations inserted in a musical phrase will make it more expressive only if they return to the fundamental pulse.

The symphony's D major first movement is marked *allegretto*. Koussevitzky conducts the $\frac{6}{4}$ meter in two and takes the somber introductory string phrase at ♩. = 69. This allows the music to pulsate with a forward motion that paints the austere grandeur of a northern landscape. Koussevitzky establishes this mood by using a subtle rubato to accelerate and retard the tempo, but he carefully adheres to the indicated crescendos and dynamics. When the oboe and clarinets enter at measure 9 Koussevitzky contrasts the original mood by taking the perky folk-like tune at ♩. = 80. In measure 13 Koussevitzky inserts a *subito ritardando* that allows the horns to enter and introduce a passionate second theme at the original tempo of ♩. = 69. Nowhere in the score are these tempo changes indicated, but by making them, Koussevitzky establishes the two contrasting moods that permeate the entire first movement.

Seventeen measures before B, Sibelius introduces one of his characteristic expansive melodies that displays Koussevitzky's exceptional sense of timing and phrasing. Koussevitzky beautifully shapes the theme at a tempo of ♩. = 63, finishes the end of the first phrase in the fifth measure with a gentle *luftpause*, and then returns with a piano dynamic that is truly breathtaking.

A good example of textural clarity occurs one measure before the fermata when Koussevitzky brings out the ♩♪♩ triplet on the second beat in the violas and cellos with just enough crescendo to be audible.

Transitional passages are often difficult to control, especially when played by pizzicato strings that have a tendency to rush. The transitional phrasing marked *poco affrettando* five measures before C̄ starts at ♩. = 63 and gradually increases in speed to arrive at *poco allegro* at C̄ with ♩. = 80, Koussevitzky and the Boston Symphony string section handle this passage so adroitly that the listener hardly notices it.

Koussevitzky possessed an uncanny ear for instrumental color and balance, as demonstrated at the *poco tranquillo* four measures before E . Here, he gradually slackens the tempo, brings out the timpani on the down beat, and makes the timpani sound like a pizzicato string bass as the rest of the strings answer with perfectly matched dynamics.

Another good example of dramatic timing occurs one measure before N , where he inserts a ritardando in the brass and timpani, an effective preparation for the noble brass choir theme that starts five measures after N .

As a colorist Koussevitzky had the ability to match the timbre of different sections so they would sound like one instrument. Twelve measures after when the quarter-note melody starts in the trumpets and then transfers to solo horn and on to bassoon and flute, Koussevitzky makes it sound like one continuous line, perfectly matched in style and volume.

At Koussevitzky achieves a remarkable textural clarity of balance and duality of mood when Sibelius combines the perky theme of the woodwinds in $\frac{6}{4}$ meter against the cut-time passionate theme in the strings.

Koussevitzky had the inexplicable ability always to arrive convincingly at a sudden change of tempo. A good example of this occurs two measures before $\boxed{S}$ when the tempo is ♩. = 108 and suddenly changes to ♩. = 69 at $\boxed{S}$. Koussevitzky makes this sudden shift to a slower tempo to emphasize the *tenuto* characteristics of the melody.

In the last three measures Koussevitzky brings the movement to a close with a beautifully timed *poco rallentando* and *diminuendo* as he broadens the tenuto quarter notes that prepare the last D major chord in the strings to gently fade away.

At the close of these final measures I am reminded of the essay Koussevitzky wrote when he received an honorary doctorate from Harvard University in 1929:

> Good interpretation transforms the crowd into one level of receptivity...the mass into one single listener. A spiritual enrichment has taken place. For the interpreter, this is the highest reward, the highest step to which interpretation may ascend. (Ewen 15)

Commissions and Premieres by Serge Koussevitzky

Samuel Barber: Symphony #2, 3/3/44; Concerto for Cello and Orchestra, 4/5/46; *Knoxville, Summer of 1915*, 4/9/48.

Béla Bartók: Concerto for Orchestra, 12/1/44.

Leonard Bernstein: Symphony #2 *The Age of Anxiety*, 4/8/49.

Benjamin Britten: Spring Symphony, 8/13/49.

Aaron Copland: *Music for the Theatre*, 11/20/25; Concerto for Piano and Orchestra, 1/28/27; Symphony #3, 10/18/46.

David Diamond: Symphony #2, 10/11/44.

Lukas Foss: *The Prairie*, 5/15/44; *Song of Songs*, 3/7/47.

George Gershwin: Second Rhapsody, 1/29/32.

Howard Hanson: Symphony *#2 Romantic*, 11/28/30.

Roy Harris: Symphony #1, 1/26/34; Symphony # 2, 2/39; Symphony # 5, 2/26/43; Symphony # 6, 4/14/44.

Paul Hindemith: Concert Music, 4/3/31.

Arthur Honegger: P*acific 231*, 5/8/24; Concertino for Piano and Orchestra, 5/23/25.

Bohuslav Martinu: Concerto Grosso, 11/14/41; Symphony #1, 11/13/42.

Darius Milhaud: Symphony #2, 12/20/46.

Walter Piston: Symphonic Piece, 3/23/28; Third Symphony, 1/9/48.

Sergei Prokofiev: Concerto *#1* for Violin and Orchestra, 10/18/23; Symphony #4, 11/14/30; Symphony #5, 11/45.

Maurice Ravel: Mussorgsky's *Pictures at an Exhibition*, 10/19/22.

Ottorino Respighi: *Church Windows*, 2/25/27.

Albert Roussel: Suite in F Major for Orchestra, 1/21/27; Symphony #3, 10/24/30.

Arnold Schönberg: Theme and Variations, Op. 43-b, 10/20/44; *A Survivor from Warsaw*, 11/4/48.

William Schuman: *American Festival Overture*, 10/6/39; Symphony #3, 10/17/41; Symphony #5, 11/12/43.

Alexander Scriabin: *Prometheus Symphony*, 3/15/11.

Roger Sessions: Symphony #1, 4/22/27.

Dmitri Shostakovich: *Symphony #9*, 6/25/46.

Igor Stravinsky: Symphony of Psalms, 12/19/30; Ode, 10/8/43; Symphonies of Wind Instruments, 6/12/21.

Randall Thompson: *Alleluia* for mixed chorus, commissioned for opening of Tanglewood, 6/40.

CHAPTER 7

The Genius of Willem Mengelberg in a Classic Strauss Recording

One of my favorite summer activities is searching for rare books and old recordings at yard sales. One summer I found a 1928 recording of Richard Strauss's tone poem *Ein Heldenleben* (A Hero's Life) by the New York Philharmonic under Willem Mengelberg (1871–1951). This legendary performance set me back fifty cents and it is a magical performance by a virtuoso orchestra and marvelous conductor. I have long admired the greatness and passion of Mengelberg's interpretations with the famous Concertgebouw orchestra in Amsterdam, but this performance of *Ein Heldenleben* with the New York Philharmonic is one of the most aesthetically satisfying recordings I have ever heard.

The Fritz Reiner recording of *Ein Heldenleben* with the Chicago Symphony is among my favorite interpretations because of the great brass playing in the battle-music section. I enjoy the tender lyrical sections in the Royal Philharmonic recording under Sir Thomas Beecham. Sir Georg Solti's recording with the Vienna Philharmonic is vigorous and dramatic, and Toscanini gave careful attention to clarity and detail in the NBC Symphony recording. After many hours of comparative listening with score in hand, I find that the Mengelberg version surpasses all others and is the definitive interpretation. It has been reissued on compact disc by Mark Obert-Thorn on Pearl Records, and I encourage all conductors to study it and to learn the art of interpretation from a true maestro.

Mengelberg was one of the great virtuoso conductors of the early 20th century, and his legendary interpretations are rightly revered for their beauty, color, and passion. Harold C. Schonberg wrote in *The Great Conductors*:

> He was a conductor of extraordinary skill and drive, one who reveled in the big-sounding, complicated scores of Mahler and Strauss. The latter dedicated *Ein Heldenleben* to him, and it was commonly held that no conductor could get such excitement, brilliance, and drama from the score. Mengelberg left a recording that bears ample witness to such a statement. As a colorist he was exceeded by none, not even Koussevitzky. The little man was an authentic force, one of the great individualists, and one of the authentic masters of the orchestra. (Schonberg 269)

The virtuoso orchestra on this outstanding recording includes principal trumpet Harry Glantz who was in his prime when this recording was made in 1928; Bruno Jaenicke, whose beautiful horn tone sends chills up my spine; Saul Goodman on timpani; John Amans on flute; and concertmaster Scipione Guidi, whose violin solos are beautiful and expressive.

For this recording session in Carnegie Hall the orchestra consisted of 124 players, and the acoustics are superb despite the sounds of subway trains during violin solos and some engineering difficulties. According to Mark Obert-Thorn, "Not even the well-known deficiencies of the original recording can shake its place in the hearts of those who have come under its sway. It remains *sui generis*, the touchstone against which all subsequent performances have been measured." (Pearl)

Richard Strauss (1864–1949) composed *Ein Heldenleben* in 1898 at age 34 and conducted the first performance in Frankfurt, Germany the following year. In six sections this symphonic poem traces the life of the hero, and Strauss portrayed himself in this work. He stated, "I do not see why I should not compose a symphony about myself; I find myself quite as interesting as Napoleon or Alexander." Later he said, "There is no need for a program. It is enough to know there is a hero fighting his enemies." (RCA 1042) However, by quoting themes from his previous tone poems in the fifth section, Strauss identifies himself as the protagonist.

Other composers wrote musical autobiographies before Strauss, including Berlioz's *Symphonie Fantastique* (1830), Beethoven's Fifth Symphony (1808), and Schumann's *Carnaval*. Music critic Virgil Thomson described *Ein Heldenleben* as "hopeless banality and stuffy elaborateness and strutting self-satisfaction." (London)

However, this opinion of the music is the exception. The majority of musicians love to perform this work, and under the baton of Willem Mengelberg, the New York Philharmonic makes *Ein Heldenleben* a moving, poignant musical autobiography.

Strauss's self-portrait starts in E♭ major with the German directive *lebhaft bewegt*, lively and animated. Mengelberg interprets these directions at a tempo of ♩ = 120–126, and the opening measures evoke a perfect musical description of what a hero should be.

The principal theme is introduced by low horns in the sweeping E♭ major arpeggio found in the low horns and strings that spans over three octaves. As one of the best orchestrators who ever lived and one of the great conductors of his time, Strauss knew exactly what worked with an orchestra. This opening theme is a masterpiece of musical logic, and Strauss develops several motives from this theme in later sections of the work.

Mengelberg was a master of artistic preparation, and his controlled rubato surges forward, falls back, hesitates, and becomes passionate and free. After a fortissimo attack followed by a slight decrescendo on the opening half note, Mengelberg brings out the horn timbre as the dominant color. The crescendo on the ascending triplets on the third and fourth beats leads into the dotted half note. He lifts the ♩. ♪ and spaces the two accented half notes in measure 5 but holds the tempo back on the four descending quarter notes and adds a crescendo for dramatic effect. The eighth-note chords in measures 6, 8, 9, and 11 are carefully balanced, and each is held for full value, accented, and lifted with a ringing release. The first and second violins add excitement with a crescendo on the quarter notes on beats one and three.

One measure before ⬚1 Mengelberg brings out the quarter-note triplet in the low strings and horns and pushes the theme forward with a crescendo. For textual clarity at ⬚1, the accented 16th notes in the trumpet, first and second violins are brought out.

One measure after ⬚1 the horn enters on a B♭ and soars over the orchestra in counterpoint against the first and second violins.

At ⬚2 the dynamic level drops to *pp* with contrasting lyrical themes reminiscent of Wagner. Strauss considered himself the rightful heir to the Wagnerian tradition and often used leitmotifs and thematic transformations. The chromatic inflections and contrapuntal texture here are similar to those in the *Meistersinger* Overture. Strauss indicated the most important themes with *hervortretend* in his lyrical juxtaposition, which is a perfect example of orchestral balance and clarity.

Mengelberg prepares for the recapitulation of the hero's theme by adding a ritard two measures before it begins four measures before 12. A codetta based on the third measure of the opening theme follows eight measures before 13. The first section ends *fff* with a dramatic augmentation of the opening motive. Five measures before the end of the section Mengelberg brings out the syncopation in the low brass then changes the articulation to emphasize the final cadence. He removes the slur and the tie to the final beat and has the full orchestra accent and separate the final two notes for a stronger cadence.

Aldous Huxley wrote that "parodies and caricatures are the most penetrating of criticisms," and in the second section of this work Strauss describes his critics and enemies as petty, grotesque, cynical, and jealous. With brilliant orchestration and acerbic wit, Strauss creates some of the most descriptive musical parodies of critics. Mengelberg captures these grotesque caricatures in the passage that begins six measures before 14 at a tempo of ♩ = 76–80.

The flutes play short staccato 16ths in $\frac{3}{4}$ meter, and the oboe and piccolo enter in the same sarcastic style to evoke visions of backbiting gossip. Two measures before 14 the basses join the dialogue with a pompous phrase in parallel fifths.

Snarling brass enter fortissimo, and the overall effect is an uncanny musical depiction of small, critical people.

The hero returns eight measures before 16 with the melancholy theme in the cellos, brass, bass clarinet, and contra bassoon. This *molto espressivo* passage conveys the hero's disbelief that critics would have the audacity to attack him. At 19 the critics return, but this attack is shorter because the hero resolves to defeat all enemies. As the music accelerates and crescendos into a fortissimo victory theme, he triumphs over all adversaries.

In the third section of the tone poem one measure after 22 a solo violin depicts the hero's beloved, who is based on Strauss's wife. In the passionate portrayal, concertmaster Scipione Guidi begins on a piano high C♯ half note two measures after 22. After a gorgeous crescendo and decrescendo on the first note, Scipione plays the violin like a master storyteller, describing the beloved as playful, seductive, mysterious, angry, and finally yielding to the hero.

After several short cadenzas the solo violin gives way as the full orchestra enters at 32 with an overwhelming opulence reminiscent of Wagner's *Tristan and Isolde*. Mengelberg artfully used rubato and phrase leading as he romanticizes the music with expressive nuances and string portamento. The music finally subsides eight measures after 40, and the closing bars fade away *ppp* on a G♭ major chord. However, this calmness is short-lived because the critics return to disrupt the reverie. This time the hero stands alongside his wife and fights his enemies.

The fourth section of the tone poem, "The Hero's Battlefield," depicts the hero fighting the adversaries in some of the most exciting music ever written. A military trumpet fanfare in $\frac{3}{4}$ time announces the upcoming battle one measure before 42. At a tempo of ♩ = 160 the effect is brilliant and perfectly describes the onset of the war. The nine measures from 42 to 43 demonstrate the virtuosity of the New York Philharmonic trumpet section led by Harry Glantz. The passage is beautifully articulated, balanced, and phrased as if by one player.

After 43 Mengelberg brings out a syncopated version of the original melody, he slows the tempo for the theme of the beloved, then returns to ♩ = 160 with the trumpet fanfare. The orchestration is brilliant and balanced as the hero battles his enemies with encouragement from his beloved.

Five measures after 49 Mengelberg slows the tempo to ♩ = 144 and brings out the percussion part. Strauss develops themes and reunites them for the climax of the battle, signaling the triumph with the *fff* return of the hero's theme. Glantz's finest hour is the soaring shift from F^5 to a fortissimo D^6, which this recording captures for all to study and appreciate. Three measures before 77 Mengelberg adds a ritard not indicated in the score for a strong transition to the recapitulation of the hero motive at the original tempo.

In the fifth section the musical quotations from earlier Strauss works underscore that Strauss himself is the hero of this tone poem. Mengelberg sets an uplifting tempo of ♩ = 132 for the trumpet entrance in this cheerful section. In this musical journey the quotes from previous compositions – *Don Juan, Death and Transfiguration, Till Eulenspiegel, Also Sprach Zarathustra*, and *Don Quixote*— are used as an integral counterpoint to the complete composition rather than as extraneous quotations. Under Mengelberg's direction these themes are perfectly balanced with the main theme of *Ein Heldenleben*, an ingenious combination that is brilliant and beautiful.

The final section of the tone poem depicts the hero's release from the world with slow horn eighth-notes before the violins signify the hero's release with a combination and expansion of the beloved theme. Once again the critics interrupt the tranquility, but at [106] the beloved theme in the solo violin returns to the serene mood. The final measures of the composition are a lovely duet between the solo violin and solo horn that depict the hero's spiritual triumph in a moment of poignant beauty. He departs with a blaze of majestic orchestral color as Strauss quotes the sunrise theme from *Also Sprach Zarathustra* before the work fades away to silence.

I encourage conductors to study the musicality, flexibility, and compelling emotions Willem Mengelberg brings to this great work. The genius of Mengelberg has never been fully appreciated, but he proves here that he was one of the greatest conductors, whose artistry will inspire all who take the time to study his performances with an open mind and heart. ✍

CHAPTER 8

Lessons in Interpretation from Bruno Walter

If a conductor's personality is unable to fulfill the spiritual demands of the works he conducts, his interpretations will remain unsatisfactory, although their musical execution may be exemplary. —Bruno Walter

In the quest for technically perfect performances many directors concentrate on fixing problems and rarely focus on the musical interpretation. Surely most directors enter the profession with the clear purpose of interpreting music, rather than becoming musical mechanics, but deficiencies in musical interpretation are the single greatest problem with performances today.

Gustav Mahler said, "What is best in music is not found in the notes." The great conductors make the leap from notes to interpretation. The generation that followed Mahler included Bruno Walter, Arturo Toscanini, Wilhelm Furtwängler, George Szell, Fritz Reiner, Guido Cantelli, and Herbert von Karajan. The recordings they left stimulate the musical imagination. Directors today can listen to these recordings while making notes on the score that will improve their interpretive skills.

Over the years I have frequently returned to Bruno Walter's probing of the depths of Mozart's music, and his work is truly a seminar on the art of interpretation. Walter's death in 1962 at the age of 85 was the end of an era. He had been a professional conductor for nearly 70 years and was the last link to a romantic school of conducting that included Nikisch, Mahler, Strauss, Mengelberg, and Furtwängler. In Vienna from 1901–1907 Mahler was a mentor to Walter, and Walter extolled Mahler as "the greatest performing musician I have ever met, without exception. Mahler taught me how to work and what to work for." It was from Mahler that Walter discovered the spiritual depths of Mozart. He wrote:

> As a teenager I was enthusiastic for the great pathos and the big emotions, and Mozart seemed to me at that time too quiet, too tranquil. Youth is much more apt to love the shout and the great gestures. It needs some maturity to understand the depth of emotion that speaks in Mozart's seeming tranquility…. Through Mahler's efforts I saw Mozart in a new light. It requires maturity to approach Mozart. I was 50 before I conducted the G minor Symphony…. (Columbia DSL)

Walter wrote that the key to Mozart's personality is found in his last letters to his father reflecting Mozart's preoccupation with death and religious feelings. Walter cites a passage Mozart wrote at age 31:

© *The Instrumentalist*, March 1993. Reprinted with Permission.

> Never do I go to bed without thinking that, young as I am, I may not see the dawn…Since it is the true end and aim of our lives, I have for the last two years worked toward an intimacy with death, mankind's best and truest friend, so that he holds for me no terror, but only tranquility and comfort. (Walter 199)

Columbia issued a recording of Walter's rehearsal of Mozart's Symphony No. 36 in C major, the *Linz* (Columbia DSL), and this gives listeners an example of music making at the highest level. Walter once said, "We can live on with our best efforts," and these recordings are eloquent testimony to his understanding of and love for Mozart's music, while demonstrating how a great conductor goes behind the notes to recreate the miracle of Mozart.

For the Adagio in the first movement Walter conducted a subdivided three at ♪ = 72. At the outset he asked for precise execution of the eighth and thirty-second note rhythms in the first measures. "Gentleman, your eighth notes are too long, and the thirty-seconds must be shorter. You must be able to say 'off' after the eighth-note release for the proper spacing." (Columbia DSL) In the fourth measure he cautioned the second violins not to accent the entrance but to think of musical lines. He asked the second violins to add a diminuendo in measure seven so the sixteenths in the first violins are audible.

Walter sought a more ringing sound and a slight crescendo on the *f* eighth-note chords in measure 8. "In Vienna we called this the accent after the note." Insisting on more of a singing quality in the eighth-note lyrical passage in the woodwinds and strings in measures 8–10, he demonstrated by singing the result he sought.

In the Allegro spiritoso section Walter conducted in two at ♩ = 96–100, admonishing the orchestra to search for the true character of Mozart in the rhythm, melody, and phrase. He tells the players, "There are puzzles to be solved in every bar, much like different characters running across the stage in an opera." To Walter each musical line and rhythm had a different character: going beyond the notes to character helps unlock the interpretation. Walter had the celli and bass establish a firm rhythm with the quarter notes to start the allegro, insisting at the same time on a true piano in the first violins with absolutely no space between the E and F whole notes to create a lyrical musical line. He told the orchestra "it is not a march here. It must sing and be lyrical."

In measure 33 Walter insisted on long quarter notes for the chords. His careful observations of durations established the correct style. In measure 68 he asked the first violins to accent the sixteenth-note F♯ slightly so it would not be lost in the texture.

Walter insisted that players match dynamics so the string entrances sounded like one instrument in measures 105–108.

In his quest for continuity Walter warned first violins against accenting the two-note phrase in measures 119–120 while building to the half note in measure 122, leaning on it before ending the phrase with a decrescendo to make a beautiful arc.

Walter asked for expressive rather than rhythmic syncopation in measure 144, with tenuto quarter notes.

In the recapitulation Walter reminded the orchestra of the melody's character, asking that they play the notes long, lyrically, and *cantare*.

For the final seven measures of the movement Walter asked the strings for precise rhythm, especially bringing out the 32nd notes. The first violins conclude the movement with ringing C major chords.

It is sometimes said that the true merit of a composer is heard in his slow movements because these reflect his spirituality. Perhaps more than any other conductor, Walter brought Mozart's slow movements to life with a poignant, lyrical eloquence that was contemplative, serene, and expressive. In the *Linz Symphony* Walter showed his interpretive genius in the Poco Adagio.

For the second movement Walter again asked the violins to heed the opening rhythm. The second violins should hear the sixteenth notes the first violins play in measure 2 before entering on beat six.

To solve the balance problem between the first and second violins, Walter began with an equal duet between the violin sections, with the seconds reducing volume to accompany the firsts in measure two. Next Walter asked the first violins to begin the movement up-bow for a singing quality. Insisting again on a beautiful arc in the melody, he used this articulation: ⌐⌐ ⸰.

He brought out the thirty-seconds in measure 4 with a slight crescendo, adding a breath pause after the two gently lifted G upbeats in the horns. Walter interpreted the *fp* in measure 5 as a phrase accent, $f > p$ instead of an accent followed immediately by *p*.

In measure 11 Walter cautioned the winds against entering with an accent, having them instead crescendo into the tone. In the next measure he tapered the phrase with a slight decrescendo, lifting on each note without staccato. A slight rubato in the triplet figure and a crescendo gave the triplets of the theme a sense of forward motion.

As in measure 4 Walter again leaned on the eighth note D in measure 15 and rehearsed the winds on the quarter note to assure the exact value was two eighths for a clean release before the first violin entrance on the sixth beat. He asked the first violins to start up-bow in measure 18 to assure starting at piano before reaching the climax in measure 19.

Walter substituted long notes in the bassoon for the staccato notations in measure 46 to match the style of the celli. Staccato markings in Mozart can be confusing because he used both a wedge marking ▾▾▾ to designate the shortened notes of today's standard staccato marks and dots ꜛꜛꜛ usually to indicate full value but with a lifted style, which is the interpretation Walter followed in the second movement.

Walter concluded the Adagio with a slight ritard and broadening of the last four notes, bringing the movement to a gentle close.

A study of Walter's rehearsal comments and nuances can be a concentrated lesson in interpretation for conductors. Emulate Walter by searching for the essential character of melodies, rhythms, and phrases. It is apparent that Walter carefully observed rhythms to establish a good style matching dynamics so different instruments sound like one. He experimented with bowings, articulations, and dynamics to achieve the desired musical effect. Walter brought out the 16th and 32nd notes enough for them to be audible. On *f* chords he added a slight crescendo after the attack to achieve the Vienna effect. Instead of using the sudden *fp* in practice today, directors might try using a *f* ≻ *p* in slow movements.

Walter did not avoid displaying emotion, and neither should conductors today. Think of the sustained musical line, underplaying or eliminating accents that interrupt it. Respect the arc of a musical phrase with its rise and fall; lean on certain notes in a phrase to bring out the climax. Even with large ensembles, work for chamber-music clarity and expressive nuance.

Research the letters, books, and compositions of a composer for clues to the personality and interpretation of his music. Walter never exaggerated nuances but used them with immaculate taste and a knowledge based on a lifetime of studying Mozart's music. For Bruno Walter, Mozart became more than a pow-dered-wig composer who wrote in the age of snuffbox royalty, and Walter's interpretations continue to inspire listeners and set an example for conductors today.

CHAPTER 9

Leopold Stokowski Explores Debussy's Orchestral Colors

Many people first heard classical music while sitting in a dark theater as they watched the larger-than-life image of Leopold Stokowski (1882–1977) projected on the screen for the movie *Fantasia* step onto the podium and give a dramatic downbeat to Bach's *Toccata and Fugue in D Minor*. This magical movie also included music of Beethoven, Dukas, Mussorgsky, and Stravinsky with Walt Disney animation. Since seeing Stokowski in this movie during my childhood, I have been in awe of his interpretations. He was the conductor who unleashed my creativity and my love of music.

Leopold Stokowski was born in London on April 18, 1882 to a Polish cabinetmaker and his Irish wife. The name on his birth certificate is Leopold Stokowski, not Leo Stokes, as is often claimed. (Daniel 5) Although the family was poor, Stokowski received an excellent education and was the youngest student to enter the Royal College of Music. He was an organ student at age 13, and in 1903 graduated from Queen's College in Oxford. He was appointed organist and choirmaster at St. Bartholomew's Church in New York City in 1905.

Stokowski's professional conducting career began in 1909 with a three-year appointment by the Cincinnati Orchestra. In 1912 he became music director of the Philadelphia Orchestra, a union that led the ensemble and Leopold Stokowski to legendary sounds and reputation. When Rachmaninoff heard the Philadelphia Orchestra under Stokowski, he said, "I don't know that I would be exaggerating if I said that it is the finest orchestra the world has ever known." (Daniel 500)

A major contribution to the Philadelphia sound and balance was Stokowski's experimentation with the seating arrangements of the orchestra. Stokowski believed that "tradition is laziness. If something isn't right, we must change it. Why should we continue to seat an orchestra just as it was done a century ago? It was formulated and frozen long before instruments had been improved, changed, and invented." (Chasins 77)

Stokowski was the first conductor to investigate the traditional seating of the orchestra since the time of Haydn (1732–1809). He experimented to find the optimum sound and balance. The result was the famous Stokowski sound. Even the *Philadelphia Bulletin* reviewed his seating ideas: "There can hardly be any doubt that this new arrangement is acoustically logical. Those instruments which stand in most need of reflective reinforcement get it, and those that need it least are out front where the power and reflection are less intense." (Opperby 126)

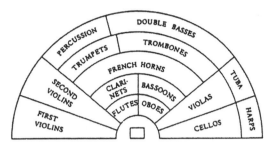

Stokowski's revised seating, from 1921.

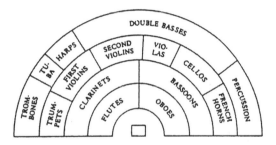

The upside-down orchestra, from 1939.

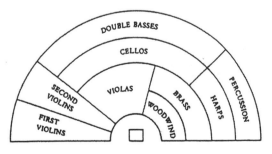

Stokowski's later seating arrangement.

Stokowski vehemently disagreed with the tradition of uniform bowing in the string section, even though its purpose was to produce even phrasing and precision. However, Stokowski believed such precision was too mechanical and disrupted the musical line: "Mechanism as one part of life is wonderful in an automobile or airplane, but not in art, which requires flexible pulsation." (Chasins 79) He was frustrated that the strings often failed to produce a seamless musical line because they changed bowing at the same time, and had them change bow strokes at different times so the musical line flowed without any break. Stokowski used this technique, called *bogen frei* (free bowing) with every orchestra he conducted which produced some of the most expressive *bel canto* string performances ever recorded.

Stokowski sought the same effect with the winds so the music would not stop when they took a breath at the end of a phrase. Stokowski introduced the concept of staggered breathing to the Philadelphia Orchestra and hired extra players so no one had to take a breath at the same time. The result was a continuous musical line.

In his 1943 book, *Music for All of Us*, Stokowski wrote, "Conducting is only to a small extent the beating of time; still more it is done through a kind of inner communication between player and conductor." (Smith 82) Stokowski often improvised and conducted without a baton, which encouraged the musicians to watch him carefully and be *noten frei* (free of the notes). Stokowski abandoned batons after he broke one during a concert in the 1929–30 season and discovered that he had greater freedom in using only his bands. In the February 1955 issue of *Musical America* Fritz Reiner stated, "Baton or no baton? I question the importance of the subject raised. In the last analysis only the musical results mean something." No one can say that Leopold Stokowski didn't get fantastic musical results with his ensembles without a baton.

Stokowski had an uncanny ability to mix and match the many different colors of an orchestra as he saw and defined music in colors. Stokowski described it as, "Each note of a scale is a different color tone: F♯ is a golden brown; G is a sticky blue. A♭ a dark rich brown, A♮ a brilliant red, C♮ a creamy white, and so on." (Opperby 132) According to bassoonist Sol Schoenbach, Stokowski thought of the orchestra as a palette of colors. "He was just like a painter who decides he wants to put a little red here, a little blue here, and he would do this right on the spot." (Daniel 301) For Stokowski there were strong parallels between painting and music, and he would often compare the music of Tchaikovsky and the paintings of Van Gogh. He said these two had "the same vivid coloring and almost pathological intensity of emotional expression." (Daniel 302) When Schoenbach played the opening bassoon solo of "*The Rite of Spring*" for the *Fantasia* soundtrack, Stokowski asked him to try many different reeds. Schoenbach played the passage over 40 times before Stokowski was satisfied with the color. (Daniel 302)

In my opinion Stokowski's greatest interpretations are the works of French Impressionistic composer Claude Debussy (1862–1918), who was a great innovator and orchestral colorist. The evocative moods, rich colors, and shimmering rays of light floating over iridescent harmonies in the *Prelude to the Afternoon of a Faun* were in part brought to life by Stokowski and flutist Julius Baker; for me this performance is the quintessential example of orchestra painting. Originally released on Capitol record SP8399 in 1957, this imaginative and creative interpretation is now on compact disc (EMI Classic 65614).

Prelude to the Afternoon of A Faun was inspired by the poem *L'Apres-midi d'un faune* by French Symbolist poet Stephen Mallarmé (1842–1898); Debussy intended to compose a suite of three pieces but between 1892 and 1894 composed only the *Prelude.* The poem is 110 lines and Debussy's *Prelude* is 110 measures in length. There is a good English translation of the poem by Aldous Huxley in *An Anthology to World Poetry,* edited by Mark Van Doren. The faun, a mythical creature that is half man and half goat, wakes at dawn in the forest and tries to recall a memory of nymphs and if they were real or part of a dream, but his memory of the nymphs grows fainter and becomes confused with swans swimming in a pool or with a garden of lilies. The harder the faun tries to remember, the more its memory fades. It basks in the sunlight on the soft grass, drinks wine, and sleeps. (Van Doren 777) Like the poetry of Mallarmé, Debussy's music evokes the impressions of the faun as it tries to recall his memory through an evanescent, suggestive, and dreamy atmosphere.

The *Prelude* opens with an exposed C# and the flutist establishes a dreamy interpretation with subtle rising and falling of the chromatic motive, which is one of the most famous flute solos in orchestral repertoire. This is a classic example of when the conductor would stay out of the way and follow the soloist. Stokowski understood that creative musicians should be given leeway. In the video *The Art of Conducting,* Stokowski explains how the musicians in his orchestra gained spontaneity and freedom under his direction. "Whenever musicians have a solo, I don't conduct them. I listen to how they phrase, their tempo, and then I follow them." This is good advice for all conductors.

The *Prelude* has no tempo indication, only the French directive, *Tres modere, doux et expressif* and a dynamic of piano. Stokowski's tempo choice for the flute solo is a deliberate ♪ = 76–80 for a sweet and expressive mood. On the recording the beauty of Julius Baker's flute tone opens up a world of impressionistic color; he enters softly on the C♯ and adds a slight crescendo to start the phrase. The phrase is then beautifully shaped as Baker plays the first three measures in one breath and adds a crescendo and decrescendo in each measure. In the third measure he puts a decrescendo on the dotted quarter note and adds a subtle break in measure four after the first B eighth note. Then he reenters and adds a ritardando on the B and C♯ eighth notes with a gentle lift before resolving to the A♯ that tapers off to silence. Within four measures Baker gives a master class on how to perform the solo.

Stokowski begins conducting in the fourth measure for the entrance of the half-diminished chord in the oboe, clarinet, and harp on beat four and then brings in the horn on beat five at a tempo of ♪ = 66; he gives these different colors prominence in the piece. For example, in measures 4–8, Stokowski seems to paint in sound as he makes each timbre stand out with wonderful textural clarity.

Another example of matching colors occurs in measures 49–58 as Stokowski juxtaposes timbres and harmonies. The horn rides above the chromatic movement of the ascending strings at the ritardando at measure 51 then blends into the harp and flute line.

At tempo of ♪ = 76 at measure 51, the clarinet sounds sweet and expressive, a mood that is enhanced by the flutes entering on an A♭ major triad. In measures 51–55 Stokowski also brings out the harmonic colors as the music modulates. Each measure has nuances of color, just as an impressionistic painting captures the changes of light and colors of the early morning hours. In measure 53 the oboe joins the clarinet and the flute enters a measure later. As the music changes into the key of D♭ major, Stokowski conducts a perfectly timed ritardando.

The B section begins at measure 55, and the tempo shifts to ♪ = 80–84. Stokowski sustains the sound by having the winds play in one breath while the strings play legato; in this diatonic harmonic underpinning the measures come alive. Denis Vaughan, who played string bass under Stokowski in the Royal Philharmonic, explained the effectiveness of this foundation.

> We did *L'Apres-midi* and he [Stokowski] said, 'Gentlemen, you know I heard Debussy play the piano, and he did things with the pedal which I've heard no other composer and no other pianist do.' He proceeded then to prolong quite a number of bass notes beyond the written length in order to get the pedal effects Debussy had written. As I was playing the double bass it touched on me. It was very original and effective too. I knew then that he was a master of sound as such there have been few if any at all. (Daniel 551)

Stokowski was a master of rubato, and he had an amazing ability to tease a tempo without breaking the musical line. One of the most perceptive statements about tempo came not from another conductor, but from playwright George Bernard Shaw:

> A conductor who takes the time from the metronome and gives it to the music is, for all conducting purposes, a public nuisance; a conductor who takes the time from the music and gives it to the band is, if he takes and gives it rightly, a good conductor. (Schonberg 181)

In measure 61 the flexibility of Stokowski's rubato is almost rhapsodic as he stretches the triplet over the third beat and puts an accelerando on the sixteenth note triplet. He adds a ritardando on the third beat for a smooth transition into measure 63.

Stokowski conducts one of the most beautiful sections of the composition beginning at measure 63. With a tempo of ♪ = 84, Stokowski disregards the *pp* markings and lets the tutti orchestra sing out and dazzle listeners with color. This section reminds me of a Vincent Van Gogh landscape flooded with sunlight; the strings sing out the melody fully as the wind triplets enhance the expression with flashes of light.

measures 63-65

One of the great contrasts in the piece occurs in measure 82–83 as the music modulates from the lyrical melody of E major ♪ = 84 to a grotesque diminution of the original flute theme played by the oboe in C major ♪ = 116. Here Stokowski emphasizes the dry quality of the oboe staccato that adds humor to the music and contrasts the lush lyrical section.

With a molto ritardando five measures from the end, Stokowski transcends the written notes, and demonstrates his exceptional ear for color and tempo. He conducts the chromatic reminiscences of the harp in a slow ♪ = 52 and places a slight hesitation between the seventh and eighth beats in measure 106 with wonderful timing.

Measure 107 is conducted in a subtle $\frac{12}{8}$ subdivision. Stokowski's tempo slows down to ♪ = 50 to balance the muted horns and violins with a slight crescendo on the sixteenth. In measure 108 he blends the flute colors and brings in the antique cymbals on the first beat and the harp on the second and fourth beats as he conducts in a very slow four. In measure 109 he continues using four slow beats to bring out the antique cymbal color on the first and third beats and the cellos and basses on the pizzicato eighth notes.

In the last measure Stokowski adds a curious nuance that is not in the score; the ensemble stops on beat one as Debussy intended, but Stokowski then prolongs the sound of the flutes for four more beats and decrescendos into silence. Perhaps Stokowski wished to convey that the faun fell asleep again in Mallarmé's poem. The prolonging of the flutes creates an impressionistic atmosphere and bring the *Prelude* to a beautiful close.

Stokowski remained active as a conductor until his death at age 95 on September 13, 1977. He had planned to record Rachmaninoff's Second Symphony on that day. Stokowski was an original musician with an insatiable curiosity for music. From his 70 years of conducting, he left us a valuable legacy of recordings to appreciate, love, and study. Stokowski had the rare ability to convince audiences that music is a living entity with colors and emotions to discover. ⟳

CHAPTER 10

Lessons from Otto Klemperer

For in much wisdom is much grief; and he that increaseth knowledge increaseth grief. (Ecclesiastes)

Otto Klemperer's parents recognized his musical talent when, at the age of eight, he could name all the notes being played by the clarinet in a military band. Klemperer was born in Breslau, Germany on May 14, 1885; his mother, a professional pianist, gave music lessons, and his father, a "wretched businessman with a small income," loved to sing the classic art songs by ear. Klemperer's first musical memory was of his father singing Schumann's *Dichterliebe* accompanied by his mother on piano. (Heyworth 22)

With early musical training from his mother, Klemperer was talented enough to enter the Hochschule für Musik in Frankfurt and later studied at the Berlin Conservatory, where he practiced piano eight hours a day and studied composition and conducting under Hans Pfitzner. After graduation Klemperer worked as a pianist and accompanist for several years before deciding to become a conductor. In 1910 he was selected to be Gustav Mahler's assistant for the Munich premiere of Mahler's Eighth Symphony. Impressed with the phenomenal conducting genius of Mahler, Klemperer considered Mahler to be 100 times greater than Toscanini. "When he [Mahler] conducted, you felt it couldn't be better and couldn't be otherwise." (Heyworth 31)

Mahler, in turn, was impressed with Klemperer and later wrote a recommendation for him. As a protégé of Mahler, the conducting doors of Germany opened for Klemperer. He became music director of the Cologne and Kroll opera theaters where he gave noted first performances of contemporary operas by Stravinsky, Krenek, Hindemith, Schönberg, and others.

Unfortunately, after such an auspicious beginning Klemperer suffered many mental and physical misfortunes. While conducting a 1933 rehearsal with the Leipzig Orchestra, he fell off the podium and hit his head. After this accident he had intense headaches, and his health was never strong again. The Nazi party came to power that year, and they forced the Jewish Klemperer to resign his conducting posts. In September 1933 he was appointed conductor of the Los Angeles Philharmonic, succeeding Artur Rodzinski who had moved to Cleveland. While in America Klemperer also conducted the New York, Pittsburgh, and Philadelphia orchestras. Tragedy struck again when Klemperer was diagnosed with a brain tumor in 1939 and had to give up his post with the Los Angeles Philharmonic.

© *The Instrumentalist*, October 1998. Reprinted with Permission.

Among the great 20th-century conductors none experienced more physical or mental grief than Klemperer. His life was one of indomitable courage, spiritual strength, and stoic endurance. This gifted musician suffered almost every calamity possible: manic-depression, brain concussion, a brain tumor operation that left him partially paralyzed on the right side of his body and transformed his face into a permanent scowl, meningitis, strokes, severe burns, deafness in one ear, kidney failure, prostate cancer, and a host of other afflictions that would have killed most men. In spite of all these misfortunes Klemperer never gave up. This 6'4" giant of a man had an iron will and gave the world brilliant interpretations of Beethoven, Bruckner, Wagner, and Mahler until his death at age 88. Through his suffering Klemperer exemplified the deep, spiritual significance of music. We can be ever thankful for his wonderful musical interpretations. According to Galkin:

> In the final analysis a conductor is more than a performer or an interpreter; by his musicianship, his insightful convictions, and the fervency of his power of persuasion projected to both orchestra and audience, he is transformed into an artistic catalyst. Poignant examples, such as Otto Klemperer in his last years, half-paralyzed, capable of making only rudimentary time-beating gestures, yet producing majestic readings of masterpieces…confirm our understanding of conducting as a force ever striving, ever spiritualizing. (Galkin 774)

Ludwig van Beethoven (1770–1827) also suffered many misfortunes. At the age of 31 Beethoven became painfully aware of failing hearing, and his impending deafness became a psychological, artistic, and spiritual turning point in his life. Believing that his career as a performing musician was over, Beethoven plunged into severe depression and contemplated suicide. In a letter to his brothers intended to be read after his death, Beethoven pours out his soul in one of the most moving, eloquent, and tragic testaments ever written. Known today as the famous "Heiligenstadt Testament," the letter was written in the village of Heiligenstadt, located outside Vienna, in the autumn of 1802:

> What a humiliation for me when someone standing next to me heard a flute in the distance and I heard nothing, or someone heard a shepherd singing and again I heard nothing. Such incidents drove me almost to despair, a little more of that and I would have ended my life—it was only my art that held me back. Ah, it seemed impossible to leave the world until I have brought forth all that I felt was within me. And so I cleave to this distressful life—a life so truly miserable that any sudden change is capable of throwing me out of the happiest condition of man into the worst. (Schmidt-Gorg 21)

As his deafness became worse, Beethoven disregarded what went on around him and turned inward to a world of silent genius. Somehow his sheer strength of will and character prevailed: "I will take Fate by the throat. My infirmity shall not get me down."

In a wild burst of creative energy Beethoven left Heiligenstadt for Vienna, where he composed some of his greatest works. One masterpiece that resulted from this spiritual struggle was the Symphony #3 in E♭ Major, which some musicians contend is the greatest symphony ever written. Finished in 1804, it breaks from the traditional musical style of the time and is as far removed from the symphonies of Haydn and Mozart as Stravinsky is from Tchaikovsky.

Because Beethoven greatly admired Napoleon and saw in him the same revolutionary idealism Beethoven had within himself, he originally wrote "Bonaparte" on the title page of the score. When Napoleon proclaimed himself to be Emperor, Beethoven flew into a rage. "Is he [Napoleon] then nothing more than an ordinary human being? Now he, too, will trample on all the rights of man and indulge only his own ambitions. He will exalt himself above all others and become a greater tyrant than anyone." (*World of Music* 135)

Beethoven scratched out the original title so violently that he made a hole in the paper. This page can be seen today at the Gesellschaft der Musikfreunde in Vienna. The work became *Sinfonie Eroica*, or Heroic Symphony, "composed to celebrate the memory of a great man" and was dedicated to Prince Lobkowitz. Beethoven conducted its first public performance on April 7, 1805 at the Vienna Theatre. The *Eroica* Symphony is heroic in every sense of the word because it depicts human greatness and heroic endurance. In retrospect many people believe that Beethoven's suffering marks the symphony with universality and spirituality.

I have seven recordings of the *Eroica* Symphony by noted conductors, and I love them all for different reasons: Toscanini's drive and x-ray clarity; Bruno Walter's nobility; Furtwängler warmth; Stokowski's colors; Reiner's drama; Koussevitzky's passion. However, Klemperer's 1961 recording on Angel (S35835) is the one I find revelatory because he captures Beethoven's majestic architecture, especially in the finale. Although Klemperer was 76 years old, in constant pain, walked with the aid of a cane, and had to be helped to the podium where he sat because he was unable to stand, this recording is an interpretation with unparalled authority, authenticity, and humanity.

Beethoven based the finale of the Eroica Symphony on a theme that he had used previously, both in his ballet *The Creatures of Prometheus*, and in *Fifteen Variations and a Fugue on an Original Theme* (for piano), Op. 35. Apparently the legend of Prometheus had strong appeal to Beethoven because it represented the triumph of the human spirit over the fate of the gods as Prometheus stole fire from heaven and gave it to man. Many people believe Beethoven, whether intentionally or subconsciously, used this theme as the symbol of his struggle against deafness. Perhaps it is closer to the truth to say Beethoven used this theme because it adapted well to the theme and variation form.

In E♭ major and $\frac{2}{4}$ meter the Allegro Molto finale begins with a brilliant, *ff* sixteenth-note string passage.

Measures 1-3

Klemperer conducts ♩ = 120 and treats this introduction almost as a cadenza, inserting a slight ritard to broaden and lift the quarter notes that come to rest on the V⁷ fermata. Throughout this movement Klemperer frequently varies the tempo in ways not indicated in the score, but these rhythmic digressions are never abrupt and always musical.

The strings introduce the Prometheus theme with pizzicato at a piano dynamic in measure 12; Klemperer's tempo is ♩ = 112. It is amazing that Beethoven creates an entire movement from this eight-measure theme, a study in simplicity itself.

Measures 12-19

When the theme repeats in measure 20 Klemperer achieves a beautiful echo effect as the woodwinds imitate the volume and style of the strings on the beat before. In measure 29 Klemperer broadens the three *ff* eighth notes with a slight ritard, but in measure 31 he does not release the 𝄐♪ but ties it to the following eighth 𝄐♪; he treats the 𝄐 fermata in the measure 39 the same way.

The second violins, marked *dolce*, play the first variation of the theme, which appears augmented in measure 44 and leads to a controversial fermata in measure 55. Some editions of the score have the fermata over the quarter note E♭ going to the D eighth note, and a few conductors compromise by putting equal stress on both notes. However, it is generally accepted that the fermata should be over the D eighth note, which Klemperer observes.

In the second variation of the theme (measure 60) the violins state the melody in augmentation, again marked *dolce*, but Klemperer also brings out the triplets in the strings. The balance is so good here that it sounds like a string quartet.

The tempo of ♩ = 116 in measure 76 brings out the principal melody played by the oboe (marked *dolce*). Accompanied by the clarinet and bassoon, the oboe melody should dominate, but frequently the clarinet harmony is too loud.

The transition to the upcoming fugato section, measures 107–116, is often rushed and the entrances to the fugal section are unclear. Klemperer solves this problem by inserting a slight ritard on the quarter-note cadence in measures 115 and 116.

From measures 117 to 175 Klemperer demonstrates an impeccable understanding of musical structure as each entrance of the fugal section is crystal clear at a tempo of ♩ = 112. Of the many marvels within this interpretation, Klemperer's handling of this richly textured fugal section is most outstanding. Through careful balance and matching articulations, the musical architecture of a complex and difficult section becomes obvious.

Another example of textural clarity occurs in measures 191 to 198, where the difficult flute solo should match the style of the violins in answer to their rapid sixteenth notes in measures 183–190. At a tempo of ♩ = 116 Klemperer gives the flute enough time to make this passage sound musical and charming instead of like an exercise in double tonguing.

Measures 191-198

In measure 211 the music modulates to G minor, as cello and bass play the Prometheus theme in half notes. The music takes on a Hungarian march flavor as Klemperer gives the ♪⃜ notes in the woodwinds and first violins full value. When the music changes from G minor to C major in measure 256, Klemperer achieves a smooth modulation with a slight ritard and lift on the G half note played by the horns. The principal melodic theme, now in the flutes and first violins, is finally established in C major as Klemperer leans on the eighth note pickup to the ♩. with a slight crescendo ⌐⌐

The oboe picks up the Prometheus theme in measure 266, but when the second violin enters beneath the oboe the principal melody hints at C minor. Klemperer interprets this melody as a four-measure phrase with a crescendo for the first two measures and a decrescendo for the last two.

Measures 266-269

When the melody passes to the violas in measures 270–273 and to the cellos and basses in measures 274–277, he treats it the same way.

From measures 277 to 348 there is a fugal development beginning in C minor. A slight accent and lift to each half-note entrance as it passes from voice to voice brings out the Prometheus motive. On top of this motive Klemperer brings out the principal melodic theme in the flutes in measures 292 to 296, the horns in measures 303 to 307, and the oboe in measures 335 to 337.

Klemperer inserts a crescendo from measures 335 to 337 in all parts, puts a ritard in the syncopated strings in measures 344 to 345, and brings out the sixteenth-note runs in the cellos and basses in measures 346 to 347. The cadence in measure 348 is emphasized by bringing out the trumpet and timpani on the sixteenth-note pickup leading to the fermata.

Klemperer conducts the abrupt mood change in $\frac{4}{8}$ and *molto espressivo* at the Poco Andante. Although Beethoven marked the tempo at ♪ = 108, many conductors believe this is too fast and take the section at ♪ = 80 to 84. Klemperer begins at an even slower tempo of ♪ = 66. The melody, based on the principal melodic theme first heard in measure 76, now appears in augmentation and takes on a profundity, tenderness, and romantic drama and grandeur that is quite over-whelming. Klemperer's curious phrasing here is different from every other inter-pretation I have heard: on the oboe pickup in measure 348 he inserts a *luftpause,* and in measure 350 he break the slur by phrasing after the third beat and using the fourth beat as a pickup to measure 351. He does the same thing in mea-sures 352 to 353. This phrasing may have its roots in the Romantic tradition of Gustav Mahler because Klemperer believed that the most important thing for a conductor is to let the music breathe. On first hearing I thought the breaking of the phrase line in measure 350 caused the music to sound disjointed, but after repeated hearings I have decided the slow tempo causes the music to stand out in bold relief.

In measure 358 Klemperer puts a crescendo under the ascending line in the clarinet and also inserts a *subito piano* on the downbeat of measure 359, which he does again with the oboe answer in measures 360 to 361. In measures 362 to 363 he leans on the eighth notes and phrases this passage in the following manner:

When the principal melodic theme returns in measure 365 Klemperer gradu-ally increases the tempo to ♪ = 84 to add life to the rhythm in the violins and oboe and to bring out the sixteenth-note triplet in the clarinet. After a crescendo-decrescendo, in the strings and a slight ritard in measure 372, Klemperer returns to a tempo of ♪ = 84 in measure 373 and brings out the syncopated melody in the first oboe and first clarinet.

In measure 380 Klemperer crescendos the sixteenth-note string triplet and inserts a slight ritard before the majestic entrance of the horns, clarinets, bas-soon, cellos , and basses. The horns are the dominant color as he broadens the theme and puts a crescendo on the sixteenth-note triplet in the strings.

For added drama he brings out the timpani and trumpet in measure 381 on the eighth-note entrance. For the climax of this majestic section Klemperer has the horns crescendo in measures 392 to 393.

The coda in E♭ major begins in measure 396, and Klemperer reduces the dynamic to piano and brings out the horns in measure 401 on the sixteenth-note triplets. In measure 474 he increases the tempo to ♪ = 80 and matches the dynamics of the woodwinds and strings. A decrescendo and ritard prepare the Presto section, which Beethoven marked ♩ = 116. Klemperer, however, takes this Presto on the slow side at ♩ = 92–96, which brings out the heroic quality of the horns and bassoon on their ♩♩ melody in measures 435 to 438.

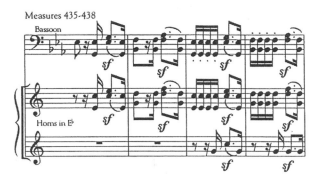

The sixteenth-note timpani rhythm is brought out in measures 457 to 460, and in measures 461–466 Klemperer achieves a nice echo effect as he matches the volume of the *ff* chords between winds and strings The E♭ major quarter-note arpeggio is brought out by the cellos and basses in measure 467, and the volume of the half note is reduced in measure 469 so the clarinet and bassoon lines are heard on the ascending sixteenth notes. In measure 470 the woodwinds and strings play an ascending E♭ major scale as the movement ends with three accented E♭ major triads of triumphant joy.

Today Otto Klemperer is regarded as one of the foremost interpreters of Beethoven symphonies in the Austrian-German tradition; any conductor interested in the interpretations of Beethoven should study his recordings. Klemperer died July 6, 1973 in Zurich, Switzerland, and like Beethoven, it was during a raging thunderstorm. His wallet still contained Mahler's recommendation from 67 years earlier: "Gustav Mahler recommends Herr Klemperer as an outstandingly good musician. In spite of his youth he is already experienced and is pre-destined for the career of a conductor." (Heyworth 37) Indeed, Klemperer's career proved Mahler's words to be very prophetic.

CHAPTER 11

The Lost Lyricism of Guido Cantelli

I love this young conductor. I think he is like me when I was young.
He will, I feel sure, be my true successor. —Arturo Toscanini

O ver half a century has passed since the internationally acclaimed young conductor, Guido Cantelli, died in a fiery airplane crash minutes after departing from Paris enroute to conduct the New York Philharmonic in a series of concerts. At age 36 Cantelli's professional career was at its peak, and he was regarded as Arturo Toscanini's protégé and chosen successor having been appointed to the post of chief conductor of the La Scala Opera House in Milan. According to Alan Schulman, a cellist who played under both Toscanini and Cantelli in the NBC Symphony, "If Cantelli had lived, he would have done with contemporary music what Toscanini did with the standard repertoire…. He was very remarkable, and his death is one of the great tragedies of our time." (Haggins 31)

Guido Cantelli was born April 27, 1920 in Novaro, a town in the Piedmont region of northern Italy. His father, Antonio, was a military bandmaster who played trumpet and horn and conducted the town band. He took Guido to band rehearsals, where the boy stood and waved his arms to imitate his father's conducting gestures. Antonio would sometimes reward his son by letting him practice his conducting skills before the band.

Cantelli's father taught him to play the trumpet, and he soon joined the town band. In later years Cantelli stated that while in the town band he learned the importance of strict discipline in making music, one of the most important lessons his father ever taught him. Antonio recognized Guido's extraordinary talent and arranged for him to study with Felice Fasola, a master teacher of piano, organ, and composition. By age 10 Guido had composed and dedicated a mass to his parents.

Cantelli entered the Milan Conservatory in 1939 and studied conducting with Antonio Votto, a former assistant conductor at La Scala under Toscanini. Votto started the conservatory's first conducting course, and Cantelli became one of his first pupils. There Cantelli had many opportunities to conduct a student orchestra that included members from the La Scala Orchestra.

Shortly after graduating in 1943 he was forced to join the Italian army, but because he refused to support Fascism he was sent to a Nazi concentration camp in Stettin on the Baltic Coast. Atrocious conditions and little food caused his health to deteriorate and his weight to drop to 90 pounds. He later said that

---

© *The Instrumentalist*, July 1999. Reprinted with Permission.

half of his stomach had been lost at the labor camp; he suffered discomfort for the rest of his life. Cantelli was transferred to Bolzano to recuperate. The hospital chaplain there helped him escape to Novaro, where he found work in a bank. The Fascists eventually caught him and sentenced him to death by firing squad, but with the liberation of Italy, Cantelli's life was spared.

The next major step in Cantelli's career occurred in 1948 when Arturo Toscanini visited Italy in search of an assistant to work with him and the NBC Symphony. When Toscanini attended a concert at La Scala conducted by Cantelli, he recognized the young conductor as a kindred spirit with the same qualities he valued: honesty, humility, and a complete mastery of the score. Toscanini was impressed with Cantelli's talent and invited him to conduct the NBC Symphony in a series of four concerts.

Cantelli's American debut with the NBC Symphony was a January 15, 1949 concert that included Haydn's Symphony #93 and Hindemith's *Mathis der Mahler*. The concert was so successful that he was asked to conduct two more concerts with the orchestra. The orchestra members were impressed that Cantelli memorized every note and rehearsal letter in the score. He was also able to *solfege* each part on pitch. After the debut Toscanini wrote a letter to Cantelli's wife, Iris, stating that Guido was the most gifted young man he ever met and that he would go very far in his career.

As Toscanini predicted, Cantelli exploded onto the international scene after this American debut. For the next seven years he conducted the New York Philharmonic, Boston, Philadelphia, Pittsburgh, Chicago, and San Francisco Symphony Orchestras, the Vienna Philharmonic, and the Philharmonia. Eventually he fulfilled a lifelong dream and became the principal conductor at La Scala.

Cantelli's final concert was with the La Scala Orchestra in his hometown of Novaro. There he conducted Handel's *Largo* as an encore. Following his tragic death Guido Cantelli was laid to rest in Novaro on December 1, 1956 as the town band played the strains of Handel's *Largo*. Because of ill health, Toscanini was never notified of Cantelli's death.

Cantelli made a brief but indelible mark in the history of great conductors, and his brilliant interpretations are incandescent landmarks of great orchestral performances. Cantelli's interpretation of *Mathis der Maler*, which was recorded with the NBC Symphony on June 13, 1950, is a shining example of his legacy. This great performance captures the essence of Cantelli's genius and reminds me of T.S. Eliot's poignant words:

> *Music heard so deeply*
> *That it is not heard at all*
> *But you are the music*
> *While the music lasts. (Untermeyer 397)*

Mathis der Maler (Matthias the Painter) was originally an opera based on the life of the German Renaissance painter Matthias Grünewald (1474–1528). Hindemith took excerpts from the opera and composed a three-movement symphony. Wilhelm Furtwängler and the Berlin Philharmonic premiered the work on March 12, 1934.

The first movement, "Angelic Concert," is taken from the opera's overture. Hindemith marks it calmly moving (*ruhig bewegt*) with a tempo of ♩. = 66; written in ⁹⁄₄ meter, the movement is conducted in three. Cantelli opens with a slightly slower tempo, ♩. = 60–63, and mixes the colors of the French horns and clarinets like in a painting. He gives the dominant timbre to the horns while the clarinets shadow the tone. When the strings enter in measure 2, the G major chord balances like a musical halo around the horns and clarinet color. As the horns hold the G concert pedal point the first bassoon and clarinets gently play a rising legato syncopated line, crescendoing to the E♭ on the third beat of measure 3.

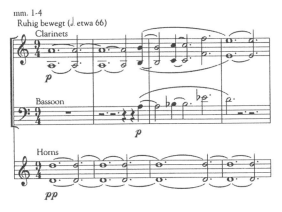

The strings repeat the G major chord on the second beat of measure 4 while the oboe and flues have the syncopated legato line and complete the 8-bar phrase.

The opening measures introduce the trombones who enter with the cantus firmus "*Es Sungen drei Engel*" (Three angels sang) at ☐1☐. Here, Cantelli conducts at a tempo of ♩. = 69–72. This melody, used throughout the opera, is the principal theme of the first movement of the symphony. It firmly establishes D♭ major, and Cantelli shapes the string line beneath it with a slight crescendo and decrescendo.

Eight measures after ☐1 the horns, bassoons, and clarinets enter with the cantus firmus, and Cantelli balances the clarinets and bassoon with the horns. The melody crescendos until the rest of the orchestra joins in on the pick-up to ☐2. Here, the trumpets play the melody forte and the glockenspiel doubles it adding new color.

In measure 27 the phrase decrescendos to piano in the trumpet and first violin, and Cantelli breaks slightly before measure 32. The next six measures mirror the introduction but start with a Db major chord in the winds as the strings play the ascending syncopated legato line.

Because of his use of counterpoint, Hindemith has often been described as a 20th-century Bach. In the contrapuntal $\frac{2}{2}$, which Cantelli conducts at $\textwon = 108$, the violins and flutes enter with a lively theme at *mf*.

Cantelli inserts a slight crescendo in the third measure of this section to bring out the tenuto on the high B and emphasizes the accents throughout the section to shape the melody and dynamics. Eight measures after ☐3 the

punctuated brass chords crescendo to move forward and then quickly diminuendo to piano to bring out the sequential string melody.

At 4 Cantelli observes the brass *fp* so the string theme can be heard. The balance throughout this section is extraordinary, and each line is heard with perfect
transparency. Cantelli's feeling for balance and clarity of articulation make this
section come alive.

At 7 the strings play piano on a contrasting second theme which Cantelli
conducts in a calm and lyrical manner.

The melody intensifies as the rest of the orchestra joins in for the romantic climax at [9] before resolving and slowing down with a plagal cadence in B♭ major.

At [10] Cantelli conducts a tempo of ♩ = 110 as the flutes play the theme. The low strings develop the tune before passing it to the first violins four measures before [11]. The melody is developed masterfully up to [16]. The fugato section before 12 is an appropriate study for textural clarity and balance; it sounds like it could have been composed in the Baroque period.

At ⬛16⬛ the trombones return with the "Angel" *cantus firmus* in $\frac{3}{2}$ while the fugato section continues in $\frac{2}{2}$. The polymeter is handled by conducting in $\frac{2}{2}$ while the trombones line up their half notes with the duple meter.

The $\frac{3}{2}$ ends at ⬛17⬛ as Cantelli broadens the tempo and the violins crescendo on their eighth-note runs. This leads to a majestic statement of the "Angel" theme played by the brass. Cantelli uses this climactic point to let the trumpets sing out at *ff*.

At ⬛18⬛ the woodwinds play the lyrical theme heard in measure 39. Cantelli again places a tenuto lift on the perfect fifth leap up to the high C. The theme ritards and calms at ⬛19⬛, then dimuendos to the fermata one measure before ⬛20⬛.

The last section starts at ⬛20⬛ and has a small theme in the flute part which Cantelli conducts at ♩ = 112. The meter shifts from $\frac{2}{2}$ to $\frac{3}{2}$, remaining intense up to the coda eight measures from the end. Cantelli conducts this fortissimo section to a joyful conclusion in G major.

Cantelli was a first-class maestro who left a lasting mark on the history of the great conductors. His interpretations and timings are universally accepted, and he will continue to influence each new generation of musicians who care about the art of conducting and feel the same aesthetic excitement as those familiar with his work. ✒

CHAPTER 12

A Conducting Lesson from Rafael Kubelik

While attending the Midwest Band Orchestra Convention in Chicago, I make my traditional walk from the Conrad Hilton to Rose (now Tower) Records to check out the latest recordings. A few years ago I found a reissue of the legendary Rafael Kubelik performance of *Pictures at an Exhibition* with the familiar red, black, and gold picture of Mussorgsky on the cover. There were three great recordings of this work made during the 1950's that were absolutely phenomenal: Arturo Toscanini's richly detailed and highly dramatic performance with the NBC Symphony in 1953; Fritz Reiner's virtuosic recording with the Chicago Symphony Orchestra in 1957, and Rafael Kubelik's 1951 recording with the Chicago Symphony Orchestra with its amazing high-fidelity sound, youthful tension, and spontaneity of performance. Under Kubelik's direction, the performance has such vivacity that it seems as if the music is being composed as it is being played.

The Kubelik interpretation continues to resonate in my memory, and I consider this performance one of his greatest achievements. The reissued recording is even better than I remembered, and it documents Kubelik's place as one of the great interpreters in music history. The final paragraph of the program notes reads, "This compact disc is dedicated to the treasured memory of Rafael Kubelik

(1914–1996), whose death occurred as *Pictures at an Exhibition* was being prepared for reissue." (Mercury)

The composer of *Pictures*, Modeste Mussorgsky (1839–1881), was one of Russia's most original musical minds. Like Dostoevsky, he was a realist whose genius was rooted in the Russian soil. Mussorgsky loved and was inspired by the folksongs and legends of the Russian peasants. He once wrote, "To trace the finer characteristics of human nature and of the mass of mankind, that is the mission of the artist. I am a realist in the higher sense; i.e., my business is to portray the soul of man in all its profundity!" (Siegmeister 514) Mussorgsky captured the rugged strength of the Russian soul better than any other composer.

However, Mussorgsky was never fully understood by his contemporaries. Largely self-taught, he refused to submit to conventional musical training. Convinced of his genius and his mission, he was uncompromising in his search for musical truth and broke many of the rules of harmony that others held sacred at the time. Rimsky-Korsakov, his friend and roommate, attempted to correct what he thought were mistakes in Mussorgsky's music. After they separated, Mussorgsky became addicted to narcotics and alcohol and suffered from epilepsy and severe depression. Friends abandoned Mussorgsky completely; his money ran out; his health failed, and he was admitted as a charity patient at a military hospital in St. Petersburg. The artist Ilya Repin visited the lonely, pathetic Mussorgsky at the hospital and painted the famous portrait that now hangs in the Tretyakov Gallery in Moscow. Mussorgsky died a few days after this sitting on March 25, 1881 at the age of 42, thinking himself a complete musical failure. It is the Repin portrait of Mussorgsky on the cover of the Kubelik CD.

Mussorgsky composed *Pictures at an Exhibition* as a suite for piano in 1874 in memory of Victor Hartman, a close friend, architect, and painter who died in 1873. After attending a memorial exhibition of Hartman's work at the Art Academy in St. Petersburg, Mussorgsky decided to honor his friend by portraying ten of Hartman's pictures in music. Unfortunately the piano suite attracted little attention and languished in obscurity for over a half century.

It was not until 1922 that Russian conductor Serge Koussevitzky was drawn to Mussorgsky's rugged, colorful piano suite and asked Ravel to prepare an orchestral version of the work. Ravel produced an orchestral arrangement that brought the music to life so vividly that the work became firmly established in the concert repertoire. Toscanini once remarked that Ravel's orchestration stands with Berlioz's book on the instruments of the orchestra as one of the two great treatises on instrumentation.

When *Pictures at an Exhibition* was recorded on April 23, 1951 at Orchestra Hall in Chicago, Rafael Kubelik was only 36 years old. He later recalled that listening to the playback of the master tapes was one of the greatest experiences of his life. The energy and exuberance of this performance makes it a great experience for all listeners.

The "Promenade" begins with a folk-like theme that alternates between $\frac{5}{4}$ and $\frac{6}{4}$ meters, suggesting the image of Mussorgsky entering the gallery and walking from picture to picture. This is perhaps the most exciting promenade ever recorded. The doors of the exhibition are flung open with the trumpet artistry of Adolph Herseth at a tempo of ♩ = 104. Herseth plays this introduction like a master sculptor, shaping each note perfectly.

   The rest of the brass join in with impeccable balance and phrasing. Kubelik relaxes the tempo when the strings enter and holds the dynamic to *mf* in contrast to the brass. The strings add a nice contour to the line with a slight crescendo-decrescendo in the second measure after [2]. In the second measure after [3], the woodwinds and strings match dynamics perfectly. Kubelik returns to the tempo of ♩ = 104 at [4] so the "Promenade" ends with a flourish as each note is separated, lifted, and ringing with orchestral brilliance.
   Next comes one of the most grotesque creatures in music, the "Gnomus," Hartman's sketch of a toy nutcracker. This hideous dwarf-like creature waddles around on legs too short for his body and twitches and jumps as he cracks the nuts between his moveable jaws. Kubelik captures the ferocity of this music as the strings dig in fortissimo. For the introduction he conducts in one beat per measure at ♩. = 104. Four measures later he relaxes the tempo and observes a major contrast in dynamics, piano, while maintaining the intensity.

   Kubelik's strict adherence to the sudden change in dynamics is a refreshing change from the usual style; under most conductors this movement has no significant color changes. At [11] Kubelik observes the *pesante* markings and creates a perfect dynamic match between the woodwinds and brass as they answer each other at a tempo of ♩ = 116 in four. At [14] Kubelik draws out the muted trumpets *ff* and the cymbal roll for additional color. Seven measures later the low brass enter in perfect response to the previous trumpet statement. Five measures after ⟨17⟩ Kubelik brings out the snarling timbre of the stopped horn and muted brass with an accent to achieve a grotesque effect. The movement comes to a close at ⟨18⟩ with an accelerando and crescendo to the end in all parts.

The return of the "Promenade" signals a change in mood with the marking of piano and *con delicatezza* as if Mussorgsky is being reflective here. The horn artistry of Philip Farkas captures the mood perfectly as his solo floats above the orchestra. Kubelik maintains the mood as the winds enter with rainbow phrases, playing a gentle crescendo and decrescendo. Kubelik slows down for the last two measures, then floats the release for a tapered ending.

"Il Vecchio Castello" is a masterpiece of mood portrayed in music. Ravel's orchestration captures the moonlit night as a troubadour sings a sad serenade to his beloved in a medieval castle in Italy. I have always considered Ravel's choice of alto saxophone to depict this doleful troubadour as a stroke of genius. This was probably one of Mussorgsky's favorite paintings because the music lasts over four minutes. Kubelik sets the sustained character of the music with a tempo of ♩. = 55–60. The cellos come in with the *sotto voce* perfect fifth on G♯ and D♯ followed by the first bassoon, which matches the D♯ and the second bassoon, which enters one beat later on the lower G♯.

The D♯ is usually a little sharp in the bassoon, but the Kubelik recording has impeccable intonation between the bassoon and cellos. The first bassoon gives a beautiful lift to the *portamento* articulation and sets the stage for the alto sax solo. Marked *vibrato, molto cantabile, con dolore*, this passage features one of the great saxophone solos in the orchestral literature. The beautiful tone, tapered phrasing, and careful attention to detail in the Kubelik recording makes it one of the most musical presentations I have heard of this movement. In the last measure the saxophone plays a true *perdendosi* in a decrescendo that floats away to nothing.

After the "Old Castle" the trumpet restates the "Promenade" theme at a confident tempo of ♩ = 112. In the next to last measure Kubelik broadens the theme in the strings with *tenuto* articulation and prepares the style of the next movement with pizzicato in the strings.

"Tuileries" depicts a noisy group of children and their nurses in a Parisian park. The children create quite a fuss as the nurses try to restrain them. Kubelik captures the capricious character of the music with a masterful use of rubato. The movement starts out ♩ = 104 and quickly accelerates to ♩ = 116 in the ninth measure. Ravel uses high woodwinds here to create the sounds of chattering children.

At 35 Kubelik slows to ♩ = 92 as if the nurses are holding on to the children as they try to escape. At 36 Kubelik begins an accelerando with the clarinet solo to ♩ = 120 as the children break free and run away.

Hartman's next picture, "Bydlo," a Polish word for cattle, depicts a large wooden-wheeled oxcart moving slowly down a muddy road. In Ravel's arrangement we hear the heavy and slowly moving oxcart from a distance while the driver sings an ancient folksong in the minor mode. The cart draws near, rambles along, and disappears over the horizon in one huge crescendo and decrescendo. The tuba depicts both the song of the driver and the lumbering progression of the oxcart. The music starts *pp* marked *pesante* and *sempre moderato*; Kubelik conducts the $\frac{2}{4}$ meter in $\frac{4}{8}$ at a tempo of ♪ = 100–104.

Because of the extreme range of the solo, G$\sharp^4$ marked *pp*, some conductors insist that it be performed on the euphonium instead of the tuba, but the euphonium timbre fails to capture the *pesante* quality needed for this music. Arnold Jacobs demonstrates in the recording that a tuba can sing with the same tonal beauty as the celebrated Russian bass singer, Feodor Chaliapin. At 42 the full orchestra plays the tuba theme at *fff*, which is enhanced by the accent on the first beat of the snare drum roll. The balance between the enormous strength of the music and the colors of Ravel's orchestration create a marvelous and spine-tingling experience. The movement ends with perfectly matched responses as the strings bass pizzicato echoes the *ppp* notes of the harp in the final two measures.

Hartman based "Ballet of the Chicks in Their Shells" on a costume design he did for the ballet "Trilby," which was staged in St. Petersburg in 1871. The *scherizino* and *vivo leggiero* music depicts the cheeping of baby chicks as they hatch. Kubelik captures this with a humorous, light style at an extremely fast tempo of ♩ = 184. Each section enters with matched dynamics and light staccato to make it difficult to discern when one section stops and the other begins.

The picture, "Samuel Goldenberg and Schmuyle," portrays two Polish Jews: one rich and pompous, the other poor and insecure. Mussorgsky liked this picture so much that Hartman gave it to him. Mussorgsky conveys the personalities of the two men so clearly that it is easy to distinguish the low voice of rich Goldenberg from the high nervous voice of Schmuyle. Kubelik starts the pompous tone of the beginning with strings and woodwinds at *ff* instead of the marked *f* at a tempo of ♩ = 54. Each note is so intense that the listener focuses on the subdivided eighth notes at a tempo of ♪ = 108. Kubelik observes the tenuto and *sf* marking so closely that it is easy to imagine the vain Goldenberg berating Schmuyle. When Schmuyle finally has a chance to respond, Ravel depicts him as a nervous, fast-talking man by using rhythmic triplets in the trumpet.

Each grace note and triplet of this trumpet solo is so cleanly articulated that it is a terrific example of triple-tonguing technique. Beneath the chattering trumpet line Kubelik uses legato woodwind sonorities as a contrast, perhaps suggesting people walking by and eavesdropping on the conversation. Kubelik broadens the tempo one measure before 60 to ♩ = 69 in preparation for Goldenberg's restatement in the strings. The furious dialogue ends at 62 as Kubelik returns to a tempo of ♩ = 56 at the *poco ritard* and *con dolore*. The *con dolore* marking (with sadness) had always puzzled me until I pictured Schmuyle walking away from Goldenberg feeling somewhat sad after losing the argument. It seems that Goldenberg has the last word as the music ends with a *ff* triplet to close this great character portrayal in music.

Another dispute occurs in Hartman's picture "Limoges: the Marketplace" with a disagreement among women over prices in the market. Ravel's orchestration connotes the bustle of the marketplace as the venders push their carts and fight for a place to sell their goods. The chattering and bickering of the market comes to life as Kubelik conducts this difficult movement at a vigorous tempo of ♩ = 126–132. This movement is especially difficult because of the fast 16th note runs that have to be articulated clearly in all parts. Kubelik and the members of the orchestra give a stunning performance, allowing the balance and clarity of the 16th notes to come through without being rushed. The movement ends at the *meno mosso* ♩ = 116 with a virtuoso display of double-tonguing in the brass.

The next picture, the "Catacombae," portrays Hartman, a friend, and a guide studying the underground catacombs of Paris by eerie lantern light. Here Mussorgsky creates ponderous, scary passages that portray light from a lantern reflecting off skulls hidden in recesses of the cave walls. The talents of the Chicago brass shine here with *ff* chords, perfectly balanced and in tune. The movement is followed by a mysterious variation on the original promenade theme, "*Con Mortuis in Lingua Mortua*" (with the dead in a dead language). Mussorgsky intends this to be a requiem for Hartman, and Kubelik mixes and matches the dark colors in these two movements as skillfully as Rembrandt did in painting.

Hartman's drawing of "The Hut on Fowl's Legs" depicts the house of the Russian witch Baba-Yaga, which takes the shape of a clock supported by chicken legs. However, Mussorgsky's music focuses on Baba-Yaga racing through the air in search of victims. We can almost hear Baba-Yaga's cackle in Kubelik's interpretation. Marked *allegro con brio feroce*, the score's indication is ♩ = 120, which is actually Mussorgsky's first tempo marking in the score. Kubelik disregards it and conducts this diabolical music at an incredible tempo of ♩ = 184–192. Kubelik kicks off this wild ride by bringing out the F♯ in the timpani on the first beat marked *ff* with the bass drum matching the intensity on the second beat. The intensity never falters as Kubelik takes us on a fantastic rhythmic rollercoaster until we reach the *andante mosso* section which he conducts ♩ = 92. The race resumes at 94 as Kubelik again conducts at ♩ = 192 and drives into the final movement with intensity.

Hartman drew "The Great Gate of Kiev" as part of a competition to commemorate the escape of Czar Alexander II from an assassination attempt. Although the gateway was never constructed, Hartman's design for the proposed entrance into Kiev was a tower shaped like a Slavonic War helmet supported by a chapel arch. The design itself appears almost wimpy in contrast to Mussorgsky's music.

If ever music surpassed the visual image, it occurs in this victorious procession through the gateway with soldiers, chanting priests, the pealing of bells, and even the vision of Mussorgsky himself as the promenade theme resonates with the other triumphant music in counterpoint. "The Great Gate of Kiev" seems tailored for the talents of the Chicago Symphony and Rafael Kubelik.

Marked *allegro maestoso and con grandezza*, Kubelik conducts in two at $\quad =$ 76–80. The grandeur of the first inverted E♭ chord is perfectly balanced in the brass and woodwinds, and in measure 4 Kubelik brings out the bass drum timbre to emphasize the accent on beat two.

Two measures before 105 Kubelik drops the dynamic level down to piano and creates a balanced crescendo as he pulls the sound from the low brass for the entrance of the full orchestra *ff* at 105. With Kubelik's meticulous handling of the relative dynamics prior to this climax, the *ff* is especially dramatic.

At 106 the clarinets and bassoons play a lyrical melody for the procession of the priests. Two measures before 107, Kubelik inserts a slight accent and lift to this line to foreshadow the sounds of bells in the distance. At 107 the high woodwinds and strings explode in cascading eighth note runs as the low brass sing the processional. Kubelik brings out the accents at 110 in the horns, low reeds, brass and chimes to imitate festive church bells. Four measures after 110 Mussorgsky creates a $\frac{2}{2}$ meter for winds over a $\frac{6}{4}$ meter for strings. However, the music continues in the same two beat pattern while the strings fit their $\frac{6}{4}$ quarter note groupings in the time of two. At 112 Kubelik increases the tempo to $\quad = 92$ as the promenade theme enters and the music drives to a climax at 114 .

At 115 the winds play in $\frac{2}{2}$, but the strings are now in $\frac{3}{2}$.

A good way to handle this polymeter is by continuing with a two-beat pattern but with a weakened second beat to let the strings fit in the triplets. Another choice is to use a definite one-beat pattern or to erase the bar line and think of two measures as one $\frac{6}{2}$ measure conducted in two. This solution resolves the problem until we get to 120 where the timpani and bass drum should be given definite cues. These measures usually create problems for conductors but are really quite simple if the three measures are considered as one complete measure.

Think of this rhythm as a subdivided three-beat pattern with each beat in the same place in front of the body, but with preparation for two coming from the rebound on the left. It helps to think of the dotted-half-note duplet as equal to one group of half-note triplets.

Phrasal conducting also works at 121; think of two measures of $\frac{2}{2}$ as one measure of $\frac{4}{2}$ but conduct in a two beat pattern at a tempo of $\circ = 56$. One measure after 122 the brass blend into the French horn color and give a beautiful bell tone answer to the woodwinds and strings. Kubelik drops the dynamics down to piano five measures from the end and leads a perfectly balanced crescendo, bringing out the percussion parts to end on a resounding E♭ chord. As the last E♭ major rings with kaleidoscopic color and grandeur we are left with a feeling of tremendous power and beauty. ✍

CHAPTER 13

The Fearless Conducting of Fritz Reiner

The best conducting technique is that which achieves the maximum musical result with the minimum effort. The only general rule is to infuse all gestures with precision, clarity, and vitality. —Fritz Reiner

I first became interested in Fritz Reiner (1886–1963) after watching a New York Philharmonic broadcast in which Leonard Bernstein paid special tribute to Reiner as a teacher and conductor by informing the audience of Reiner's recent death and dedicating the performance to him. Afterwards I went to a record store and bought all the available recordings of Reiner and the Chicago Symphony Orchestra from 1953–62. After listening to his legendary interpretations of Richard Strauss and Bela Bartók, I knew that this was the optimum level of orchestral performance. Many years later I studied the Fritz Reiner memorabilia at the Northwestern University Library. His score markings reflected a conducting genius who knew the purpose of every instrument and what the composer wanted from it.

As a piano student of Bartók and a conducting protégé of Richard Strauss and Arthur Nikisch Reiner developed a small, precise baton technique that was one of the best. "It was Nikisch who told me that I should never wave my warms in conducting and that I should use my eyes to give cues." (Schonberg 335) Musicians who played in his orchestras documented Reiner's virtuosity with a baton: "In some of these complicated modern pieces the tip of the baton would be beating three, the elbows would be beating four, his hips would be beating seven and his left hand would be taking care of all the other rhythms." (Schonberg 336) Perhaps bassoonist Leonard Sharrow said it best: "Anybody who couldn't follow precisely what he wanted had something missing." (Papp 21)

Fritz Reiner never had the charisma of Bernstein, the warmth of Walter, or the commanding presence of Toscanini, but he followed his inner conviction of each

---

composer's musical intent with ruthless tenacity. Reiner was of the old European school that imposed an iron-willed discipline through fear and intimidation. According to Harold Schonberg, "One malevolent glance from those slitted Reiner eyes, and musicians would be turned into whimpering blobs of protoplasm." (Schonberg 16)

> Philip Farkas agreed:
> He had a reputation for being strict and tyrannical. When trumpeter Frank Kaderabek first came to the Chicago Symphony, Reiner saw him backstage and said, 'Well, Kaderabek, how do you like it here?' 'I love it: I'm having a wonderful time,' Kaderabek replied. 'We'll fix that,' Reiner snarled. (Stewart 27)

Although many described Reiner as a tyrant on the podium, his orchestra gave inspired performances. Conductors today should strive for this level of performance by studying Reiner's recordings with the Chicago Symphony. These historical documents display the impeccable standards of another era.

A 1955 recording by Reiner and the Chicago Symphony of Bartók's Concerto for Orchestra was reissued on CD. Alan Rich's comments about this performance are still true today.

> The combination of passion, fantasy, and rhythmic surge is altogether remarkable in this performance, and the execution of the Chicago Symphony, at the height of its resurgence under Reiner, is little short of fantastic. (Russcol 63)

Not many people know that this monumental work would never have been composed without Fritz Reiner. Bela Bartók (1881–1945) is recognized as one of the greatest composers of the 20th-century, but this recognition was not given during his lifetime. Bartók spent the last years of his life in poverty and ill health. After escaping Nazi-occupied Hungary in 1940, Bartók brought his wife and son to New York. During the war all royalties from music composed in Europe were cut off. Bartók was unable to support his family by composing because Americans did not accept or appreciate his music. Bartók entered Mt. Sinai Hospital in 1943 in a severe state of depression and was diagnosed with leukemia. An article by Irving Kolodin in the *New York Sun* describing Bartók's ill health alerted Fritz Reiner to his former teacher's plight. Reiner and violinist Joseph Szigeti approached the Koussevitzky Foundation to suggest commissioning a new work by Bartók. Serge Koussevitzky immediately visited Bartók in the hospital and offered $1,000 for a new composition in memory of his wife Natalie, who had died in 1942. At first Bartók accepted only $500, believing that he would not live long enough to finish the work, yet his spirits lifted and he left the hospital to work all summer on what became one of the greatest compositions of the 20th-century. Koussevitzky and the Boston Symphony Orchestra premiered the Concerto for Orchestra on December 1, 1944 at Symphony Hall, not at Carnegie Hall, as stated on the score. Bartók was unable to attend the performance because of his illness, but he made it to Boston for the repeat performances on December 29 and 30. Bartók later wrote, "…the performance was excellent. Koussevitzky is very enthusiastic about the piece and says it is the best orchestral piece of the last 25 years." (RCA VICS) Bartók died nine months later in New York.

The Concerto for Orchestra has five movements and lasts approximately 37 minutes. The October 1955 recording from Orchestra Hall is vintage Reiner, who at 69, was at the height of his artistic powers. This monumental recording captures the greatness of Bartók's genius with precision, clarity, and Hungarian vitality.

Bartók's metronome markings for the opening *Andante non Troppo* are ♩ = 63–64, and the score indicates sectional timings to clarify metronome indications throughout the movement. For example, Bartók's instructions indicate a duration of one minute and 38 seconds for the first 34 measures and that the length of the first movement should be 9 minutes 48 seconds. Reiner's performance lasts 9 minutes, 51 seconds.

The mood of the introduction is somber and introspective, as if Bartók were reflecting on his terminal illness. Reiner's tempo on the beginning phrase in the low strings is approximately ♩ = 60–62, a little slower than Bartók's marking. This gives beautiful shape to the phrase as Reiner leans on the top B♮ in the third measure and lingers on the F♯ in the fifth measure before resolving to C♯. Bartók opens a world of kaleidoscopic tonal color in measure 6 as the pedal C♯ in the low strings clashes with the muted violin C♮ tremolo. As the remaining strings enter the harmony evolves into whole-tone clusters with flutes ending the phrase that sets up the next F♮ – F♯ clash in the strings. Reiner and the Chicago Symphony Orchestra achieve remarkable textural balance and clarity as the tone clusters resolve.

Measures 12 to 22 are similar to the first phrase except now the quartal harmony is expanded. Again the strings play through the whole-tone clusters with impeccable intonation. From measures 22 to 30 Reiner phrases a beautifully timed accelerando to the high D♮ and gracefully returns to the original tempo in perfect symmetry.

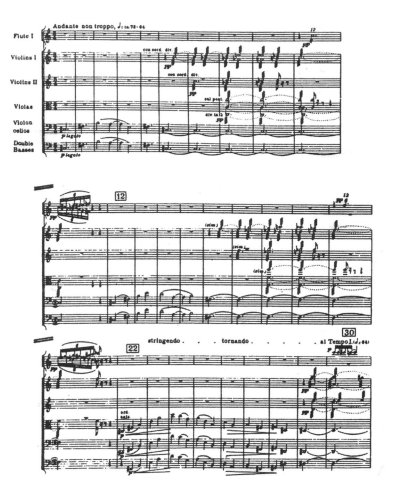

Great conductors make transitional passages sound convincing as the tempo accelerates, but the problem is complicated when moving from a slow three-beat pattern to a fast one-beat. Perhaps the most neglected beat in a conductor's arsenal is the subdivision of one to a bar as the tempo quickens. Many a conductor has met disaster by trying to show all the nuances in a Strauss waltz, finding out too late that his stick technique is inadequate. At measures 63 to 75 a conductor should have a clear musical conception and the technical expertise for a convincing tempo increase. Reiner was a master of transitions and starts the *poco a poco accelerando* at 63 with a three-pattern of ♩= 73. He controls the gradual increase in tempo by phrasing the groups as 4 + 3 + 3 + 3. The pulse for the first seven measures is in three as Reiner brings out the augmented 4ths on the third beat of the strings and bassoon motive and controls the trumpet syncopation in measures 67 to 69. He then conducts in one at measure 70 for a perfect accelerando to ♩.= 76. This makes musical sense because the flute entrance in measure 70 prepares the theme in the violins at the allegro vivace.

There is another tempo transition from a fast to a slower tempo between bars 149 and 155 that calls for a precise beat. Reiner broadens his one to a bar at measure 149 and gives a small two-beat for the oboe entrance, returning to one at measure 155. Another example of textural clarity that is rarely heard is found in the way Reiner brings out the harp part in measure 157.

When the passage in measures 456 to 462 is conducted in one to a bar at $\textstyle\frac{}{}$ = 70, the legato woodwind theme and staccato 16ths in the violins are seldom together. Reiner seems to emphasize the natural hemiola by conducting a three-pattern in measures 456 to 457 and 459 to 460 and a basic one in 458 and 461.

Measures 494 to 509 are perhaps the most difficult to control, and the slightest rhythmic uncertainty here will lose an orchestra in the mixed meters. The rhythmic value of the eighths is constant but the beats are asymmetrical. Farkas said Reiner's beat "…was small but accurate; if he conducted a fast $\frac{5}{8}$ bar, you could see all five beats perfectly." (Stewart 27) He showed an uncanny precision with subdivisions by a flick of the wrist. Most conductors would relax the beat in these measures and use a lopsided one-pattern, expecting the ensemble to count the subdivisions. Conducting in one does not bring out the phrase groupings or give a convincing interpretation. Reiner teaches us that good interpretation is the result of understanding the phrase groupings. These fifteen measures are grouped into the following metrical sequence: 3, 3, 2; 3, 3, 2; 2, 3, 2; 2, 3, 2; 2, 3,3. After studying these measures on the recording, I believe Reiner used a three-pattern of long-long-short, long-long-short, short-long-short, short-long-short, and short-long-long.

The final spine tingling measures of the movement remind me of the Hungarian word *vege*, the end. Reiner's legacy of uncompromising standards and consistent excellence was the end of an era. Many conductors cherish these old RCA recordings that originally sold for only $2.50. Never has so little bought so much beauty.

CHAPTER 14

The Often Cantankerous, Creative Artur Rodzinski

Throughout history there have been many creative artists who have been inspired by the great loves of their lives, from Elizabeth Barrett Browning in the romantic poetry of Robert Browning, to Zelda, the quintessential 1920s flapper in the novels of Scott Fitzgerald. Gala was the model for the surrealistic paintings of Salvador Dali, and Cosima influenced Wagner. We know of the effect of the mysterious, immortal, beloved on Beethoven and the support of the patroness of Tchaikovsky, Nadezhda von Meck.

Conductors have the valuable biography of Artur Rodzinski, written by his wife of 25 years, Halina Rodzinski, as a tribute to Artur, whom she calls "her terribly volcanic musical hero." The book offer candid recollections of the period from 1925–1960, which many consider to be the golden age of conductors in America.

Artur Rodzinski was born of Polish parents in Spalito, Dalmatia in 1894 and received formal education at the University of Vienna and earned doctorates in law and music. In the First World War he was wounded while fighting on the Eastern front but went on to a career in music rather than law. Initially a pianist in Lvov, Russia, he soon became the conductor of the Lvov opera house. Here Rodzinski began carrying a loaded revolver in his back pocket, even while conducting. According to Mrs. Rodzinski, the revolver became a good luck token when "Artur's conducting debut at Lvov was a great success and because he was superstitious he refused to conduct unless that particular charm was in the seat of his pants." (Rodzinski 111)

In 1919 Rodzinski moved to Warsaw to become director of its opera and Philharmonic Orchestra. His work there so impressed Leopold Stokowski that he invited Rodzinski in 1926 to become his assistant at the Philadelphia Orchestra. Rodzinski also conducted the Curtis Institute Orchestra and directed the Philadelphia Opera Company.

Rodzinski's gratitude to Stokowski for these American appointments was offset by his critical assessments of Stokowski's Polish accent, which seemed false, and excessive showmanship on the podium. Rodzinski also felt his creativity was being suppressed and believed his role was nothing more than that of a musical traffic cop. Mrs. Rodzinski wrote:

> Stoki would sit in the gilded and red plush emptiness of the Academy of Music while my husband took the orchestra through a Varèse or Webern score. While watching the notes and players Artur was also obliged to keep

> an eye on a traffic-light arrangement rigged upon the stage. When Stokowski wanted to stop, a red, green, yellow, or blue light on the podium blinked to cue Artur of his chief's intentions. (Rodzinski 109)

Rodzinski left Philadelphia in 1929 to become conductor of the Los Angeles Philharmonic. In 1933 he was appointed conductor of the Cleveland Orchestra, a position he held until 1943 and which was the longest and best tenure of all his appointments. Rodzinski is generally credited as a great orchestra builder because his efforts with the Cleveland Orchestra made it comparable with the New York Philharmonic, Boston, and Philadelphia orchestras.

In Cleveland Rodzinski made notable recordings of Rimsky-Korsakov's *Sheherazade* and Shostakovich's First Symphony, but his many disagreements with the orchestra board and fights with the manager ultimately led to his departure. Orchestra members increasingly disliked him, and the concermaster resigned after a falling out with Rodzinski. Regardless of these disagreements, it was Rodzinski's success with the Cleveland Orchestra that inspired Toscanini to recommend Rodzinski as the person to organize and select the musicians for the new NBC Symphony being created specially for the Maestro in 1937. Rodzinski accepted his idol's request with enthusiasm and auditioned 700 musicians over eight months until he was satisfied.

Toscanini was extremely pleased with Rodzinski's selections after hearing them perform Brahms's Fourth Symphony: "Bravo, bravo Rodzinski. Magnificent orchestra and magnificent concert. What beautiful work," he shouted.

In 1943 Rodzinski became director of the New York Philharmonic and was able to restore discipline and raise standards that had fallen under the pervious conductor, John Barbirolli. However, Rodzinski's tenure with the New York Philharmonic was extremely controversial. His first move was to fire fourteen musicians. Other members became bitter, and things degenerated. Rodzinski became exhausted from this strife and frequent battles with the management about programming. He resigned in January 1948. Virgil Thompson wrote in the *Herald Tribune*:

> Artur Rodzinski has done more for the orchestra than any other conductor in our century has done. Mahler and Toscanini were greater interpreters, were not great builders…Today the Philharmonic for the first time in this writer's memory is the equal of the Boston and Philadelphia Orchestras and possibly their superior. (Rodzinski 292)

After New York, Rodzinski became conductor of the Chicago Symphony Orchestra in 1948. Despite rave concert reviews by music critic Claudia Cassidy, Rodzinski had conflicts once more with orchestral management and resigned in the middle of the season because of tremendous nervous strain.

Rodzinski never received another major conducting post and toured as a guest conductor. Believing his career as a conductor in America and Europe was over, he became depressed and attempted suicide by overdosing on sleeping pills, but a doctor found him in time to save his life. Artur Rodzinski died in a Boston hospital of heart failure Thanksgiving Day, November 27, 1958 at age 64.

Peter Ilyitch Tchaikovsky (1840–1893) was another musician who also battled nervousness and fits of depression. Tchaikovsky never felt a deep affection for any woman other than his mother, but he formed associations with two women in 1877. Nadezhda von Meck became his patroness and inspiration for 13 years, and Antonia Milyukova brought him misery and disaster as his wife. Antonia was a pupil of his at the Moscow Conservatory and threatened suicide if he did not marry her. The tragic marriage on July 18, 1877 ended after a few weeks. Tchaikovsky could not bear the sight of his wife and in desperation tried to kill himself by standing up to his neck in the ice-cold water of a nearby river. He failed but had a nervous breakdown and eventually left his wife and went to Italy and Switzerland to regain his health. Antonia also suffered from metal disorders and was confined to an institution the last two decades of her life.

Tchaikovsky composed his way out of this emotional crisis by writing the Fourth Symphony in F minor. At this time he received a letter from Madame von Meck, a wealthy music lover who expressed great admiration for his work. When she heard of his difficult situation, she paid all of his debts and offered him a salary of 6,000 rubles a year but stipulated that they never meet. Their correspondence lasted for 13 years until 1890, when she could no longer afford to pay the salary. Tchaikovsky was devastated when von Meck terminated the relationship and never heard from her again. Tchaikovsky did not know for some time that the real reason for her decision was that she and a son were slowly dying of tuberculosis.

Madame von Meck was the inspiration for one of Tchaikovsky's greatest works, the Fourth Symphony in E minor, which he dedicated to her. The symphony was written in 1878, and Tchaikovsky regarded it as his finest work.

In a letter to Madame von Meck, Tchaikovsky explains his parallel feelings of being an ordinary human being and also a creative artist:

> Those are mistaken who think that the creative artist can express his feelings through his artistic medium while he is experiencing them. Sad as well as joyous feelings are always expressed, as it were, in retrospect. Without any particular reason for joy, I can immerse myself into a gay creation; on the other hand, in happy circumstances I can execute a piece full of the gloomiest and most despondent feelings. In short, the artist leads two lives; that of the ordinary human being and that of the artist; and those two lives do not always run parallel. (Kalmus)

Tchaikovsky's disastrous marriage produced one of the gloomiest periods in his life, yet the Fourth Symphony is one of his most optimistic works. In correspondence with Madame von Meck he referred to the Fourth Symphony as "their" symphony and sent her complete program notes. He described the finale as "the picture of a folk-holiday; see how it feels to be jolly. Scarcely have you forgotten yourself before untiring fate again announces its approach. The other children of men are not concerned with you. Rejoice in the happiness of others, and you can still live." (Kalmus)

One of the most joyful interpretations of the fourth movement is by the New York Philharmonic under Rodzinski from a performance recorded from a radio broadcast on January 13, 1946. It was reissued in 1998 on a CD made in Italy, called *The Radio Years.*

Under Rodzinski the fourth movement explodes with a crash of cymbals as the exposition begins *ff* at a blistering pace of ♩ = 168, without a doubt the fastest I have heard. Marked *allegro con fuoco* the opening four notes are reminiscent of a variation of "Joy to the World" as the strings and woodwinds whirl through descending sixteenth-note runs.

This is indeed a fiery demonstration of outstanding orchestral virtuosity unleashed by a great conductor as the first phrase ends *ff* with a dominant to tonic low brass, string, and timpani cadence.

Rodzinski repeats this motive with the same dazzling brilliance as the preceding four measures. Remarkably, the tension in this introduction does not let up on the repeat but gives full dramatic and dynamic intensity to each descending sixteenth. The pizzicato cellos and basses in measure 8 establish the new tempo of ♩ = 160 as the horns join in *ff* in half note octaves at measure 9 and quickly diminuendo to *mf.*

The principal theme in the flute, clarinet, and bassoon at measure 10 is actually the old Russian folk tune, "In the Field There Stood a Birch Tree." Stravinsky once said Tchaikovsky "was the most Russian of us all." This use of a folk tune is an example of the Russian soul in Tchaikovsky's music.

Rodzinski then crescendos to the first quarter in measure 11 and decrescendos the second quarter note on beat two. For an additional sense of forward motion he brings out the sixteenth notes in measure 11 with a crescendo in the strings.

The music sounds alive here, much like the wind blowing through leaves of a tree. For dynamic contrast Rodzinski inserts a piano marking to the main theme in measures 18–21 and does not return to the *mf* indication until measure 22.

The music become more animated and grows dynamically four measures before measure 30, where Rodzinski conducts two beats to a measure for the sweeping sixteenth-note runs that alternate between woodwinds and strings. Although the color changes between the woodwinds and strings, the volume stays the same and sounds as one instrument in the passage leading once more to the exposition.

Rodzinski returns to four beats at measure 30 as the tempo returns to ♩= 168. In measure 38 Rodzinski once again slows to ♩= 152 for one measure to emphasize the entrance of a dance-like theme. After the theme is introduced, Rodzinski accelerates *ff* back to ♩= 168, perhaps because he wanted to call attention to Tchaikovsky's background in ballet, and the tempo change is characteristic of a Slavic dance.

In measure 60 the birch tree theme in B♭ minor enters at a much slower tempo, ♩= 126–132, in the oboe and bassoon. Rodzinski inserts a crescendo in measure 60 and a decrescendo in measure 61 to give melodic lift to the theme. For additional color he also brings out the triangle starting in measure 61.

As the theme played by the flute is passed to the horns and bassoon, Rodzinski brings out the ascending runs in the strings, perfectly dovetailed to sound as one instrument. In measure 69 he accents the F minor horn chord with a quick decrescendo so the ascending string passage can be heard.

In measure 76 the horn melody grows in intensity and has a martial quality as the tempo returns to ♩= 152. Trombones and tubas emphasize the *ff* theme in the horn as the strings and woodwinds crescendo for added excitement.

In measure 92 the dynamic changes to piano as the oboe and flute sing above a delicate *pp* sixteenth-note string accompaniment in the next measure, which has a sparkling, chamber music quality that is reminiscent of ballet music.

The mood returns to a martial flavor in measure 100 as Rodzinski accents the sixteenth-note entrances in the woodwinds and strings. The music grows in intensity and builds to the transition in measures 115–118 with sweeping sixteenth-note runs, which Rodzinski conducts in two beats per measure. The recapitulation in measure 119 is at a fast ♩ = 168.

For measures 173–199 Tchaikovsky breaks the theme into sixteenth-note fragments and tosses them around the orchestra. Rodzinski accents the first note of each fragment, which creates a remarkable balance between each section. This is one of the most difficult sections of the movement because orchestras typically rush each fragment and leave too much space before the next entrance. Rodzinski solves this problem by keeping each sixteenth note clearly audible, which allows each fragment to dovetail into the next entrance.

Two measures before the restatement of the fate theme, which is first heard in the introduction of the first movement, Rodzinski adds a major ritard not marked in the score. The fate theme begins at ♩ = 80, exactly half the tempo at which he starts the recapitulation. For dramatic effect Rodzinski inserts a piano dynamic marking in measure 203 and crescendos to *fff* by measure 205. From measure 210 to 223 the previous tempo is resumed and creates a remarkable blend of colors between horns and strings. In measure 216 Rodzinski inserts a forte to the descending bassoon and string quarter notes, which Tchaikovsky marked piano. The string basses play the transition as quietly as possible and return back to tempo one which Rodzinski conducts at ♩ = 152.

The coda starts in measure 223 with a muffled timpani roll on the dominant of F major to which the string basses join in measure 225. This section starts *p* and is marked *poco a poco crescendo*: this is very difficult because most conductors let the tempo run away too soon and most orchestras crescendo too rapidly. When the horns enter with the joyful theme in measure 225, the articulation has to be clear because it is a model for other instruments to imitate.

Often the horns are too loud here and play with unclear articulation, so when the woodwinds enter in measure 227, their clean, and light articulation causes the horns to sound louder. However, in this recording the horns enter with a lightness and clarity that is a superb model for the other instruments to imitate. The joyful little theme is passed off from instrument to instrument and slowly grows in volume and excitement until reaching a tempo of ♩ = 168 in measure 249 for the Joy to the World-like theme over repeated triplet figures in the brass.

Measure 263 is another difficult spot because three rhythms occur simultaneously.

Rodzinski brings out the low brass, winds, and strings to be a musical anchor and gives an accent to emphasize notes on the beat.

Measures 266–268 are also tricky with syncopation at a fast tempo. Too many conductors beat the syncopation, which causes an orchestra to rush and leaves the brass unsure when to enter at measure 268. Rodzinski demonstrates that there can be no syncopation unless there is something to syncopate against. He keeps the rhythm steady by emphasizing the beat in the strings.

The final measures of the finale literally jump off the page as Rodzinski inserts a piano dynamic marking and quickly crescendos to end at a fiery tempo of ♩ = 184 mm. Some conductors lose control of the final few measures, and the ending becomes too noisy. Under Rodzinski the movement is brilliant and powerful, perfectly balanced and articulated, and breathtaking. It is truly one of Tchaikovsky's and Rodzinski's shining moments of joy that the audience shares with a thunderous ovation. In this performance an outstanding conductor and a great composer remind us that even in sorrow we can always find the inspiration to be joyous. ⪥

CHAPTER 15

Exploring Holst's *Planets* with Adrian Boult

The 20th century will be remembered as the golden age of conductors. There were masterful interpretations of Verdi by Toscanini, legendary performances of Mahler by Bruno Walter, and wonderful Fritz Reiner renditions of the music of Bartók. The aristocratic Karajan is remembered for his interpretations of Mozart, and George Szell left us some remarkable Beethoven performances.

Another notable conductor was Adrian Boult (1889–1983), who championed British music and earned the respect of musicians in his orchestras. He was a superb interpreter of Gustav Holst, Ralph Vaughan Williams, and Edward Elgar and collaborated with all three as a friend and colleague.

Boult did not exude the glamorous and volatile personality of some modern conductors but was content to spend most of his time in England, where he avoided any displays of narcissism or histrionics on the podium. He had the refreshing concept that a conductor should appeal to the eyes of the orchestra and gratify the ears of the audience. On the podium Boult was austere and reserved, and he came to rehearsals impeccably dressed in a suit and tie. He looked, "a bit like the long stick he wielded," and hid his intelligence "behind the stiff British bristle that decorated his upper lip." (Lebrecht 41)

Gustav Holst recognized these exceptional conducting talents when he asked Boult to conduct the premiere of *The Planets* for a private performance on September 29, 1918. In letter to friends Boult wrote about the sequence of events leading up to this event.

> One day in mid-September there was a sudden visit from Gustav Holst. The subject was his unperformed masterpiece, *The Planets*. (Holst said,) "I've been ordered to Salonika in a fortnight, and Balfour Gardiner has given me a wonderful parting present. It consists of Queen's Hall, full of the Queen's Hall Orchestra, for the whole morning on Sunday week. We're going to do *The Planets* and you're going to conduct!" (Northrop Moore 32)

The Sunday morning concert was a tremendous success for the 29 year-old Boult as well as for Holst. Holst inscribed Boult's score of *The Planets*: "This score is the property of Adrian Boult, who first caused *The Planets* to shine in public and thereby earned the gratitude of Gustav Holst." In 1967, at the age of 78, Boult recorded *The Planets* with the Philharmonic Orchestra (Angel S36420). This fourth and final recording of the work by Boult outshines his earlier efforts.

It was during the summer of 1914 that Holst wrote "Mars, The Bringer of War," in a broad ABA form. The first of seven movements, it captures the horrors of war although it preceded the First World War by several years.

© *The Instrumentalist*, November 1994. Reprinted with Permission.

For the mysterious opening Boult chose a tempo of ♩ = 160 that generally sounds faster because it was so cleanly articulated. Some conductors perform this movement as fast as ♩ = 176 but Boult's tempo emphasizes the natural pulse of the music.

> I well remember the composer's insistence on the stupidity of war as well as all its other horrors, and I feel the movement can easily be played so fast that it becomes too restless and loses some of its relentless, brutal, and stupid power. (Angel)

Boult's choice of tempo, approved by Holst, fits the rhythmic *ostinato* 𝄴 ♫♩ ♩ ♫♩ throughout the movement.

A director should experiment to find a suitable conducting pattern for the $\frac{5}{4}$ meter. The geometric patterns of the baton will be more significant to the orchestra if the music is interpreted well. A cardinal rule of conducting states the movements of the baton should reflect the music and Boult said, "If one watched the cinema film of a good conductor at work, one would tell what he was conducting without hearing the music." (Boult 4) A 3 + 2 grouping defines the $\frac{5}{4}$ meter in "Mars" but the textbook diagram of:

is too academic, lacks intensity, and drags the tempo. Instead, Boult followed the technique he learned from Hungarian conductor Arthur Nikisch (1855–1922), who advocated simplicity. Using small beats with the focal point directly in front of his body, Boult superimposed a 5-beat pattern on a 3-beat frame:

Beats 1, 4, and 5 were given on the same vertical plane.

The entire movement follows this pattern and should begin with a precise and rhythmic preparatory beat, after which the beats can be melded and the conductor should be an artistic monitor of sound instead of a time beater.

From the first measure Boult's ear for textual clarity and timbre is evident. The *col legno* effect of the back of the bow bouncing on strings is enhanced by wooden sticks on timpani playing the same rhythm. The eerie and mysterious sound is perfectly balanced and rhythmically exact. Boult defines the rhythm by placing a slight accent on the first and fourth beats 𝄴 ♫♩ ♩ ♫♩ that suggests a thrown pebble skipping on water. With crisp, clean articulations the rhythm presses forward and transcends the bar lines.

Boult adds vitality to the opening passage, marked piano, using crescendos and decrescendos to connect the movement. The first crescendo begins on the downbeat of the third measure in bassoons and horns. Holst wrote to Boult that the passage should sound "unpleasant and far more terrifying." (Northrop Moore 34) A member of the orchestra wrote that Boult "seemed hardly to be moving, but we could see how he was almost foaming at the mouth." (Kennedy 297)

Boult approaches the climax at ⟨2⟩ with subtle crescendos and decrescendos leading up to the abrupt crescendo that sounds like a snarling animal in a cage. The whip-like sixteenth note fanfares in the bass and woodwinds are rhythmically distinct but not rushed. The timing of these figures and crescendos add brilliance to the climax.

At *fff* Boult punctuates the motif in brass, strings, and timpani without creating noise.

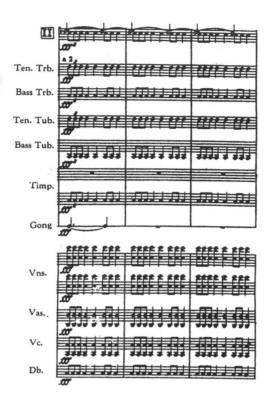

The euphonium enters *ff* at $\boxed{4}$ with staccato articulations on a military theme and Boult cues rapid crescendos and decrescendos while the strings diminish volume. The volume between the euphonium and trumpet remains constant and the rhythm is exact and not rushed; this can be a trouble spot if ♩♪ is played instead.

Boult reduces the volume of the horns and bass trombone on the sustained chord three measures before $\boxed{6}$ to hear the articulations of the woodwinds. At the $\frac{5}{2}$ meter, Boult concludes the first A section without any dramatic hesitation before beat two. The timpani color dominates the start of the chord, but Boult quickly balances the sound before the release.

The slow B section at 6 retains the time of the A section (♩ = 160) with a tempo of ♩ = 80. Despite the style change the sinister rhythmic motive echoes in the percussion. Later, Boult stretches and releases the phrases with a subtle rubato and creates a tight musical line with the *molto legato* effect by giving the eighth-note its full value.

Holst instructed Boult to use many crescendos and decrescendos and the decibel gradations are easily heard.

The A section returns at ♩ = 160 fifteen measures later as the orchestra, except for the double bassoon, hammers out the rhythm at *fff*. The powerful entrance, audible and balanced, makes a tremendous impact. The driving ostinato propels this section with intensity and emotional excitement.

A *ffff* marks the final $\frac{5}{2}$ section and Boult balances the orchestra around the organ for an overwhelming effect that will cause speakers to shake. Holst gave Boult specific instructions concerning these measures:

> In the last $\frac{5}{2}$ in the second bar the brass have to shorten the last note of the first phrase in order to take a breath. The organ chord should also have been shortened—it was careless of me to have made it a minim (♩.) Would you make it a crochet (♩) followed by a crochet rest so that the organ and brass finished the phrase more or less together. (Northrop Moore 34)

A clean break occurs in the second measure so the brass and organ chords do not overpower the woodwinds and strings. In the fourth measure Boult stresses the horn chord with an accented *ffff* entrance and the trombones and tuba enter *ff* and echo the horn.

Measures 11 and 12 in the $\frac{5}{2}$ section may be difficult to perform well because its massive texture contrasts the light texture of the $\frac{3}{4}$. To prepare the entrance of the crisp staccatos in the strings and pointillistic phrases in the woodwinds, a small subdivided preparatory beat should be given on the last half note in the section. Boult's technique allowed him to make this difficult transition with ease.

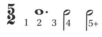

The sixteenth notes stand out at ⬚11⬚ because Boult does not begin the crescendo in the sustained horns and percussion until three measures before ⬚12⬚; then the timpani leads the rapid crescendo into ⬚12⬚. Again Boult follows Holst's suggestions: "Whenever there are semiquavers (sixteenths) it might be well to pull back a little so that they come out clearly and heavily." (Northrop Moore 35)

Finally at ⬚12⬚ the famous ending of the movement culminates the movement on war. Boult drives each quarter and eighth note to a rest with full intensity and lengthens the rests with each passing measure. By stressing this motive one final time and adding a crescendo on the fermata, Boult adds drama and excitement to the ending.

Adrian Boult's final recording of "Mars, The Bringer of War" has subtle instrumental colors and rhythms that are performed with clear articulations and impeccable taste. Like all great interpretations, this performance moves the listener both emotionally and intellectually. 🖎

CHAPTER 16

Tyranny on the Podium

I want this phrase to sound completely spontaneous. However as the result of meticulous planning. —George Szell

Following in the tradition of autocratic conductors of the past, George Szell was a disciplinarian who often exhibited a startling degree of cruelty and harshness in the pursuit of musical perfection. The Cleveland Orchestra became recognized as a great ensemble under his direction, one with absolute clarity and precision. In doing so, Szell regularly terrorized the musicians. When a critic wrote, "The Cleveland Orchestra performed as if the players' very lives depended on it," orchestra members responded, "They do, they do." (Rosenberg 18)

During the reign of Szell (1946–1970), audiences for Cleveland Orchestra concerts heard outstanding performances, but few in the audience realized the extent of intimidation that emanated from the podium. After hearing a performance conducted by Szell, Arturo Toscanini invited him to guest conduct the NBC Symphony. As he usually did when a guest conductor was on the podium, Toscanini paced back and forth in the balcony of the Studio 8H and

 was horrified as Szell ripped and snarled at his musicians, especially the horn section. Toscanini never invited Szell back.

George Szell was born in Budapest in 1897 but grew up in Vienna from age three. He was a musical prodigy and could sing forty folk songs by age three. At four he conducted as his mother played the piano and gently tapped her wrist with a pencil when she played wrong notes. His debut as a composer-pianist was a performance of his own *Rondo for Piano and Orchestra* with the Vienna Symphony, at age eleven. At age seventeen he appeared with the Berlin Philharmonic as conductor, pianist, and composer, performing

---

© *The Instrumentalist,* January 1999. Reprinted with Permission.

Beethoven's *Emperor Concerto*, Richard Strauss' *Till Eulenspiegel*, and his own symphony. (Stoddard 237)

With such enormous talent at an early age Szell became a protégé of Richard Strauss and the piano coach of the Berlin State Opera. With a recommendation from Strauss, Szell succeeded Otto Klemperer as conductor of the Strasbourg Opera at age twenty. Klemperer was so impressed with Szell that he recommended him to the Prague Opera in 1919.

As Erich Kleiber's assistant at the Berlin State Opera from 1924 until 1929, Szell learned about string technique. Szell also taught at the State Academy of Music, where he was known as an outstanding and demanding teacher of conducting.

Szell returned to Prague at the age of 32 as the general music director of the German Theatre but left the European mainland to become conductor of the Scottish National Orchestra when the Germans occupied Czechoslovakia. With the outbreak of World War II the Scottish Orchestra was disbanded, and by 1939 the 42-year-old Szell was in New York City without a job.

Within the year Szell became head of the theory department at the Mannes College of Music, where he also guided young conductors.

> A conductor must have not only a good memory, a faultless sense of rhythm, and preferably, absolute pitch, but also a thorough training in all the disciplines of music such as harmony, counterpoint, form, orchestration, and score reading. He should have the insight and imagination which will enable him to slip into the skin, as it were, of each composer he interprets, in order to transmit the composer's message to the listener. Above all, he must have that not easily defined power of communication which will carry through to the orchestra as well as to the listeners. (Stoddard 241)

In time Szell conducted the major American orchestras, including Boston, Philadelphia, Chicago, Detroit, Los Angeles, New York, and the Metropolitan Opera. A two-week engagement with the Cleveland Orchestra in 1945 led to a second engagement a few months later for a standing-room-only concert. Afterwards Szell was offered and accepted a three-year contract that gave him complete authority over all artistic matters.

Although the Cleveland Orchestra played well under its first three conductors, Szell's stern leadership developed the ensemble into one with an international reputation. Szell's goal was to make the Cleveland Orchestra a combination of the best elements of American and European orchestral playing. He explained, "I wanted to combine the American purity and beauty of sound and virtuosity of execution with the European sense of tradition, warmth of expression, and sense of style." (Stoddard 241)

Szell's ears were so keen that he could discriminate between instruments tuned at 440 or 442 vibrations per second. His performances of music by Dvořák are some of the best, especially his recording of Dvořák's Symphony #9 in E minor, Op. 95 with the Cleveland Orchestra.

While in New York serving as the director and teacher of composition at the National Conservatory, Dvořák observed that American composers went to

Europe for training and returned sounding like poor imitations of Brahms and
Wagner. Dvořák believed that Americans should not imitate the Europeans
but develop an American style that included the folk-like melodies of African-
Americans and Native Americans. Dvořák issued a challenge to American composers to stop imitating and start creating. "These beautiful and varied themes
are the product of the soil. They are American. They are the folk songs of America,
and your composers must turn to them." (Chase 391)

The New York Philharmonic Symphony conducted by Anton Seidl premiered
The New World Symphony at Carnegie Hall on December 15, 1893. Composed
as a model for American composers, the New World Symphony was Dvořák's
tribute to America, incorporating American folk tunes in modified form, using
pentatonic scales and modes. Said of his adaptation of folk melodies, "It is the
duty of composers to reflect in their music the spirit of the folk tunes of the people to whom they belong; not by using these tunes badly as themes, but composed in their vein." (*World of Music Encyclopedia 962*) This symphony had an
effect on American musical nationalism and demonstrated the intrinsic value
of indigenous American tunes. Later, composers such as Charles Ives, George
Gershwin, and Aaron Copland followed Dvořák's example.

The Cleveland Orchestra under George Szell captured the excitement of the
New World Symphony on a CBS Great Performances recording (37763). This
exciting and emotional recording continues to receive critical acclaim; the finale
is the most impressive I have ever heard.

The first nine measures of the finale burst forth with great energy, at exactly
the indicated tempo of ♩ = 152. Szell's precision is especially noticeable in measures 4 and 5, where the second violins and violas overlap eighth and sixteenth
rhythms and sound as one musician playing consecutive sixteenth notes.

In measures 10–25 the trumpets and horns enter *ff* on a bold, modal theme
in four-measure phrases that is reminiscent of American Indian melodies, on
which Szell accents the quarter-note chords in the background.

This theme is repeated in measures 18–25 with the trumpets one octave higher for added brilliance. For a sense of forward momentum Szell adds a crescendo under the sixteenth-note E minor string arpeggios before they finally play a harmonized version of the melody in the dominant key of E minor.

At ⟦2⟧ the excitement increases as Szell brings out the triplets in the strings against the syncopated horn parts.

The woodwinds take over seven measures after 2, and Szell emphasizes the timpani downbeat and the accented *ff* eighth note in the first violins on the second beat, characteristic of a back beat in jazz.

Three measures before 3 the tempo slows with a ritard in the ascending eighth notes in the bassoon and cellos. This tempo change to ♩ = 126 prepares for the second most important theme of the movement, a lyrical clarinet melody.

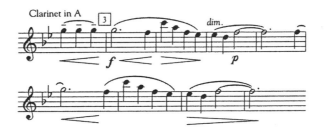

Here Szell and principal clarinetist Robert Marcellus demonstrate the art of rubato in a wonderful interpretation of the lovely melody.

Four measures before 4 the first violins take the melody as Szell increases the intensity by accelerating back to the original tempo of ♩ = 152. Reminiscent of the American minstrel style found in New Orleans, the violin melody uses sequences and accented grace notes.

Twelve measures before 5 the three-note motif from "Three Blind Mice" appears in flutes, oboes, clarinets, and then in the bassoon two measures later.

The theme is passed from one instrument to another and finally to the string bass. Because Szell insisted on good balance, all the instruments sound as one. The section closes with flute and oboe trills on the final note. As with many Romantic era and 20th-century symphonies, the themes from other movements are repeated in the finale. Dvořák often repeated themes rather than developing them. Thirteen measures after 6 the Largo English horn theme of the second movement returns in an augmented form in the flutes and clarinets.

Beneath this melody the first violins play a rhythmic staccato motive from the third movement, which is answered by cellos and basses. Dvořák builds to a wonderful *ff* at 8 by sequencing the Largo theme from the second movement. Once at 8 Szell emphasizes the syncopated themes from the first movement that Dvořák puts in the bassoon, horn, cello, and bass parts. This section of themes from previous movements is conducted at ♩ = 144 and leads back to the Indian theme in the trumpets nine measures after 8 at a tempo of ♩ = 160. Now played *fff* in the brass with punched accented chords in octaves, this theme closes the section six measures before 9.

At 9 Dvořák indicates *Meno Mosso* and Szell slows to ♩ = 96 for the clarinet and horn melody that is a nostalgic revision of the Indian theme played *molto legato* and piano. For good phrasing Szell adds a crescendo in the first measure of 9 to balance the decrescendo in the second measure. Seven measures after 9 the first violins enter *mf* and accent the first beat of the melody before

diminishing in a smooth modulation from E minor to E major using an enharmonic V⁷ of V at the close of the ritard.

The melody in the violins fourteen measures after 9 is broad, expressive,
and full of beauty as Szell mixes and matches the wonderful colors of the string
melody with horn and bassoon counterpoint. In this perfect example of subtle
rubato and phrasing Szell allows the music to be both passionate and flowing
without interrupting the phrase.

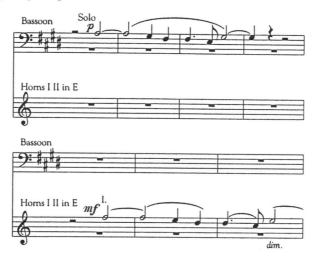

Fifteen measures before 10 Szell accelerates from ♩= 96 to ♩= 112 as the flutes
and oboe play a singing melody in octaves that is reinforced by the first violins.
Although Szell slows down slightly two measures before 10, once at 10, marked
un poco sostenuto, the tempo is ♩= 116. The violas and cellos play the sixteenth
notes three measures after 10 with a crescendo and decrescendo, and in the
ninth measure after 10 the dance-like theme in the bassoon, again reminiscent
of a melody that could be heard on the streets of New Orleans, is heard over the
sixteenth-note violin passage.

In the twelfth measure before 11 Szell brings out the ascending and descending overlapping figures found in the bassoon, violas, and cellos as he inserts a
crescendo and decrescendo. Eight measures before 11 are some of the most difficult measures in the symphony. The first horn has an exposed solo, which is
a rhythmic alteration of a theme from the first movement, while the clarinets,
oboes, and flutes enter with a theme heard previously at 4. At the same time
the first and second violins play sixteenth notes marked *ppp*. Near the end of

the first horn solo the other horns overlap the first horn line, descending to the extreme low range while sounding like a continuation of the first horn solo. After only three beats of rest, the first horn reenters with the second horn in a fanfare that starts slowly and gradually accelerates to ♩ = 160. The clarity, balance, and skill of the Cleveland Orchestra is truly remarkable in this difficult passage.

At ⑪ Szell brilliantly captures the hustle and bustle of the American scene as he conducts the syncopated motive heard in the first movement at a tempo of ♩ = 160. However, when the horns and trombones enter *fff* playing a modification of the Indian theme, the music become exciting, and Szell increases the excitement by bringing out the trumpet fanfare and the fast triplets in the violins. Ten measures before ⑫ Szell emphasizes the syncopated melody in the trombones along with the dotted-eighth-sixteenth fanfare in the trumpets, which includes accents on the sixteenth notes.

One measure before ⑫ Szell inserts a ritard on the quarter notes to slow the tempo from ♩ = 160 to ♩ = 152 and draw attention to the woodwind and brass harmony, which is from the second movement.

In the fifteenth measure after ⑫ the clarinets enter with the Largo theme from the second movement, which they slur, but it is five measures later that Dvořák marks *legato* which causes interpretation questions. The new Prague edition of Dvořák's score indicates that the first four measures should be tongued in the clarinets and only the last two measures slurred. Szell has his clarinets slur all eight measures. Eventually, the flutes enter over the clarinet melody with the theme from the Scherzo, which is answered perfectly in the strings and timpani.

After a reiteration of the main first movement theme by the solo horn at the *poco a poco ritard* a new tempo occurs as the strings play ascending sixteenths notes *con fuoco* with a fast crescendo. The main theme returns *meno* in woodwinds and strings, and Szell has them play *molto marcato*.

The entire orchestra enters *ff* and modulates to E major eighteen measures from the end. It is a climactic moment as the E major tonality sounds for two measures like a magnificent sunrise. The next four measures are marked *un poco meno mosso* and Szell slows down to ♩ = 96. In these measures Dvořák quotes and combines themes from all movements, which can easily be heard because of the clarity and power of the Cleveland Orchestra.

Twelve measures from the end is marked *allegro con fuoco* which Szell conducts at a tempo of ♩ = 176, faster than any other recording I have heard. Dvořák incorporates a boogie-woogie bass line nine measures from the end that is reminiscent of the folk tune "Shortnin' Bread." In the last three measures Szell broadens the tempo and begins the last E major fermata *ff* but has the winds slowly decrescendo to *ppp*. It is an interesting ending that seems to look back upon the completed symphony with nostalgia.

The musical legacy of George Szell is universal and indelible. When I listen to great recordings of Szell conducting the Cleveland Orchestra on the works of Haydn, Mozart, Beethoven, Richard Strauss, and especially Dvořák, I am transported back to the spirit of an era of uncompromised and unparalleled art-istry. Perhaps Szell's credo can best be summarized by his own words: "I am a musician who loves music. I want to make music to the best of my ability. My happiest moments have been those in which I have succeeded in doing some justice to the great works I am permitted to perform." (Stoddard 236) ⬿

CHAPTER 17

Conducting Lessons from Pierre Monteux

Just as the splitting of the atom altered the course of the 20th century, so did The *Rite of Spring* unleash a new energy that completely changed the future of music. With this composition the 30 year-old Igor Stravinsky (1882–1961) began a rhythmic revolution that unshackled the symmetrical and poetic meter of the 19th century and introduced into music the asymmetrical and iconoclastic prose rhythms that became characteristic of the 20th century. That is analogous to a shift from the smooth, iambic pentameter of John Keats to the jagged rhythms of James Joyce's *Finnigan Wake*. On of the most famous compositions of the early 20th century, *The Rite of Spring* is a tour-de-force now recognized as a classic.

Pierre Monteux (1875–1964) conducted the premiere of the ballet on May 29, 1913 in Paris at one of the wildest concerts in history. The revolutionary, barbaric rhythms of this new ballet stirred the first-night audience into savage outbursts. Within minutes after the curtain rose the performance was drowned in shouts, whistles, and raucous laughter. Monteux ignored the commotion and ensuing riot, which the police finally quelled by clearing the hall. Despite all this, Monteux, with curly black hair and an enormous walrus mustache, kept his eyes on the score and conducted to the very end without deviating from the tempos Stravinsky had specified.

Monteux himself had been shocked the previous summer when Serge Diaghilev (1872–1929), director of the Ballet Russe, took him to hear Stravinsky play the piano sketch of *The Rite of Spring*, a work, Stravinsky explained, inspired by an unusual vision:

> One day when I was finishing the last pages of the *Firebird Suite* in St. Petersburg I had a fleeting vision, which came to me as a complete surprise, my mind at the moment being full of other things. I saw in my imagination a solemn pagan rite: sage elders seated in a circle, watched a young girl dance herself to death. They were sacrificing her to propitiate the god of spring.

Such was the theme of *Le Sacre du Printemps*. I must confess that the vision made a deep impression on me...In Paris I told Diaghilev about it, and he was carried away by the idea. (Stravinsky 310)

Monteux had expected the new work to be colorful and melodious like *Firebird*, which he had first heard in 1911. Monteux described his surprise on first hearing Stravinsky's latest work:

The old upright piano quivered and shook as Stravinsky tried to give us an idea of his new work for ballet. I remember vividly his dynamism and his sort of ruthless impetuosity as he attacked the score. By the time he had reached the second tableau, his face was so completely covered with sweat that I thought he would surely burst or have a syncope. My own head ached badly, and I decided then and there that the symphonies of Beethoven and Brahms were the only music for me, not the music of this crazy Russian! I must admit I did not understand one note of *Le Sacre du Printemps*. My own desire was to flee the room and find a quiet corner in which to rest my aching head. Then my director (Diaghilev) turned to me and with a smile said, 'This is a masterpiece, Monteux, which will completely revolutionize music and make you famous, because you are going to conduct it,' and of course, I did. (Monteux 89)

Stravinsky chose Monteux to conduct the premiere because he was not interested in calisthenics exhibition for the entertainment of the audience but was only concerned with giving clear signals to the orchestra. Monteux studied the score to *The Rite of Spring* throughout the winter of 1913, with Stravinsky at the piano, and by spring was ready to try the music in sectional rehearsals. Monteux described how the music jolted the players:

The musicians thought it was absolutely crazy, but as they were paid, their discipline was not too bad. When at last I put the whole thing together, it seemed chaotic, but Stravinsky was behind me pointing out the little phrases he wished heard. We rehearsed over and over the small difficult parts, and at last were ready for the ballet. We had in all 17 rehearsals. (Monteux 89)

Nijinsky (1890–1950), recognized as one of the world's greatest dancers, may have been responsible for much of the adverse reaction because he choreographed the ballet so exotically. However, after weeks of preparations, including 135 dance rehearsals, the composer, conductor, producer, and choreographer were unprepared for the opening night pandemonium. As Monteux said, "the public reacted in a scandalous manner," and the demonstration became so violent that Stravinsky feared for his safety and dashed backstage. The shouted insults were so loud that the dancers could not hear the music. Nijinsky was beside himself with anger and called out the beats to the dancers. Diaghilev ordered the electrician to blink the hall lights to settle the audience, but the riot continued. Four renowned composers were in the audience. Saint-Saens yelled, "*Mais il essst fou, il est fou!*" (He is crazy, he is crazy.) and left the hall in disgust. Puccini said "the choreography is ridiculous, the music is sheer cacophony...

taken altogether it might be the creation of a madman." Debussy and Ravel stood and cheered, declaring it to be a work of genius. (Kaufmann 132)

There were five more performances, but each was treated with hostility. Monteux explained, "Their reaction amazed me, as the Parisian usually considers himself a real connoisseur of the arts, adoring everything a bit avant-garde...." (Monteux 90) The public rejection of the ballet was so strong it was shelved for a year until Monteux suggested that *The Rite of Spring* might be more successful as a concert piece and conducted the concert premiere on April 5, 1914 at the Casino de Paris. Stravinsky attended and heard the work in its entirety for the first time. The performance was such a huge success that Stravinsky was carried from the hall on the shoulders of the crowd.

The triumphant concert premiere soon led critics and the public to revise their opinions of the work. Through the tireless efforts of Pierre Monteux, *The Rite of Spring* is now recognized as one of the most important compositions of the 20th century. He made the first recording of the work in 1929 with the Paris Symphony and later with the San Francisco Symphony and Paris Conservatoire orchestras. In my opinion, however, his recording with the Boston Symphony Orchestra in 1951 when Monteux was 75 years old, is the most outstanding. This historical masterwork is now available as a CD in the Pierre Monteux Edition. Every conductor could benefit by studying Monteux's imaginative interpretation, which captures all the nuances of Stravinsky's complex score.

The introduction begins with an eerie bassoon solo in the high register and evokes the mysteries of Spring. Stravinsky explained:

> In *The Rite of Spring* I wanted to present the continuous renewal of nature, the fear and the joy of the essence of life which streams through plants and all living things. In the introduction I made the orchestra express the fear which overwhelms everyone who is faced with elemental forces. The whole introduction is played *mezzo forte*. The melody develops in a horizontal line, which is only strengthened or weakened by the number of instruments and the intensive dynamics of the orchestra – not by the melodic line itself. I wanted to reproduce some of Man's panic-stricken fear of eternal beauty, and his awed trembling before the shining sun; his cry of terror seemed to hold new musical possibilities. In this way the whole orchestra reproduces the birth of Spring.... (*The World of Music Encyclopedia* 1189)

Stravinsky borrowed the haunting bassoon melody from a collection of Lithuanian folk music.

It would have been interesting to see the shock on the bassoonist's face in 1913 when he first saw the part, which starts on C[5]. This is now a standard excerpt for all symphony bassoon auditions. A wise conductor stays out of the way and lets the bassoonist play it alone. In the second measure, however, the conductor should indicate the horn entrance and coordinate the rhythm of the horn trip- let against the two eighth notes of the bassoon. It helps to mark this two-against three rhythm in the parts as well as the score. Monteux puts a decrescendo on the horn D concert so the bassoon's high D can sound. He does not hurry the bassoon quintuplet in measure 3, and then stresses the C♯ concert in the horn. After a clear release from the horn and bassoon on the fourth beat, he waits for the bassoon's high C on the second half of that beat before bringing in the clari- nets against a background of bassoon crescendos and decrescendos.

In measure 5, Monteux follows the *poco accelerando* direction and slightly emphasizes the solo clarinet entrance. Stravinsky described the introduction as portraying the "violent Russian spring that seemed to begin in an hour and was like the whole earth cracking. That was the most wonderful event of every year of my childhood." (White 172) Under Monteux's direction, the seemingly effortless performance of the introduction sets the mood perfectly.

The barbaric dances in "The Augurs of Spring" burst out at exactly the tempo Stravinsky marked, ♩ = 50, which Monteux conducts in two, at ♩ = 100; many con- ductors take this movement too fast and it becomes ragged.

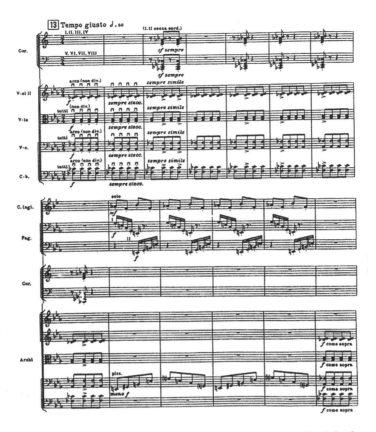

Monteux hammers out the polytonal string ostinato as all eight horns inject short, biting off-beat *sfz* accents that seem to make the notes jump off the page. Strictly adhering to Stravinsky's forte marking, Monteux clearly juxtaposes the E♭ chord in the violins and violas against the F♭-C♭-A♭ (enharmonic E major) one half step away in the cellos and basses. The articulation of the entering English horn and bassoons at 14 sparkles with the clear precision of a Swiss watch. Too many conductors try to increase excitement in this movement by pumping up the volume, but succeed only in losing clarity. With clinical precision Monteux perfectly tunes and balances the clashing polytonalities.

Because Monteux learned this score from Stravinsky his performance is authoritative, and perhaps the greatest revelation is his control of the many meter changes. Although at first the various meters appear confusing, the solution is to keep the eighth-note values constant and to conduct the irregular meters using asymmetrical variants of the basic conducting patterns.

One of the first asymmetrical problems occurs at 41 in the "Ritual of Abduction" where Stravinsky groups $\frac{9}{8}$ meter as $\frac{4}{8} + \frac{5}{8}$ and reverses it to $\frac{5}{8} + \frac{4}{8}$ in the next measure. The tempo is marked presto ($\quarternote\!\cdot = 132$), which Monteux follows exactly, conducting at 41 in an asymmetrical two-beat pattern with an extended second beat and the next measure with an extended first beat.

For the $\frac{6}{8}$ measures beginning at 43 Monteux conducts in a small, precise two-beat pattern, extending the second beat for the $\frac{7}{8}$ measure. The $\frac{3}{4}$ measure is taken in one, as is the $\frac{2}{4}$ measure, the eighth note remaining constant while the size of the beat changes to accommodate the variable number of eighth notes.

The rhythmic polyphony at 70 in the "Procession of the Sage" troubles many conductors because the percussion section has four pulses against six in the rest of the orchestra. The danger in such a passage is over conducting; the conductor should simplify as much as possible so players can fit their parts against each other. Stravinsky marks this movement ♩ = 166, but Monteux conducts at ♩ = 152. After listening to the passage many times, I think Monteux conducts the two measures before 70 in four and changes to $\frac{3}{2}$ at a tempo of ♩ = 76, keeping the quarter note equal, at 70. To help the percussion section, the conductor should think the four-against-three rhythm as he conducts this passage with a precise downbeat on one and smaller second and third beats.

This technique also occurs at ⬚134⬚ in the "Ritual of the Ancients." Here, Stravinsky has marked the score in $\frac{6}{4}$ ($\downarrow$ = 52), but a divided three pattern works best for the horn and oboe melodic line.

The second measure after ⬚103⬚ has the unusual meter of $\frac{11}{4}$ at $\downarrow$ = 120. Some conductors rebar these measures as 4 + 4 + 3, but most conductors will use straight downbeats, placing the first ten beats in a focal point directly in front of the body with the eleventh beat coming up in preparation for the next measure.

At ⬚104⬚ in "Naming and Honoring of the Chosen One" the fortissimo indication on the fourth eighth note of the $\frac{5}{8}$ measures dictates a 3 + 2 grouping. Because of the rapid tempo (vivo $\downarrow$ = 144) these measures are conducted in an asymmetrical two with an extended first beat, the $\frac{9}{8}$ measure in an asymmetrical four pattern with the extended beat on one, and the $\frac{7}{8}$ bar in three beats with the extended beat again on one. The $\frac{3}{8}$ is in one and the $\frac{4}{8}$ measure is in two. Because of the horn *sf* in the $\frac{7}{4}$ measure, it is conducted in 3 + 4.

In the final section, "Sacrificial Dance": ($\downarrow$ = 126), many of the complicated time signatures can be simplified by combining measures. For example, the second, third, and fourth measures may be merged into one and conducted as an asymmetrical three beat pattern, short-long-long. The $\frac{2}{8}$ measure is conducted in a regular two-beat pattern.

At ⬚149⬚ in the same movement, combine the $\frac{3}{8}$ and the first $\frac{2}{8}$ into one measure of $\frac{5}{8}$ and use an asymmetrical two-beat pattern, extending beat one. Merge the next four measures into two $\frac{4}{8}$ bars, and conduct in two. Soften the second beat of ⬚151⬚ a little to help the trombone fit the quintuplet into the measure.

Pierrre Monteux conducted the world premieres of Stravinsky's *Petrouchka*, *Rite of Spring*, and *LeRossignol*; Ravel's *Daphis and Chloe*; and Debussy's *Jeux*. When he died at his home in Hancock, Maine on July 1, 1964 he was 89 years old. His legacy of brilliant recorded performances will continue to illuminate and inspire us to become better conductors.

CHAPTER 18

A Lamb Among Lions:
A Profile of Dimitri Mitropoulos

A good musician should try also as much as possible to be a first-rate human being. Possessing a certain talent is no excuse for him to be arrogant and presumptuous. —Dimitri Mitropoulos

Like the many immigrants who came before him, Dimitri Mitropoulos (1896–1960) fell in love with American ways and culture. The deeply religious Greek conductor first set foot on American soil at the age of 40 after Serge Koussevitzky had invited him to be the guest conductor of the Boston Symphony in 1936.

The orchestra members were impressed that Mitropoulos had memorized every note on his program of Beethoven's *Leonore Overture #2*, Debussy's *La Mer*, and Richard Strauss's *Domestic Symphony*. When asked why he memorized scores, Mitropoulos replied, "You don't expect an actor to come on stage to play Hamlet while still carrying a script." (Trotter *Journal* 6) The concert was an outstanding triumph, and some even hailed Mitropoulos as the next Toscanini.

Mitropoulos returned to America the next year for another successful appearance in Boston and went on to conduct the Minneapolis orchestra in Beethoven's Symphony # 2 and Leonore *Overture #2*, Bach's *Fantasia and Fugue in G Minor*, and Respighi's *Toccata for Piano and Orchestra*, which Mitropoulos conducted from the piano. This concert in 1937 received rave reviews from critics and led to his appointment as music director after Eugene Ormandy had moved on to lead the Philadelphia Orchestra. Mitropoulos remained in Minneapolis from 1937 until 1949 and turned the orchestra into an internationally recognized ensemble particularly noted for its brilliant performances of romantic and contemporary music which he conducted with missionary zeal.

Because of his intense religious beliefs and spiritual commitment, he treated members of the orchestra as musical equals: "In the history of music there are only the two types of conductor: the tyrant and the colleague. For myself, I chose to be the second type…a great interpretation represents a communal effort, and in no case does it move from the conductor's baton to a pack of subjugated slaves." (Trotter *Journal 7*). Mitropoulos carried two of his golden rules in his wallet:

> God grant that I may seek rather to comfort than to be comforted, to understand rather than be understood, and to love rather than be loved.
> —St. Francis

> If I must choose between doing an injustice and being unjustly treated, I will choose the latter. —Socrates. (Trotter *Journal 9*)

Members of the Minneapolis orchestra respected and responded to Mitropoulos's altruism, and his tenure there produced golden years of music making. His accomplishments in Minneapolis were recognized everywhere, and in 1949 he was offered the position of music director of the New York Philharmonic. Although Mitropoulos had proven that he was one of the world's outstanding conductors, he was temperamentally unprepared for what awaited him in New York. After Toscanini left the New York Philharmonic it became known as the graveyard for conductors. George Szell described it as murderers' row because the Philharmonic was merciless on conductors it did not respect.

After agonizing on whether to leave Minneapolis, Mitropoulos wrote these prophetic words: "It is like a moth to a flame. Now I will go to the middle of intrigue and struggles…it is not going to be easy in New York. I have to go even though I know I am probably going to my doom." (Trotter 252). Surprisingly, his first years with the Philharmonic were ones of mutual cooperation, about which Mitropoulos wrote, "I treated them as equals; I worked just as hard and harder than they did because a conductor's job requires that he do so. When I first came to the Philharmonic, they were untamed lions. Now they are lambs." (Trotter 312)

Unfortunately, the altruism and ideals that were so successful in Minneapolis fell upon deaf ears in New York. After a few months his relationship with members of the orchestra began to deteriorate, and soon the philosophy of St. Francis did not work for Mitropoulos; after each rehearsal he felt more like St. Sebastian. The lions were out of their cages, and Mitropoulos was a lamb going to artistic slaughter. According to Trotter, "By 1955, instead of responding to their conductor's decency, kindness, and tolerance, many in the orchestra were openly taking advantage of those very qualities and behaving like spoiled children and petty thugs." (Trotter 382).

Despite recalcitrant players and a New York press that crucified his choice of contemporary literature, Mitropoulos remained true to his beliefs. This ultimately cost him his job and his health. Box office receipts determine the longevity of any conductor, but Mitropoulos's commitment to performing contemporary music caused many people to stop attending his concerts. His American dream turned to ashes. His last full season as music director of the New York Philharmonic was 1955–56, after which Leonard Bernstein became associate conductor with Mitropoulos. In 1958 Bernstein succeeded Mitropoulos as music director.

Mitropoulos returned to Europe for a series of engagements to guest conduct. This vulnerable, gentle, and generous man, who believed that "only life suffered can transform a symphony from a collection of notes into a message for humanity," died of a heart attack on the podium at the age of 64 while rehearsing Mahler's Third Symphony in Milan. One of the musicians in the orchestra drew a cross in the margin of the Mahler score at measure 80 and wrote: "Maestro Dimitri Mitropoulos died at this point of the symphony on the morning of November 2, 1960." (Lebrecht 264)

One of my favorite Mitropoulos recordings is his passionate interpretation of Arnold Schönberg's *Transfigured Night* (Odyssey #32160298). Although many only think of Schönberg as innovator of twelve-tone music and teacher of Berg and Webern, his earliest music was profoundly influenced by Wagner and Richard Strauss. Schönberg, one of the leaders of the post-Romantic movement in Austria, said, "I write what I feel in my heart and what finally comes out on paper is what first coursed through every fiber of my body." (Kaufman 117)

Perhaps the quintessential culmination of this Romantic influence is *Transfigured Night*, which Schönberg composed in 1899. After initially scoring the work as a sextet for two violins, two violas, and two cellos, he transcribed it for chamber orchestra in 1917. In 1943 he made a few stylistic revisions. The work was inspired by the poem "Women and World," by Richard Dehmel (1863–1920), and the programmatic music describes two lovers walking by moonlight in a park on a cold winter night. The woman confesses that she is pregnant but he is not the father. When the man forgives the woman, the night is transfigured through the warmth of their love. Although the premier was a failure and evoked fist fights because of the controversial and moral implications of Dehmel's poem, *Transfigured Night* is now recognized as Schönberg's first musical masterpiece.

It is important for conductors to study the original sextet version because Schönberg left helpful markings in it that do not appear in later transcriptions. In the 1943 revision Schönberg indicates passages of primary importance with a capital P that should not be interpreted as a dynamic marking. Likewise a capital S indicates passages of secondary importance with the graphic ⌐ indicating the end of the passage. Schönberg did not depict the action of the poem, but rather the moods and emotions surrounding the events and characters. In his interpretation, Mitropoulos has musically emphasized each of these emotions in turn.

The opening sound is the reiteration of four low D♮s that Mitropoulos interprets with a slight accent and a decrescendo. The beginning is marked *grave* with a dynamic indication of *pp* and hints at D minor. Mitropoulos conducts a slight crescendo on the eight-note pick-up to measure 3 giving the music a wonderful sense of forward motion. The sixteenth-note pick-up in measure 6 is carefully placed as Mitropoulos adjusts the balance to the lower strings. The music becomes more animated in measure 8 with a faster tempo, and Mitropoulos inserts a slight ritard in measures 9 and 10 for the expressive crescendo and decrescendo. As I listen to this brooding opening and Mitropoulos's direction, I can easily imagine the hidden emotions of two people walking together, afraid to speak.

In measure 13 Mitropoulos follows Schönberg's phrase markings and inserts a small break with a *luftpause*, but the intensity quickly returns with the chromatic sequence in measures 18–21. Mitropoulos enhances the shape of the plaintive melody found in measure 22 of the first viola part by placing a crescendo on the sixteenth notes. As the promenade theme from measures 3–6 returns in measures 24–25, the first violas have a drop of a descending fifth, made more poignant when Mitropoulos inserts a crescendo that sounds like a musical sigh.

The music becomes agitated at measure 29 as Mitropoulos increases the tempo and brings out the viola melody. Measure 33 builds from *p* to *f* and to ♩ = 84 at measure 34, where the woman reveals her painful secret. This is one of the most dramatic confessionals in all music, and Mitropoulos conducts with uninhibited emotion that perfectly conveys the intensity of the moment. Mitropoulos interprets the unbearable tension with exaggerated crescendos, decrescendos, and a ritard that finally subsides at the *calando* in measure 41.

The next section, measures 50–74, describes the woman's remorse for her sin as she tells the man she has lost any hope of happiness and is lonely in her marriage. In the original sextet Schönberg wrote that this section should be performed with extreme grief, which is exactly how Mitropoulos interprets it. A slight crescendo on the descending cello line in measure 50 and a *tenuto* on the dotted eighth note on beat two, along with the same treatment of the answer, bring the passage to life.

In measures 135–188 of this confessional the music parallels the poetry that describes the woman's grief as she walks beside the man she truly loves. The orchestration is interesting as Schönberg has violins 1, violas 2, and cellos 2 play without mutes while violins 2, violas 1, and cellos 1 use mutes. Mitropoulos interprets this section as turbulent and passionate and brings out the heavily accented quarter-note pick-up in the low strings on the fourth beat of measure 136 and emphasizes the precise dotted rhythm.

In the original sextet Schönberg indicated that this section should be performed "wild with abandonment." Mitropoulos's interpretation of the ritardandos, dynamic contrasts, and texture is a fascinating study for all conductors because the music sounds improvised, yet perfectly in control. Measure 153 becomes more agitated, faster, and passionate and builds to a climax in measure

175. Schönberg wrote in the sextet version that the music should become very broad at this point, which Mitropoulos does by starting a *molto ritard* and inserting accents on the first and third beats of measure 178.

Part II of the tone poem describes the man's forgiveness, which leads to a night of transfiguration instead of a night of tragedy. This section, beginning at measure 229, is marked *adagio* and sounds like a romantic segment from a Sibelius symphony as the man speaks his forgiveness for the woman. The *agitato* melody from measure 29 returns in measure 236 in counterpoint to the first violin line. With several active lines Mitropoulos adjusts the balance so that the agitato melody stands out.

In measure 266 the tempo broadens to reflect the warmth of their love, and the man explains to the woman…"a special warmth flickers from you into me, from me into you." The *ppp* measures 226–269 build in intensity to a passionate climax in measure 337. Mitropoulos brings out the *fff* ascending quarter notes and crescendos on the descending triplets in 339 to a D major cadence marked *pp* in measure 343. The atmospheric sound of the introduction returns in measure 401 to describe the lovers as they resume walking in the moonlight.

Today Dimitri Mitropoulos is recognized in Europe with Toscanini and Furtwängler as an all-time great conductor. In America his historic recordings with the Minneapolis and New York orchestras are reissued on compact disc. Through these recordings we can study Mitropoulos's greatest interpretations and paraphrase Mahler's confident declaration, "*Meine zeit wird noch kommen.*—My time will yet come." There are many indications that for Mitropoulos, his time is now.

CHAPTER 19

The Legacy of Eugene Ormandy

Many important Hungarian conductors, including Nikisch, Reiner, Szell, Solti, Dorati, Fricsay, and Ormandy, contributed their talents to American orchestras. Of these conductors, Eugene Ormandy (1899–1985) had the longest tenure, with 42 years from 1938 to 1980 as the music director of the Philadelphia Orchestra. At the end of the 1979–80 season he was appointed conductor laureate.

Ormandy was a precocious child who could sing over 50 compositions from memory by age two and play the violin at three. With absolute pitch and absolute time he had the ability to hear a work in his head and measure the precise duration. He entered the Budapest Musical Academy at the age of five, the youngest student ever admitted, and gave his first public performance two years later. After receiving a master's degree at age 14, he was named to the highest violin position at the academy at the age of 20.

He toured Europe as a violin virtuoso and was offered a lucrative concert tour in New York. Ormandy went there, but the tour never materialized so he took a position as a violinist in New York's Capital Theater, the city's largest movie house for silent movies. After only a week Ormandy was promoted to first violin and soon became the conductor. This was great training because he

had to draw sounds from the orchestra that matched whatever emotions were shown on the screen.

When Ormandy traded the violin for the baton, his father burst into tears saying, "If I had only disciplined you more severely, you might have been a great violinist." Ormandy's conducting talent soon brought requests for him to lead the orchestra in radio broadcasts and to conduct summer programs in Robin Hood Dell (Philadelphia) and in the Lewisohn Stadium (New York). With his remarkable memory Ormandy quickly learned new scores. Arturo Toscanini chose him to conduct three concerts by the NBC Symphony in Philadelphia, an opportunity to prove he was conductor of the first rank. He conducted the Minneapolis Symphony for five years, which led to a number of engagements as guest conductor of the Philadelphia Orchestra. In 1936 he was named co-conductor with Leopold Stokowski and took over as music director in 1938.

Music critic Paul Henry Lang described the Philadelphia Orchestra under Ormandy as "the solid gold Cadillac" for rich, opulent sound, which became his trademark. No other orchestra has ever quite duplicated the rich sonorities he drew from the Philadelphia strings.

> Ormandy described the Philadelphia sound very simply: It's me. My conducting is what it is because I was a violinist. Toscanini was always playing the cello when he conducted, Koussevitzky the double bass, Stokowski the organ. The conductors who were pianists nearly always have a sharper, more percussive beat, and it can be heard in their orchestras. (Schonberg 340)

Some of Ormandy's greatest accomplishments were his passionate interpretations of music by such late Romantics as Tchaikovsky, Sibelius, and Rachmaninoff. Ormandy shaped melodic lines with subtle rubato inflections that allowed the phrase to breathe and become alive. He knew the emotional landmarks of each composer so well that the sounds he drew from the orchestra gave a master class in musical architecture.

Critics sometimes overlook Ormandy's skill at accompanying fine soloists, including Sergei Rachmaninoff, Fritz Kreisler, Lauritz Melchior, Kirsten Flagstad, Artur Rubinstin, and Isaac Stern. He could lead the orchestra and follow the soloists at the same time with such flexibility that his technique never became apparent. He knew exactly when to let a singer breathe or when to speed up or slow down to keep the ensemble exactly with the soloist and with flawless dynamic balance between them.

Eugene Ormandy has been praised for his performances of late Romantic composers, but I find his interpretations of the music of Sergei Rachmaninoff (1873–1943) to be his best. Ormandy had a special affinity for this Russian master and gave his music warmth and spiritual depth.

Rachmaninoff was a dedicated disciple and student of Tchaikovsky and continued to write Romantic music even when other contemporary composers frowned upon it. Rachmaninoff received wide recognition for his Prelude in C♯ Minor, but other early works such as the Symphony # 1 and the Piano Concerto

1, were considered failures by the music critics, who allowed that Rachmaninoff could write lovely themes but lacked the talent to develop them.

After these early failures Rachmaninoff became unable to compose and sought psychological help for three years to regain his confidence. Rachmaninoff wrote to a friend in 1907 that he had no great sympathy for modern music and believed that many composers of the day had upset the laws of music before they had mastered them. Rachmaninoff contended that "a composer's music should express the country of his birth, his romantic life, his religion, the books that influenced him, and the pictures he loves—in short the sum total of his experience." (Kaufman 106)

Rachmaninoff said,

> I try to make music speak simply and directly that which is in my heart at the time I am composing. If there is love there, or bitterness, or sadness, or religion, these moods become part of my music…. For composing music is as much part of my living as breathing and eating. I compose music because I must give expression to my feelings, just as I talk because I must give utterance to my thoughts. (Ewen 610)

Rachmaninoff was an extraordinary musician, gifted as a composer, conductor, and virtuoso pianist. Today his music is a reminder that Romanticism will never die as long as you have immortal melodies that speak to the soul of mankind.

Rachmaninoff completed the *Symphonic Dances*, his last major work, during the summer of 1940 while in Huntington, Long Island. He died in Beverly Hills, California in 1943. Eugene Ormandy and Sergei Rachmaninoff were kindred spirits who believed in the expressive power of music. On the title page Rachmaninoff dedicated the *Symphonic Dances* to Eugene Ormandy and the Philadelphia Orchestra, and they gave the world premiere on January 3, 1941. Ormandy's 1960 Philadelphia Orchestra recording of Rachmaninoff's *Symphonic Dances* for Orchestra, Op. 45, has been reissued on Sony Classical (CDSBK48279). The sound of the orchestra is simply magnificent in capturing every romantic nuance of Rachmaninoff's music.

The three movements were originally subtitled "Midday," "Twilight," and "Midnight," but he later removed these, not wanting his music to be associated with any extra musical suggestions. The name *Symphonic Dances* is derived from the waltz rhythm of the second movement.

The first page of the score lacks any tempo markings beyond the Italian direction of *Non Allegro*. Ormandy chose a tempo of ♩ = 100–104, at which the opening staccato eighth notes in the first violins establish a rhythmic foundation for the English horn entrance in the second measure, later imitated by clarinet, bassoon, and bass clarinet. This motivic fragment becomes the rhythmic basis for the first movement. Each instrument comes in at the same volume and almost sounds like a single instrument but with different colors.

The orchestra enters on the second beat with a series of marcato eighth-note chords marked *ff*, a dramatic transition of six measures. One of Ormandy's great talents is reflected in the ringing, full sonority of the strings as they punctuate marcato chords with accented down bows. Ormandy augments the cadences in the fifth and sixth measures after $\boxed{1}$ with a timpani crescendo on the *ff* 16th notes.

After this dramatic introduction bassoons, cellos, string basses, and the contra bassoon enter with the rhythmic motive established by the English horn in the second measure. The *molto marcato* low reeds and strings outline the key of C minor two measures before $\boxed{2}$. Ormandy also brings out the French horns two measures before $\boxed{2}$ and slightly accents the horns' fourth-beat quarter notes to lift and space this beat before the next measure. The violins and violas establish rhythmic drive by accenting beats one and four on the eighth-note pattern two measures before $\boxed{2}$.

At $\boxed{2}$ Ormandy emphasizes the rhythmic motive in the oboes, clarinets, and trumpets by driving the two 16th notes to the accented ♩. notes. These rhythmic fragments are tossed about the orchestra and are finally joined in a continuous 16th-note melody in the third measure after $\boxed{2}$ in the flutes, oboes, and clarinets. Here Ormandy brings the orchestra down to *mf* for the woodwinds to be heard.

Rachmaninoff develops the 16th-note motive *molto marcato* throughout the orchestra. The flute has a graceful little melody marked *mf* three measures after $\boxed{9}$, a transition to bring back the melody motive in the English horn, clarinet, and bass clarinet that is similar to the first measures of the composition.

After slowing the tempo six measures after $\boxed{10}$ Rachmaninoff wrote a poignant and eloquent alto saxophone passage that is one of the lyrical jewels in the saxophone orchestral repertoire. One of Rachmaninoff's most beautiful melodies, this reflective music is rich with expressive nuances ideally suited to the saxophone timbre.

At $\boxed{14}$ the strings play a lovely theme that soars lyrically. This grand moment epitomizes the famous Philadelphia string sound. For sheer lushness the marvelous Philadelphia sound is unmatched. Ormandy's is one of the most passionate interpretations of this melody I have heard, a perfect embodiment of Romantic melody as phrases are stretched with a flexible rubato that lets the music soar upward, fall back, hesitate, then surge forward, pulsating with life. With passion and musical conviction Ormandy holds nothing back.

Four measures after $\boxed{17}$ the mood changes to *piu mosso*, which Ormandy conducts at ♩ = 100. This *misterioso* section starts with a bass clarinet solo playing staccato eighth notes *pp* with string harmony, and later is imitated by second bassoon, then by first bassoon. As the tempo accelerates Ormandy brings out the 16th-note fanfare by trumpets and woodwinds much like the beginning.

Four measures before $\boxed{22}$ a staccato eight-note transitional passage in the woodwinds and strings alternates from $\frac{4}{4}$ to $\frac{2}{4}$ meter to lead back to the key of C minor at $\boxed{22}$. Six measures after $\boxed{26}$ the music modulates to C major with arpeggios in the piano, harp, flute, and bells. The broken chords accompany another inspired Rachmaninoff melody, worthy of music from a Tchaikovsky ballet. The cantabile string melody is built around a descending C major scale and demonstrates what a great composer can do with the simple harmonies of a C major scale.

The coda starts at 28 as the oboe brings back the 16th-note motive and the bassoon answers. The flute and clarinet exchange short solos in a transition to a 16th-note English horn motive answered by the second violins.

In the last two measures of the composition the first violins play the final eighth and quarter notes with a tenuto bow stroke instead of the indicated pizzicato. This is in keeping with the Italian directive *perdendo* meaning to let the sound vanish and fade away.

The *Symphonic Dances* are particularly well suited to the conducting style and skills of Eugene Ormandy, who earned a reputation for developing velvety and opulent sonorities, a trait often found in the compositions of Sergei Rachmaninoff.

CHAPTER 20

The Haunting Beauty of Tchaikovsky in the Hands of Herbert von Karajan

One of master conductor Herbert von Karajan's most impressive interpretations is the deeply moving but controlled performance of the Tchaikovsky Sixth Symphony with the Vienna Philharmonic. Karajan recorded this symphony more often than any other, and this performance was filmed by Sony Classical in January 1984. The *Pathétique* symphony has been subjected to many hackneyed performances by podium posers who turned it into a showpiece of slobbering melodrama.

Under Karajan's baton the music depicts loneliness, confusion, and alienation from the rest of the world. Music critic Lawrence Gilman wrote that the *Pathétique* is among the most touching disclosures in art, a thing of deep and terrible sincerity, of an eloquence that at times is overwhelming, that is filled in its richest moments with a searching and unforgettable beauty."

Karajan was born in Salzburg, Austria in 1908 and studied piano at an early age. He attended the Mozarteum in Salzburg and took conducting lessons from Bernard Paumgartner, the director of the Mozarteum, and later studied conduct-

© *The Instrumentalist*, July 2002. Reprinted with Permission.

ing at the Vienna Academy with Franz Schalk. Karajan first conducted a concert on January 23, 1929, a performance with the Mozarteum Orchestra in Salzburg that included *Don Juan* by Strauss, a Mozart piano concerto, and Tchaikovsky's Fifth Symphony. The concert was so well received that Karajan was appointed music director of the opera in Ulm.

In 1934 he went from Ulm to Aachen, where he conducted opera and symphony concerts. He conducted every score from memory, including the complete Ring Cycle of Wagner. During World War II he remained in Germany and in 1955 succeeded Wilhelm Furtwängler as music director of the Berlin Philharmonic.

During his tenure as artistic director, the Berlin Philharmonic became one of the great orchestras in the world. Karajan also was music director of the Vienna State Opera, the Salzburg Music Festival, the Vienna Symphony, the London Philharmonic Orchestra, and La Scala Opera in Milan. Without a doubt, Karajan was the busiest maestro on the continent. Harold Schonberg wrote in *The Great Conductors* that when asked by a cab driver where he wanted to go, Karajan responded, "It doesn't matter; I've got something going everywhere."

Karajan excelled at everything he undertook from conducting great masterworks and racing sports cars through the mountains to flying an airplane across the Alps, or skiing the slopes of Salzburg. He was a conductor larger than life, "the epitome of the artist as hero," according to *Time* magazine. Above all he was the quintessential virtuoso conductor.

Karajan was indeed a strong personality and demanded absolute perfection from musicians. His dogmatic opinions prompted controversy at times; but beneath a stern expression and a brusque manner, was the rare conductor who combined technical precision with a phenomenal awareness and vision of orchestral sounds. Karajan had extraordinary baton techniques despite his refusal to use the conducting diagrams found in textbooks. He considered it more important for a conductor to have inner rhythm than a fancy baton technique.

> I have no theories about stick technique: a baton, a pencil, it makes no difference. You can tie my wrist to my side, and the orchestra will still get the beat. I tell my students, 'You must feel the tempos and rhythms, and then the orchestra will feel them.' (Schonberg 326)

Karajan conducted with his eyes closed to project the image of the music he conceived in his mind. At first this bothered members of the Berlin Philharmonic until they grew accustomed to the intuitive communications between conductor and orchestra. Karajan believed that there is a sense in which the greatest art in conducting is to know when one should not conduct. When the eyes are open, a musician is chained to the printed page in front of him. The film of Karajan conducting the *Pathétique* is a study of the art of conducting at its finest because he shows us that it is what happens between the beats that controls the musical interpretation. Karajan had the ability to create seamless and beautiful musical lines.

Tchaikovsky began work on a sixth symphony upon his return from America in 1891, but aborted the partially orchestrated work in 1892, transforming one movement into the Third Piano Concerto. At the time he wrote to a nephew, Vladimir Davidoff, that "it contained little that was fine, an empty patter of sounds without any inspiration." Tchaikovsky thought of the *Pathétique* while on a train to Paris composing it in his mind and then finishing the first movement at home in less than four days.

The subtitle, *pathetique* in French, should be translated as passionate or emotional, not pathetic. This was suggested by Tchaikovsky's brother, Modeste, but not given to the symphony until Tchaikovsky wrote *Pathétique* on the front page of the score after the premiere.

Tchaikovsky first conducted the symphony in St. Petersburg October 1, 1893. Pianist Ossip Gabrilowitsch said of the event, "Everyone was visibly disappointed. This was due, in part, to the unaccustomed style of the work, the tragic gloom of the first and last movements, and the very somber ending, and in part to Tchaikovsky's unsatisfactory rendering. He was a poor conductor."

Tchaikovsky was profoundly depressed by the poor impression the symphony made, but he insisted that it was his most important work. Tchaikovsky died only nine days after the performance. In a letter to his brother Tchaikovsky wrote, "I am a little embarrassed by the circumstance that my symphony, which I have just finished, is in its mood very close to a requiem." Although the official ruling of his death was that he contracted cholera from drinking un-boiled water, later research suggests that Tchaikovsky may have committed suicide.

There was a national outpouring of grief at Tchaikovsky's funeral and schools were closed. The *Pathétique* was performed in St. Petersburg in his honor and conducted by the great Russian maestro Eduard Napravnik. Only then did people realize the value of this symphony.

Karajan takes the first movement of the *Pathétique* at ♩ = 48, although the score is marked *Adagio* ♩ = 54. This melancholy movement unfolds slowly, almost like the curtain going up at the beginning of a Greek tragedy. Karajan gives an anticipatory beat and the basses enter on a perfect fifth after the beat before he starts conducting. The principal motive is a solo bassoon against droning bass lines in the development section, a difficult passage because the bassoon comes in *pp* and has to match the E♮ in the string basses. Instead of conducting the bassoon entrance, Karajan waits for the bassoon to sound the low E before conducting the fourth beat. In this slow introduction Karajan creates an atmosphere of despair and depression.

The exposition is based on the opening bassoon solo and begins in the strings on the fourth beat of measure 19. Although marked *Allegro non troppo* (♩= 116), Karajan conducts it at a slower tempo (♩= 112), but the music is so cleanly played that it gives the impression of being faster. Karajan begins each section at the same volume and exaggerates the hairpin crescendos and decrescendos. This turns the exposition into an animated dialogue between the instruments.

The intensity builds as Karajan connects 16th-note ascending and descending scales of the entering sections, sounding as though they are played by one instrument. As thematic fragments are tossed from instrument to instrument, Karajan creates a seamless musical line with a remarkable balance and conveys his extraordinary concentration to the orchestra. The intensity of the opening exposition subsides into a beautiful melody in measure 89 that begins with three eighth-note pick-ups in muted first violins and cellos.

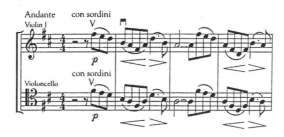

Karajan conducts this section at ♩ = 72, and the sheer beauty he draws out of the players is amazing. A master at writing enduring melodies that pull at the heartstrings, Tchaikovsky's passionate and inspired theme exemplifies Russian melodic and instrumental lyricism. Karajan captures the yearning intensity of the melody without resorting to melodrama; he uses rubato effectively without exaggerating the tempo.

After a canon between flute and bassoon in measure 101 the famous theme returns at measure 131 as the now un-muted $\frac{4}{4}$ strings sing over a restless wind accompaniment in $\frac{12}{8}$.

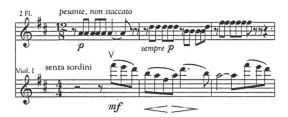

After the climax in measures 139–140 the melody dies to a *pppp* clarinet solo. Tchaikovsky dovetails the descending eighth notes in the clarinet into the bassoon part, which goes down to a fermata on low D marked *ppppp*. Few conductors besides Toscanini follow this orchestration and instead have the bass clarinet play the final four notes of the bassoon part. Karajan also chose this bass clarinet timbre, which blends well with the A clarinet.

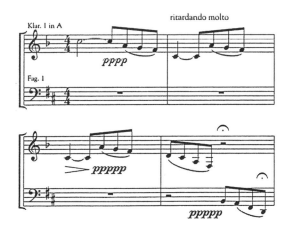

The development section begins *Allegro vivo* (♩ = 144) in measure 161 before exploding to *ff* at a tempo of ♩ = 152. Karajan assaults the listener with a ferocious, relentless sound, but the music never spins out of control and captures the genius of Tchaikovsky using simple orchestration on the fourth beat of measure 170 to create enormous power. The violins take over the bassoon theme from the introduction with fugue-like variations while other strings play scale fragments as a countersubject. The development explodes with ferocious fury:

the first bassoon theme plays ascending and descending scales in the strings and woodwinds with a dash of syncopation added in.

The main theme returns when the fury dies away in measure 305 and echoes the beautiful theme first played in measure 89 by the violins. The music grows in intensity and reaches a climax in measures 313–314 before dying away with a solo clarinet playing *pppp*.

The coda in measure 335 starts with a descending pizzicato scale in the strings to accompany the brass chorale in measure 336. The *Andante mosso* (♩ = 80) floats away to nothing and ends with a brass B major chord punctuated by soft timpani.

Karajan described the art of conducting:
In our profession someone can be very brilliant and acquire total technical mastery. Yet in the last resort, the only thing that really counts is his quality as a human being. For music is created by man for man. And if someone sees nothing more than notes in it, this can perhaps be very interesting, but it cannot enrich him. Music should exist for one purpose only: to enrich him and give him something he has lost in most respects. (Osborne)

When Herbert von Karajan died in Salzburg on July 16, 1989 he left a legacy of more than 800 recordings and CD's and over 50 hours of video recordings. He was one of the finest conductors to ever take the podium and with over 100 million recordings sold over the years, his interpretations have influenced conductors the world over. His recordings of Mozart, Beethoven, and the opera productions of Verdi and Puccini document the creative insights of Herbert von Karajan.

CHAPTER 21

The Legacy of Leonard Bernstein

In the beginning was the note and the note was with God. And whosoever can reach for that note, reach high and bring it back to us on earth, to our earthly ears, for he is a composer. And to the extent of his reach partakes of the divine. —Leonard Bernstein

Leonard Bernstein's life as a conductor, composer, pianist and educator continues to resonate in the new millennium with a greater poignancy than any of us who were raised in the turbulent 60's could have expected. When we look back at his enduring legacy we remember that it was Leonard Bernstein's music and conducting that gave us hope and inspiration during our formative years, and served as an emotional anchor through those volatile times. Who can forget after the assassination of President John F. Kennedy when Leonard Bernstein conducted an emotionally draining performance of the Mahler *Resurrection Symphony* on television? A few years later when Robert Kennedy was struck down by an assassin's bullet, Bernstein conducted the Adagietto from Mahler's Fifth Symphony. Many years later, when the Berlin Wall came down, Bernstein traveled to Berlin to lead an inspired performance of Beethoven's Ninth Symphony by an orchestra composed of musicians from all over the world. Bernstein made this performance even more poignant when he substituted the word *freiheit* (freedom) for *freude* (joy) in the choral finale.

This prodigiously gifted all-round musician was born in Lawrence, Massachusetts August 25, 1918, the son of middle-class Jewish immigrants. His father, Samuel Bernstein, had a beauty-parlor business and expected later that Lenny would go into the business. His father allowed Bernstein to take piano lessons with Helen Coates in Boston after he exhibited early musical talent but when his son decided he wanted to major in music in college they had many bitter arguments. Eventually his father relented and Bernstein entered Harvard in 1935 to study music. His professor of counterpoint and fugue was Walter Piston. Bernstein graduated with highest honors in 1939 and was accepted to the Curtis Institute of Music where he studied piano with Isabelle Vergerova, orchestration with Randall Thompson, and conducting with Fritz Reiner.

Legend has it that Leonard Bernstein was the only student to ever make an A in Reiner's demanding conducting course at Curtis. Bernstein described Reiner's teaching method as "tyrannical in the extreme. He demanded total knowledge. You had no right to step on the podium unless you knew everything about what every member of the orchestra had to do; and if you didn't God pity you…" (H. Burton 90)

© *The Instrumentalist.* Reprinted with Permission.

In the summer of 1940 at Tanglewood, Bernstein's conducting career started to grow. As a conducting student of Serge Koussevitzky, Bernstein began a life-long association with the Boston Symphony orchestra and its esteemed conductor. Koussevitzky took special pride in helping Bernstein. As Koussevitzky's protégé, Bernstein developed into a professional conductor and made important contacts with Aaron Copland, Dimitri Mitropoulous and Arthur Rodzinski, who was appointed as conductor and music director of the New York Philharmonic in 1943. When Bernstein was only 25, Rodzinski asked Bernstein to become Assistant Conductor of the New York Philharmonic. When asked why he chose the young Bernstein to be his assistant, Rodzinski replied, "because God told me to." It was in this post that Bernstein made his historic conducting debut as a substitute for the ailing Bruno Walter at a Carnegie Hall concert November 14, 1943. The performance made Bernstein an overnight success and he received invitations to conduct orchestras all over the world.

Bernstein's early successes in conducting opened the door of American music to the world: he was the first American to become music director of a major American Orchestra (the New York Philharmonic); the first American to conduct the Berlin Philharmonic, the London Symphony Orchestra, and the Concertgebow, and the first American to conduct at La Scala. However, critics who favored the classical conducting style of Toscanini and Reiner did not appreciate Bernstein's podium mannerisms. Bernstein would leap all over the podium in an orgiastic frenzy, swiveling his hips in such fashion he was nicknamed the Presley of the Podium. A critic wrote:

> Bernstein is the most choreographic of all contemporary conductors. He is a specialist in the clenched fist, the hip swivel, the pelvic thrust, the levitation effect that makes him hover in the air in defiance of the laws of gravity, the uppercut, the haymaker. (Schonberg 357)

Bernstein's movements pantomimed the music so closely that Stravinsky, after watching Bernstein's podium gymnastics, accused him of "giving a performance of a performance." (Schonberg 18) However, beneath all that charismatic showmanship was a profound musician who conducted with passion and intensity. His interpretations were highly emotional, sentimental and untraditional and he communicated his ideas with complete conviction. What the critics failed to see in all these podium antics was that Bernstein was a Romantic throwback to the past, much like Liszt, Wagner, and Furtwängler.

To me, Leonard Bernstein was one of the most gifted music educators and one of the most influential musicians of the second half of the 20th century through his nationally acclaimed television series of Young People's Concerts. Bernstein considered the Young People's Concerts among his favorite and most highly prized activities of his life. Viewed nationwide on CBS television, and eventually telecast around the world, the Young People's Concerts were on the air from 1958–1973. Leonard Bernstein and the New York Philharmonic touched the lives of millions of people with their knowledge and musicality. Dave Brubeck once said, "I daresay that he (Bernstein) has educated more young minds to become receptive to all kinds of music than all the world's conservatories put together." (Brochure 3) As an educator Bernstein was a Maestro with a mission as he packed Carnegie Hall and Lincoln Center year after year with fabulously successful concerts that unlocked the door to the secrets of the world's greatest symphonic music to children of all ages.

Bernstein reminded us why we wanted to become musicians and taught us that it was okay to feel music deeply when he wrote, "There are feelings so deep and special that we have no words for them, and that's where music is especially marvelous. It names the feelings for us, only in notes instead of words." (Brochure 7)

A few years before his death in 1990 at age 72, Leonard Bernstein remarked, "God knows, I should be dead by now. I smoke. I drink. I stay up all night. I'm over committed on all fronts. I was told that if I didn't stop smoking, I'd be dead at 35. Well, I beat the rap." (Peyser 1) He was wrong about this, but managed to live for 22 years after being diagnosed with lung cancer at age 50. In his later years Bernstein became a caricature of his former self and wore flowing capes, rode in limousines, drank scotch at the intermissions of his concerts, and would kiss his concertmaster and anyone else within reach.

Andre Previn wrote that "Lenny Bernstein skipped middle age and went from being Lenny to the grand old man in one jump." (Chapin 167) Bernstein hated getting old and lived life at a flat-out pace, refusing to slow down, and tasting everything life had to offer. He slept only a few hours each night and often attended all-night parties. These overindulgences finally caught up with him and he died of severe emphysema and a pleural tumor on October 14, 1990.

Many of us found his self-destructiveness and ostentatious lifestyle to be evidence of his superficial side, but perhaps it was an outgrowth of how he thought a celebrity conductor should behave. Despite this side of him, Bernstein had prodigious musical talent, suffered from depression and considered his life to be a complete failure.

Michael Walsh wrote in *Time* magazine (October 29, 1990) that "His tragedy was that he had too many talents and not quite enough genius. He wanted to be Mahler but had to settle in the end for being Leonard Bernstein, but that in itself was a dazzling achievement." (Walsh 113)

Like George Gershwin, Bernstein was equally at home in the classical and popular fields. Both wrote popular theater music the public loved, but critics scorned their serious compositions. Bernstein was influenced by the music of Copland, Stravinsky, Mahler and Richard Strauss but this eclecticism never pleased music critics who found something lacking in his music and this rejection by critics was the major disappointment of Bernstein's life. One of the most severe critics was Harold Schonberg, of the *New York Times*, who described Bernstein and his Mass as "an overblown, rather preposterous exercise in self indulgence whose ego was getting in the way of his music-making." (W.Burton 33) Olin Downes described Bernstein's Second Symphony, *Age of Anxiety*, as a masterpiece of superficiality." (W.Burton 48) Mstislav Rostropovich declared,

> I think he had great possibility as a composer. I also think that without him the United States could not have existed musically because he is a portrait of United States music. When Lenny tried to become a deep composer, like Mahler, or, for example, Beethoven, then it was perhaps not so successful…, but when he tried to make a portrait of himself, his emotion and temperament, then he was a good composer. (W.Burton 137)

Many people believed that Bernstein wanted to be a composite of Mahler, Koussevitzky, Gershwin, pianist, educator, and author, all rolled into one. Harold Schonberg thought that if Bernstein concentrated only on Broadway, he could have been America's Offenbach. Yet, his crossover eclecticism is what made Bernstein larger than life and popular to such a large audience.

Leonard Bernstein was such an integral part of the international musical scene we sometimes took him for granted. But when he died, the world was in shock and deeply mourned his passing. One European critic wrote: "when Karajan died the year before, corporations mourned. When Bernstein went, men and women wept in every metropolis as they recalled his extravagances and whistled tunes from *West Side Story*." (W.Burton 1)

Because Bernstein composed music with deep feelings, he touched our hearts with his humanity and vulnerability. His biographer, Schuyler Chapin, wrote, "The Danes have a wonderful expression: To live in hearts we leave behind is not to die." Leonard Bernstein could never die. He lives in too many hearts. (Chapin 17) Conductors will still be performing *Overture to Candide* and Bernstein's masterpiece, *West Side Story*, years from now.

Of all Bernstein's achievements as a composer, I think that the *Overture to Candide* is one of his greatest. The music is brilliant, witty, and bubbles like good champagne. This delightful and original music is now among the most frequently performed orchestra works by a 20th-century composer. Only four minutes long, it is great as a curtain-raiser or as an encore. Bernstein once wrote, "*Candide* was written as a kind of personal love letter to European music. It's an American Valentine to Europe…a kind of salute to everything I love in Gilbert and Sullivan, in Offenbach, and Bellini, even." (Bernstein-*www*) The overture is a true American classic still sounding as fresh, rousing and spontaneous as it did when first composed in the 1950's. The New York Philharmonic Orchestra with Bernstein conducting gave the first concert performance of the overture in New York on January 26, 1957.

Since the overture was composed I have listened to many interpretations, most by Bernstein, but the most poignant was one played without a conductor in 1997 by the New York Philharmonic as a memorial to Bernstein to open its 150th anniversary concert. Concertmaster Glen Dicterow walked on the stage, turned the light on the conductor's stand, gave a downbeat, sat down, and the orchestra performed an inspired *Candide* overture. It was almost as if the spirit of Bernstein had stood on the podium leading once more. This performance is included in the CD collection "An American Celebration."

The performance is outstanding for many reasons but I think the most important reason is that I have never heard it performed with so much love and tenderness.

The Philharmonic's performance of the overture lasted 4:35 seconds which was much slower than the snappy tempo usually heard lasting only four minutes, as indicated on the score. But I prefer the slower tempo because it allowed the music to breathe and phrase together instead of the noisy unarticulated performance usually heard.

The musical form of the overture is that of a sonatina with three major themes, then a restatement of the same material without development and a closing coda. Bernstein marks the opening boisterous fanfare *ff* theme *allegro molto con brio* with ♩ = 152, however the Philharmonic takes this opening at a ♩ = 144, but the articulation of the brass is so clean that it sounds much faster.

It is one of the greatest introductions ever composed for an overture, right away capturing the sparkle and gaiety of the comic operetta based on Voltaire's book, *Candide.* The opening fanfare theme is a six-measure phrase with the trumpets and trombones demonstrating excellent blend, balance and intonation on the half note chords. With non-professional brass, these openings chords are usually pinched sharp and held over too long instead of releasing exactly on the second beat so that the low reeds, tuba and timpani can be heard on their entrance on the end of the second beat.

Starting in measure 32 there occurs a robust theme in the woodwinds, horns, and strings, which perfectly described the hustle and bustle of New York City. With accented quarter notes and noisy glissandos this march-like theme paints a picture of downtown Manhattan better than any other composer I have ever heard. (The only other composer that I know whose music captures the excitement of New York City is George Gershwin's opening clarinet glissando in *Rhapsody in Blue.*) This section may be phrased as 7 + 7 + 1.

The second major theme starts three measures before 50 in Bb major and is reminiscent of a can-can theme composed by Offenbach. It can be outlined as a 15 measure phrase (8 + 7) with the trumpets and trombones having the melody over a rhythmic quarter note driving accompaniment by low strings, tuba, and timpani playing the tonic and dominant in Bb major with added color by the cymbals.

The transition section from measures 63 to 83 features the Philharmonic woodwinds as Bernstein takes material from the introduction and passes it back and forth to different sections. Starting with a happy little solo by the first flute in measure 63 the solo clarinet picks it up in measure 65 and passes the solo off to the 1st bassoon in measure 67. Then Bernstein breaks these two-bar solos into smaller fragments that pass from flute, Eb clarinet, 2nd oboe, finally giving over to the piccolo solo in measure 75. The piccolo continues the transition with a perky little staccato melody imitated by the first flutes in measure 80 with the Eb clarinet completing the transition starting in measure 81 playing descending quarter notes staccato leading into the third major theme in measure 83. What is unique about this transitional passage is that all woodwinds sound like one instrument as they do perfect imitations of each other.

Starting in measure 83 is one of Bernstein's greatest melodic achievements. The broad sweeping melody fits into a septuplet pattern of 2 + 2 + 3 and is worthy of Stravinsky and Brahms. The melody lasts for 51 measures and may be broken up into the following phrase groupings: 12 + 12 + 12+ 4 + 11. The conductor may think of this melody as being in an asymmetrical $\frac{7}{2}$ by erasing the bar lines of the given meter of ♩. ♩♩♩ ♩♩♩ ♩ and conducting the melody in an asymmetrical 3 pattern with an extended 3rd beat. ♩ ♪ ♩ ♪ ♪♩ ♪ ♩. The conductor's function here is not to be a time beater but to shape the melody and let it come alive *con amore*. This melody is derived from a lyrical duet in the operetta called *Oh Happy We*.

Following this beautiful melody there is a restatement of the fanfare theme found in the introduction. The coda starts in measure 207 right after the Grand Pause. The material for this exciting coda is in the tonic key of E♭ major and is taken from one of the best songs in the score, *Glitter and Be Gay*. The next 24 measures may be phrased in 1 + 8 + 8 + 7 starting with the staccatissmo accompaniment found in the bassoon and celli marked *pp*. In measure 208 the flute and oboe enter with the bouncing little tune again. The music becomes more excited when Bernstein shows off his compositional skills by having the clarinet and 2nd violins enter in canon, one beat behind the same melody found in the high woodwinds and 1st violins. Then, in measure 224, Bernstein increases the excitement by adding the French horns as a third voice in the canon.

In measure 231 the tempo is marked *piu mosso* ○ = 96 one beat per bar but the New York Philharmonic's tempo is felt in two at ♩ = 168 as they land on the tonic E♭ major chord marked *ff* which quickly drops to *piano* as the excitement starts to build all over again. The next 24 measures may be phrased 8 + 8 + 8.

With non-professional groups the percussion may have trouble with their entrances occurring on different beats. A good solution for accurate precision is to have the percussion read off the score so that they can see that even though they enter at different times the rhythm should actually come together sounding four equal quarters.

Measures 255–260 are a variation on the introduction with horns and trombones inserting some nasty glissandi on the second beat. Bernstein's polydynamic markings are important here and should be observed as the horns predominate over the trombone's *ff*. Measures 260–270 may be phrased 6 + 4 as the notes are flying by fast and furious and it helps for the conductor to think in phrases.

In measure 271 the can-can theme returns *fff* and the New York Philharmonic performs this theme with uninhibited sparkle and ferocity.

One measure before 280 the horns and trombones enter on an A♭ major whole note chord marked *fff* recalling the lyrical theme *Oh Happy We.* Four measures from the end woodwinds and strings fly up ascending eighth notes runs with the glockenspiel coming in on high B♭ in measure 285 to top off the run. For contrast the orchestra enters *pp* on a V^7 chord with the triangle adding color and the composition ends *ff* on an E♭ major chord with an added grace note sounding from the piccolo. ≈

CHAPTER 22

The Mahler Fifth Symphony Became Georg Solti's Trademark

ustav Mahler once told Sibelius that music should capture and reflect the emotions of the world, and essentially Mahler's music does just that. To know the music of Mahler is to remember and rediscover our inner selves through a long spiritual journey that reflects on nature, the innocence of childhood, adolescent yearning, first love, loss, despair, farewells, death, redemption, and resurrection.

Conductors Bruno Walter, Willem Mengelberg, Otto Klemperer, Jascha Horenstein, John Barbirolli, and Herbert von Karajan gave outstanding interpretations of the Fifth Symphony, but in the last decades of the 20th century Mahler's music reached a wide audience under the baton of Sir Georg Solti and the Chicago Symphony Orchestra. The Fifth Symphony became their trademark.

A neurotic, high-strung bundle of energy, Mahler lived in a thin, sickly body. He looked at the world through rimless glasses with fanatical morbid pessimism and a defective heart filled with spiritual doubts and longings. His life was marked by many personal tragedies: his brother committed suicide, his mother buried 8 of her 14 children, and the 1907 death of his daughter left an indelible emotional scar on his psyche.

Mahler followed the lineage of Beethoven, Brahms, and Wager and wrote music that is profound in its grandeur as well as having overwhelming emotion and elegance. Mahler captured and immortalized his tortured and tragic life while reflecting on the soul of humanity. Conductor Rafael Kubelik described Mahler as "a sufferer who forces man to look into a mirror and expose his own naked nerves." (Klaus 143)

Bruno Walter, a prodigy of Mahler's, stated that Mahler's music reflects his belief that death was the door to God and to eternity. Certainly Mahler's morbid preoccupation with death dominated much of the music of his final years, including his *Kindetotenlieder* song cycle ("Songs of Dead Children") and *Das*

Lied Von Der Erde ("Song of the Earth"), which bids a sorrowful farewell to the world. The closing moments of the Ninth Symphony also bid the world farewell with peace and resignation.

During his lifetime (1860–1911) Mahler was highly regarded as a conductor but not as a composer. From 1897–1907 he conducted the Vienna Royal Opera, and from 1908–1911, he conducted the Metropolitan Opera in New York and the New York Philharmonic Orchestra. Otto Klemperer thought Mahler to be one hundred times greater than Toscanini, but unfortunately Mahler and Toscanini did not respond sympathetically to each other while they were co-conductors of the Met and the New York Philharmonic. Toscanini was hostile to Mahler and described his music as "not fit for toilet paper." Despite turbulent feelings between the two conductors, many regard their tenure there as the golden age of the Met.

When Solti took over as conductor of the Chicago Symphony, his energy and temperament were a perfect match for the music of Mahler. With the Fifth Symphony, Solti experienced some of his greatest musical triumphs. He said,

> It was part of the program on our first tour of Carnegie Hall in New York, and we arrived with a certain trepidation, unsure how the New Yorkers would receive us, and we were still an unknown quantity. The reception at the end of the performance was overwhelming! When we finished the last movement, the audience stood up and screamed hysterically, as if it were a pop concert; they had fallen under the spell of our exceptional performance. The applause seemed endless. I had never experienced such a reception in my life and probably never will again. (Solit 168)

Without a doubt, Georg Solti (1912–1997) was one of the superconductors during the final quarter of the 20th century. At the Liszt Academy in his native Budapest, he studied piano, composition, and conducting with such notables as Bartók, Kodály, and Dohnányi. Solti was the last great conductor to have worked with Toscanini, Walter, Erich Kleiber, Furtwängler, Richard Strauss, and Stravinsky. Bruno Walter once told Solti that he was the link that will carry on the tradition of the great conductors and pass it on to the next generation. Solti observed,

> I only really learned how to conduct by watching the great conductors Erich Kleiber, Fritz Busch, and Bruno Walter, when I was a coach at the Budapest state opera in the 1930s. My experience with Toscanini at Salzburg in 1937 was also a revelation, for the magnificence of his interpretations and for the clarity of his conducting. (Solti 200)

What Solti learned from Toscanini and Furtwängler is that conducting technique is less important than a thorough knowledge of the score and that a conductor must develop his creative imagination and then convince an orchestra to play what he imagines.

Solti used large gestures on the podium and never had the grace of a Giulini. He once told the orchestra that even if he beat *forte* using large gestures that they must play *piano* where indicated. Solti's genius was not his baton technique but his disciplined presence on the podium. He combined a demonic energy with a conviction about how the music should sound after thoroughly mastering the score.

His large angular slashing gestures sometimes got so extreme that he twice stabbed himself with the baton. Ronald Blum says,

> People still talk about Sept. 8, 1976, when he conducted the *Marriage of Figaro* with the Paris Opera Orchestra at the Met. During the third act, Solti accidentally stabbed the baton into his forehead, opening a cut above his right eye. With blood streaming down his face, he left the podium for about a minute—as the performance continued—slapped some cold water on the cut and hopped right back on the podium. (Blum)William Furlong writes that sometimes Solti "looks like nothing so much as a spastic stork, bending and rearing convulsively, elbows pumping, knees popping, torso laboring until it seems almost as if he is going to tear the music from himself in a Dionysian frenzy." (Furlong 80)

> Solti sums up his baton technique by saying:
> Aside from wielding the baton, the basic necessity for a conductor is to know exactly how a certain passage should sound. If your imagination is clear, then you will communicate with the orchestra even though your beat and technique are not first-rate. If a conductor believes in what he is doing, if he is convincing and does not vacillate, the musicians will always follow him. (Solti 207)

Solti did not care about being pretty on the podium and came to rehearsals in baggy pants, an untucked shirt, and a towel wrapped around his neck, something like a boxer in training for a championship fight. No one doubts that Solti worked his magic on the Chicago Symphony Orchestra and communicated his visions of the music with power and energy.

I find his interpretation of Mahler's Fifth Symphony to be absolutely stunning and magnificent. His first recording of this work with the Chicago Symphony Orchestra in 1970 is one of the best Fifth's ever recorded. I also find his performance on March 26, 1986, in Tokyo (Sony SHV 46377) to be exciting because of its intensity and spontaneity. Solti's interpretation as recorded on film and video gains significance with each passing year, and young conductors could benefit greatly by watching Solti make music with the Chicago Symphony.

As a composer and conductor Mahler always gave detailed instructions about how his music should be performed. For the first movement of his Symphony #5, Mahler directed that the *Trauermarsch* (funeral march) be at a measured pace, strict tempo, like a funeral procession (*In gemessenem Schritt, Streng. Wie ein Konduk*).

Mahler writes, "not a single note points to the influence of extra musical thoughts or emotions upon the composition of the Fifth." But in a rehearsal of the movement with the Cologne orchestra, which gave the world premiere in 1904, Mahler said, "Think about someone who has had his ideas shattered." (Painter 299)

Whether the opening funeral march depicts the death of some great hero, or the shattering of Mahler's dreams, or even, as some say, the Christ bearing the cross, we will never know. We do know, however, that for Mahler composition was highly subjective, an intense experience, as he tried to understand the deeper meaning of life. Mahler stated "the creative act and actual experience are one and the same," and perhaps this is the key to interpreting this first movement. It may also be that the idea of opening his symphony with a funeral march had origins in his subconscious as a small boy when he lived near a military base and often heard bugle calls and march music.

The opening solo trumpet introduces the theme in C♯ minor. The legendary principal trumpet of the Chicago Symphony, Adolph Herseth, plays the opening fanfare as no one else could. In itself it is a masterclass on the art of tone production, inspired musicianship, and his uncanny ability to tell a story with the music. Herseth's performance on this work has become the standard by which other trumpet players measure themselves. With a few notes Herseth captures the sorrowful mood of a funeral procession as it passes slowly by.

1: first page

Although the score has no metronome markings, Solti gives two silent prep beats at a tempo of $\quad$ = 63 in $\frac{2}{2}$ meter. These first few measures are a painting in sound that sets the dark mood for the underlying sorrow in this music. Mahler instructs that "the upbeat triplets of this theme should always be executed somewhat hurriedly (*quasi accel*), in the manner of military fanfares." Herseth starts the triplet pick-up at the indicated dynamic of *piano*, but it has a presence and quickly crescendos to the half note (marked *sf* with an accent). There is an edge to the passage, a sense of granite-like strength communicated through the perfectly controlled crescendo on each triplet.

In measures 9 and 10 the trumpet changes from triplets to dotted rhythm ♩. ♪♩. ♪ and here Herseth adds power and grandeur by observing the accents on the double-dotted notes, creating a sense of energy by sustaining them for full value. Mahler once said, "The best part of the music is not found in the notes," and Herseth adds a lifetime of trumpet artistry to these notes.

The horns and cymbals join the trumpet in measure 12 leading up to the tutti *ff* orchestra entrance in measure 13. With enormous power on the A major chord in measure 13, the orchestra captures the power and intensity of this tragic movement with a dark, Germanic sound.

In measure 27 the trombones enter at *piano* with a rhythmic motive ♩ ♪ ♩ ♪♩♪ ♪ ♩⌐ marked *p,* and the passage sounds like the shuffling feet of men slowly moving down a dusty road carrying a coffin.

The first violins and cellos enter with a pickup to ⟨2⟩. Mahler marks this *etwas gehaltener* (somewhat slower), which Solti conducts ♩ = 60. This contrasting lyrical and almost folk-like theme evokes the image of a cortege marching slowly behind the casket. Mahler brings the same theme back at ⟨4⟩ but this time in the first clarinet, bassoons, and first and second violins in canon with the violas and cellos following one beat behind.

At ⟨7⟩ the mood, key, and tempo change suddenly to ♩ = 92, marked *Plötzlich Schneller. Leidenschaftlich* (suddenly faster, passionately, wild). Music critic Lawrence Gilman writes, "the music, grown suddenly and passionately vehement, breaks in upon the measured tread of the funeral music like an uncontrollable outburst of shattering maniacal, wild-visage grief." (Ewen 453)

Solti and the Chicago Symphony Orchestra capture perfectly the wild, passionate outcry as the first trumpet plays the main theme above the orchestra and stopped horns add color on chords marked *ff.* The first violins add intensity and agitation with fast-moving eighth notes over syncopation in the trombones. Solti adds extra weight with a trumpet part which is not in the Dover score.

After the fury subsides, a tuba solo softly connects the bridge passage leading to ⟨12⟩. With a four-measure solo, the master Arnold Jacobs adds his glorious tuba sound to this poignant moment.

Hearing a Mahler Symphony is something like entering a room full of mirrors that reflect back to us many different nostalgic memories and moods. An example of these changing moods is the music between ⟨12⟩ and ⟨18⟩ as the mood quickly changes from silent lamentation to anguished pain and on to passionate sorrow. A great Mahler conductor captures these moods by shaping the music with just the right inflection and with the restraint and subtlety to not indulge in exaggerated mannerisms. Solti captures the tragic pathos of these funeral moods without any affectations or exaggerations. He creates a fluid musical line with sufficient flexibility to bring out the drama and humanity of the music without going overboard. His interpretation is a classic example of how music can have depth and feeling without jerky tempos or syrupy nuances that distort the musical line.

Mahler marks the emotional climax at ⟦18⟧ with the German directive *Klagen* (plaintive or sorrowful) at a dynamic of *fff* and with bells up for added emphasis. The stopped horns add a plaintive edge to the sound of this final dramatic outburst before the coda. Solti and the Chicago Symphony attack this spot with an intensity and power that create an overwhelming emotional effect on the final cry of grief for the deceased. I am reminded of the Edvard Munch painting, "The Scream."

The trumpet solo returns with the triplet fanfare in measure 387, this time with a sense of finality as the procession ends. After the drum rolls in measure 403, the trumpet ends with a few muted notes that the flute echoes. A soft bass drum roll and a *sf* pizzicato ♩ in low strings conclude the movement sounding like someone closing the coffin lid.

The movement closes in a tragic, haunting mood that foreshadows the rest of Mahler's life. His eldest daughter, Maria Anna died a few years later of diphtheria and scarlet fever at age five. His wife Alma writes, "Mahler loved the child devotedly: he hid himself in his room every day, taking leave of her in his heart. Weeping and sobbing, Mahler went again and again to the door of my bedroom where she was; then fled away to be out of earshot of any sound. It was more than he could bear." (Mahler 121)

Mahler was diagnosed with heart disease a few days after his daughter's death, and according to his wife, "this verdict marked the beginning of the end for Mahler." Always a fatalist Mahler brooded over the inevitability of his death and died of pneumonia in 1911 at age 50 after being weakened by recurrent heart attacks and overwork. ❧

CHAPTER 23

Carlos Kleiber:
The Elusive Maestro with the Magic Baton

Perhaps the most eloquent and articulate hands ever to serve the art of conducting ceased in their reach to create beauty with the passing of Maestro Carlos Kleiber (1930–2004). *The New York Times* wrote that Carlos Kleiber was the "most venerated conductor since Arturo Toscanini." Many musicians also regard Kleiber with the same reverential respect and I happen to be one of them because I believe that his interpretations will become legendary similar to Toscanini's. Kleiber was truly an interpretive genius whose baton technique was exceptional and deeply moving. His outstanding and supple technique allowed him to show each nuance of the music with a clear and eloquent beat that was magical, alive, and, above all, deeply expressive and communicative. Watching him conduct reminded me of Charles Ives' statement "technique is style's liberator." Indeed, the major characteristic of Kleiber's conducting was that his music making evoked a sense of freedom and spontaneity that sounded as if the music was being composed at the time of hearing. But more than a conductor with a great technique, Kleiber was a great maestro whose artistic insight and vision expressed the very soul of music.

Kleiber was a shy and quiet man who never wrote or spoke about conducting, but he did more to freeing conducting technique than any other conductor of his time. He did this by getting away from the standardized patterns found in most conducting textbooks and using gestures that came from the music. By looking like the music his technique was there without one being aware of it. Watching him conduct was fun because he was having fun. Like some magic sorcerer he could convey his vision to the musicians through a sequence of motions that reminded me of a great artist painting in sound. That was his secret. His vision turned the music into an expressive and meaningful motion and that is the hardest of all things for a conductor to do. Sometimes his motions were sweeping, sometimes seamless, and sometimes he would stop conducting altogether and be delighted to let the musicians play alone, giving the music an intimate chamber music quality. No one was better at shaping a phrase because the subtle variations in his patterns expressed the inflections and directions between the beats. And, as all conductors know, it is the preparation between the beats that make the music and Kleiber was a master at this.

Like Pablo Casals, he believed that "all music is a rainbow." Kleiber understood how to phrase within the phrase and bring out all the different colors of the music with a beat that had more variety, intensity, and flexibility than any conductor that I know.

As the son of another great conductor, Erich Kleiber (1880–1956) Carlos was exposed to music all his early life. At first, he was discouraged by his father to pursue a career in music. Reluctant to disagree with his father, Carlos chose to study chemistry in Zurich but later gave up the test tubes for a baton and followed in his father's tradition of mastering both the operatic and symphonic repertoire. Like his famous father, Carlos advanced his career by conducting opera in Munich, Potsdam, Zurich, Stuttgart, Vienna, Bayreuth and Convent Garden. He made his American debut conducting Verdi's *Otello* with the San Francisco opera in 1977. Only later in his career, after many years conducting opera, did he become known as an orchestra conductor. His talent was quickly recognized, however, and he had guest appearances with the Berlin Philharmonic, Vienna Philharmonic, and in 1979, he guest conducted the Chicago Symphony Orchestra.

Unfortunately, the world saw only a glimpse of his remarkable talent because he would conduct only rarely and never gave interviews. He once said, "When I talk, it's rubbish." Herbert von Karajan called Kleiber a genius, but unlike Karajan, Kleiber never sought any type of publicity and preferred to be a private and reclusive individual. Kleiber was somewhat of a maverick distrusting all those in authority and was hypersensitive to any type of criticism. He once said to Karajan, "I only conduct when I'm hungry."

A perfectionist, he would demand endless hours of rehearsals for his opera productions and if his demands were not met he would walk out and never come back. Although he was the first conductor approached for the Berlin position after Karajan's death, he refused the position and preferred to guest conduct only occasionally.

Because of his reluctance to accept a permanent post and to record, he left us only a few recordings. He once said, "every unproduced record is a good record." But what he did leave behind will insure his legacy among the exclusive company of the great maestros because each recording is considered a masterpiece of interpretation.

A recording of Kleiber's that I treasure is his extraordinary performance of Beethoven's Seventh Symphony on VHS with the Concertgebow Orchestra in Amsterdam in 1983 (Philips VHS 070200–3). I encourage all conductors to study this tape in order to appreciate Kleiber's outstanding baton mastery that communicated unparalleled control and beauty. He shapes every detail of the Beethoven's 7th with a revealing insight that is truly magnificent and inspirational. The video is a master class on how a great conductor draws amazing sounds from a great orchestra through a prism of his extraordinary technique and inspiration.

The first performance of the 7th symphony took place on December 8, 1813, at the University of Vienna as a benefit for soldiers wounded in the war against Napoleon. Critics were somewhat divided in their opinions. In Vienna it was well received, but in Germany critics were of the opinion that Beethoven must have been intoxicated when he wrote it. No less a musician than Weber is said to have expressed the opinion that Beethoven was now ripe for the madhouse. Beethoven himself was the conductor for the first performance in spite of the fact that he was losing his hearing. Beethoven's conducting that day was described by an eyewitness as somewhat exaggerated:

> The orchestra had to take great care that they were not disturbed by their leader. He had feelings only for his own works and was incessantly absorbed in expressing his requirements with an endless variety of gesticulations. … He would express diminuendo by making himself smaller and smaller behind the podium and pianissimo by virtually crawling under the stand. As the volume increased he reappeared from his hiding place and grew in stature assuming almost the proportions of a giant. When the orchestra reached full volume, he would raise himself up on his toes…in fact a veritable perpetual mobile. (Schonberg 60)

The first movement of Beethoven's Seventh Symphony in A major starts with an introduction that is 62 measures long, the longest introduction of any Beethoven symphony. Marked *poco sostenuto* and a tempo of $\quarternote$ = 69 the symphony is usually played too slowly by most conductors. Beethoven intended the introduction to be *poco sostenuto*, not andante nor adagio. The challenge for conductors in this intro is not to break the musical line with exaggerated tempo fluctuations. As I listen to Kleiber's interpretation of this intro with my metronome set on $\quarternote$ = 69, I was amazed that the fundamental pulse remained at $\quarternote$ = 69 as indicated by Beethoven. Kleiber demonstrates that it is not necessary to destroy the musical line in order to make it more expressive.

INTRODUCTION   Ludwig van Beethoven, Op. 92.

The opening of the symphony starts with a brilliant A major *forte-piano* chord for all the instruments brought in by Kleiber with an anticipatory preparation indicating the style and tempo which allows the orchestra to play after the beat. An anticipatory preparation is very common with European orchestras and allows for absolute precision if it is done correctly. Along with Karajan, Kleiber was a master of this technique.

After the A major chord is sounded the oboe starts the first two bar theme in half notes and the clarinet responds with the same theme on the second *fp* chord while the oboe continues. After the clarinet states the theme the horns enter with the same theme. What is unique with Kleiber's interpretation of these measures is the instrumental balance between these instruments. The matching of dynamics by the oboe, clarinet, and horns is truly remarkable because it creates an unbroken line sounding like one instrument.

In measure 10, Kleiber brings in the strings with ascending 16th notes staccato scale passages starting with the first and second violins in thirds. The violins are added on the third beat changing the thirds into consecutive chords of the sixth. These passages are marked *pp* without crescendo but some conductors add a crescendo for added excitement. It is refreshing to hear that Kleiber follows

Beethoven's directions and does not add the crescendo. The *pp* scale passages should only be a gentle hint of what is to come. The clarinet and bassoon enter in measure 11 with the half note themes previously stated by the oboe in the first measures of the composition but this time, for contrast, Beethoven marks the theme *dolce* which Kleiber interprets as *poco expressivo*.

Kleiber follows Beethoven's instructions and does not start the crescendo until the 14th bar realizing that if the crescendo is started too soon the excitement of the *ff* climax on A major chord in bar 15 is spoiled. The strings continue the ascending scale passages *fortissimo* against sustained harmonies in the winds.

Under Kleiber's direction, the scale passages never degenerate into musical insignificance to sound like someone practicing scales from an exercise book. Kleiber gives them a dramatic intensity and direction reminding us that scales can and should sound musical.

Another nuance brought to life by Kleiber's insight occurs in bar 23 when the oboe introduces a graceful little melody marked *dolce* and *piano*.

With this melody Kleiber gives a master class to conductors on how to shape a melodic line with a touch of rubato. While keeping a definite pulse of ♩ = 69, Kleiber never breaks the musical line because his rubato happens within the pulse and was as imperceptible as leaves blowing high in a tree from a gentle summer breeze. By taking more time with the sixteenths and holding back slightly on the staccato eights on the fourth beat the melody by the oboe achieves a dance like quality as the notes are lifted off the page.

In measure 29 the graceful little theme first heard in the oboe is taken over by the strings with pulsating 16th notes in the oboe and bassoon. Here Kleiber demonstrates his amazing ambidexterity by conducting legato in the right hand for the melody in the strings and a precise 16th note staccato beat with his left hand for the winds.

The short transition occurring six measures before the exposition's new tempo of vivace ♩. = 104 is one of the most difficult transitions for a conductor to accomplish. These sections must join without being obvious. Conductors must establish the new tempo of ♩. = 104 coming from a tempo of ♩ = 69 without a break in the musical line. This transition to the *vivace* starts in measure 57 with the flutes and oboe alternating with the violins first on 16th, 8th, and finally quarter and 16th notes.

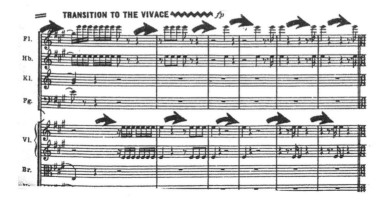

   I've heard this passage interpreted three different ways by some of our leading conductors. The first way is that the quarter notes in measures 61 and 62
of the $\frac{4}{4}$ meter are taken as the equivalent to ♩. at the entry of the $\frac{6}{8}$ meter. If the
transition is done in this manner it necessitates that a ritard be inserted at least
three measures before the *vivace* so that the tempo slows down from ♩ = 69 to
♩ = 52 which equals ♩. = 104. A second way is for the conductor to arrive at the
vivace at a slower tempo than the indicated ♩. = 104. Kleiber, Toscanini, and
Reiner choose the first way which makes for a smoother transition. Furtwängler,
Walter, and Klempner choose the second way which makes for a more romantic interpretation but is not as smooth as the first one. A third choice is for the
conductor to not put in the ritard and go directly from $\frac{4}{4}$ ♩ = 69 to ♩. = 104. To me
this is too abrupt but it is what Beethoven indicated. Whatever interpretation a
conductor will choose for this transition is a matter of personal taste but these
measures should give a feeling of suspense and expectation.
   The rhythmic motive of the *vivace* $\frac{6}{8}$ ♪. ♫ ♪. ♫ commonly known as the
"Amersterdam rhythm" should not be too fast otherwise the movement loses
its strength and cleanness. It should be remembered that ♪. ♫ ♪. ♫ in itself
gives a very animated meter. If the tempo is too fast the natural pulse of the
music is lost and does not have the $\frac{6}{8}$ lilt to make it swing and bounce.
   The Seventh Symphony was nicknamed by Wagner as "The Apotheosis of the
Dance" and under Kleiber's baton it becomes a rhythmic tour de force; a viva-
cious swaying dance, not too fast, but always graceful with sweeping phrases
and swing.
   The main theme is stated by the solo flute in the fifth measure of the exposition over the accompaniment of the other woodwinds and horns. In the sixth
measure of the exposition the dance-like theme in the flute has a grace note to
embellish the melody. The interpretation of grace notes in Beethoven's symphonies still remains controversial. While some conductors insist on playing
the grace notes on the beat, other conductors insist that grace notes in later
Beethoven should be played before the beat. Such noted Beethoven interpreters as Toscanini and Walter prefer to play them before the beat and Furtwängler

and Kleiber prefer to play them on the beat. While a comparison of how the great conductors interpret grace notes in the Beethoven symphonies is extremely interesting, the final criteria is does the music come alive without the grace notes becoming obvious and sounding academic.

I find it interesting to observe that when the flutes enter with the dance-like theme in the fifth measure Kleiber stops conducting altogether which automatically gives this section a chamber music quality. He doesn't start conducting again until he brings in the strings in measure 84 for the crescendo leading into the V⁷ chord fermata in measure 88. Most conductors put a break after the fermata to prepare for the ascending scale passage leading up to the main theme played fortissimo. What Kleiber does is unique: he does not cut off the fermata but after sustaining it with the left hand, he goes directly into the second beat with the baton without a cessation of sound. This makes the ascending scale passage sound even more brilliant because no energy is lost.

Another conducting innovation effectively used by Kleiber occurs in measure 128 when the strings come in *sf* followed by a decrescendo. To achieve the *pesante* effect on the *sf* Kleiber interlocks his fingers and quickly drops both hands as if catching a heavy object such as a rock. This is another effective example of how Kleiber's conducting technique comes from the music and not from a conducting textbook.

To give the music direction in measure 172 Kleiber uses a circular clockwise motion which is very effective. Toscanini was another conductor who used circles to build up intensity and phrase direction.

After two measures of silence, the coda starts in measure 389 and contains some of the greatest pacing I've ever seen from a conductor. Starting with the *pp* chromatic motive in the violas, cellos, and bases which is repeated many times in the manner of a basso ostinato, Kleiber gradually lets the music grow in volume and intensity which allows this final section to unfold in all its richness and splendor. It is truly a tremendous and compelling experience to watch Kleiber's control of this prolonged crescendo come alive without reaching the climax too soon. When the horns enter in measure 442 singing out in their high range, it is a moment of exultant joy.

As the final three chords of this movement ring out we know that Carlos Kleiber's legacy of recordings will substantiate his genius.

CHAPTER 24

The Elegant Lyricism of Giulini

*Every time you conduct you start from silence and from the first note
starts the mystery of the music.* —Carlo Maria Giulini

Among the finest conductors of the 20th century, Carlo Maria Giulini (1914–2005) was especially noteworthy. His first American performance in 1955 came at the invitation of Fritz Reiner, then conductor of the Chicago Symphony Orchestra. After his first concert in Chicago the *Chicago Tribune* music critic Claudia Cassidy wrote: "This tall, slender, young Italian from Milan's La Scala has sensitivity, imagination, and skill, and he has that extra enkindling thing, the promethean gift of fire." (EMI 8)

The concertmaster at the time said that Giulini's "approach to music was so honest and sincere; he was so clear and so knowledgeable… that the whole orchestra fell for him. From then onwards it was a longtime love affair with him." (EMI 7)

Giulini was born on the east coast of southern Italy in the town of Barletta, first studying violin and later switching to viola. At age 16 he entered the Rome Conservatory and joined the Augusteo Orchestra in Rome where he played under such conductors as Richard Strauss, Bruno Walter, Mengelberg, Furtwängler, and Klemperer. These conductors inspired Giulini to pursue a career in conducting.

When World War II started Giulini was drafted into the Italian Army but hated the fascists so intensely that he soon deserted and went into hiding. While he was in seclusion his wife brought him scores to study. When Rome was liberated by the Americans in 1944, Giulini was engaged to conduct the Augusteo Orchestra in a concert celebrating Rome's freedom. His conducting career developed after a very successful concert, and in 1952 he became assistant conductor to Victor de Sabata at La Scala. Two years later he became the principal conductor.

While in Milan, Giulini lived close to his conducting idol, Arturo Toscanini, but was too shy to knock on the maestro's door. However, after hearing Giulini's performance of Haydn's opera *Il Mondo della Luna*, Toscanini invited Giulini to his house and they became friends. Giulini wrote of Toscanini:

> I always tried to seek out his ideas, his conversations, his experience of music, and not to ask him favors. He was not only unbelievably gentle, but also very kind. Of course he could be incredibly rude as well and he often terrified the orchestra, but he was also kind, which is often forgotten by people who talk about him now. (Sachs 300)

© *The Instrumentalist*, April 2008. Reprinted with Permission.

Giulini followed in the lineage of Toscanini, Cantelli, De Sabata, and Serafin, all eminent Italian conductors during the golden age of conducting. Unlike these volatile maestri, Giulini was always soft spoken in rehearsals and showed respect for the orchestra members. Giulini believed that the conductor is only an interpreter in the service of the geniuses of music. He was beloved by orchestras for his knowledge of the scores and his humble approach to making music.

Giulini's concept of orchestral sound was based upon the strings being the primary color. "I think I played very good viola," Giulini said, "with good love and very good technique, and I think I wanted to produce the same sound in the other strings."

Giulini, Stokowski, and Karajan, and other great conductors invariably bring out of an orchestra the sound they hear in their heads. Their ability to do this with an orchestra is almost mystical but stems from the conductor's knowledge and deep understanding of the score. The gestures they use emanate from the sound they want to achieve. Giulini sought a sound that was warm, lyrical and seamless and he used horizontal gestures to convey a smooth sonority.

Principal trumpet Adolph Herseth commented: "Giulini's gestures with his hands and arms, the look on his face and his entire body movement delivered his ideas of the music to the orchestra in a beautiful fashion." (EMI 10)

Giulini's lyricism is captured on the reissued compact disc *Carlo Maria Giulini: The Chicago Recordings* (EMI 7243) The four-disc set includes music by Mahler, Berlioz, Beethoven, Bruckner, Stravinsky, and Brahms and demonstrate the warm sound that many conductors tried to imitate but could never duplicate.

His passionate and spine-tingling 1971 interpretation of Mahler's First Symphony with the Chicago Symphony Orchestra glows with warmth and elegance. I have eight recordings of Mahler's First by noted conductors but I return most often to the grace, warmth, and pacing of the Giulini recording. It surpasses all of the others.

Mahler's music captured his metaphysical yearnings for answers to life's questions. He struggled with manic depression and Mahler had a session in 1910 with Sigmund Freud, who recalled Mahler's visit in a letter to a friend.

> I had plenty of opportunity to admire the capability for psychological understanding of this man of genius. No light fell at that time on the symptomatic façade of his obsessional neurosis. It was as if you would dig a single shaft through a mysterious building. (Schonberg 434)

According to Harold Schonberg, "Mahler's basic trouble was that in his passionate desire to achieve his ideal, which does not exist, Mahler neglected to live as other men did. While he was lost in his work, life passed him by." (Schonberg 434)

Frequent mood changes characterize Mahler's music. The finale of the first symphony expresses anger, rebellion, inner conflict and chaos, and these contrast with moments of nobility, triumph, and a dreamlike state. Giulini's interpretation captures the depths of Mahler's tortured soul. On this recording the tempi are perfect, the transitions seamless, and Giulini's pacing graceful and elegant.

Mahler started writing the First Symphony in 1883 but did not complete it for five years. He conducted the premiere in Budapest a year later. The symphony was inspired by Jean Paul Richter's novel *Titian* in which a youthful hero philosophizes about love, friendship, death and eternity.

Bruno Walter, a student of Mahler's, claimed that the source of inspiration for this symphony was a failed love affair. Mahler found an expression for that fateful period in his life, and so this work may be considered a kind of personal confession in music.

As one of the world's greatest conductors, Mahler marked his scores in great detail. The finale to his first symphony starts with the German directive *stürmisch bewegt* (stormily, moving) at a tempo ♩ = 92. Giulini's tempo for this turbulent opening is ♩ = 96–1000 which seems to capture Mahler's description of this movement. The finale opens with a *fff* cymbal crash that expresses Mahler's anguish. It is the only symphony that I know that begins this way. Mahler wrote,

> The last movement, which follows the preceding one without a break, begins with a horrible outcry. Our hero is completely abandoned, engaged in a most dreadful battle with all the sorrow of this world. Time and again he – and the victorious motif with him – is dealt a blow by fate whenever he rises above it and seems to get hold of it, and only in death, when he becomes victorious over himself, does he gain victory. Then the wonderful allusion to his youth rings out once again with the theme of the first movement. (Floros 18)

To add intensity Mahler follows the cymbal crash with an augmented 6th chord to set the mood. While other conductors often let the brass dominate here, under Giulini the strings enter in the third measure with remarkable clarity and balance. Giulini's dramatic pacing of the movement gives each motive a sense of drama, and a sense of pacing and lyrical quality that stems from his operatic conducting experiences.

Like other great opera conductors such as Toscanini, Walter and Furtwängler, Giulini transferred his understanding of the inherent drama found in opera to the orchestral repertoire and this is the key to his dramatic pacing. Like the many characters in an opera, the finale is made up of different motives - sometimes augmented, sometimes shortened – that modulate through different keys. Mahler juxtaposes fanfare, birdcalls, canons and *ossinati*, against each other in a drama of turmoil, sadness, passion, yearning and anguish.

In measure 6 of the finale, trumpets and trombones enter *forte* with an abbreviated form of the victorious motive.

Mahler contrasts this theme with a fate motif in measure 8 with woodwinds playing *fff* descending triplets and detached staccato notes. Mahler described this motive as "triplets from hell." The first 24 measures of the finale contrast the victorious theme against the fate theme connected by arpeggiated runs in the strings.

A rhythmic shift five measures before 4 adds intensity as the orchestra enters *ff* on a syncopated, tutti passage. Most conductors start this passage at a slower tempo and accelerate to add excitement, but Giulini maintains a steady tempo and gives us a master class on the art of syncopation. To be effective syncopation needs something to syncopate against. Only by maintaining a steady tempo will it be effective, once more proving Toscanini's statement "it is easy to conduct a *piacere* but difficult to conduct *a tempo*."

Mahler gives specific instructions for the syncopation to be held back (*Zuruckhalten*) at 9 before arriving at *a tempo* five measures later. Giulini follows but does not exaggerate Mahler's instructions. Under Giulini the intensity and urgency grow without destroying the musical line.

Another mark of great conductors is how they handle transitions. Effective transitions must embody how the entire work fits together instead of as a collection of sections. Starting at 15, Giulini demonstrates his knowledge of this structure of the score as he leads the strings into 16 in a seamless transition nothing short of miraculous. The first and second violins move in octaves with impeccable intonation and tenderness as the passage slows without sentimentality or exaggeration.

At 16 the tempo slows down to ♩ = 50 and the key modulates to D major as the strings enter with an expressive lyrical theme much like the majesty of a large, flowing river. Here Giulini's restraint and modesty are reflected in a rubato that brings out the melodic inflections without breaking the musical line. Giulini's masterful rubato reminds me of Chopin's definition: "Rubato is gently blowing against the flame of a lighted candle without putting out the flame." Giulini's interpretation of this melodic section is also remarkable as it alternates between nobility and melancholy and reflects Mahler's moods in a natural ebb and flow of the musical line. The music intensifies as Giulini subtly increases the tempo, then slows a bit to bring out the expressive phrasing in a contrast of tension and relaxed tenderness.

Just before 34 a *luftpause* adds drama to the modulation to D major. Mahler said, "This D major chord had to sound as if it had come from another world." Although many conductors exaggerate this silence in what it says to me, "Watch out, here it comes," Giulini demonstrates his uncanny sense of timing and musicality by inserting only a very short pause and then quickly dropping the downbeat to achieve the effect Mahler wanted. Giulini conducts this triumphant section at 34 with a tempo of ♩ = 96–100.

At 38 the music slows down (*Sehr langsam*) to ♩ = 66 and the dynamic is *ppp* as it modulates to D minor. The second violins enter with the celli on a theme of descending fourths in half notes that is very reminiscent of the slow movement of Beethoven's Ninth Symphony. This section from 38 to 41 includes fanfares in brass, birdcalls in woodwinds, and fragments of other themes heard in the first movement of the symphony depicting the awakening of nature at early dawn.

The recapitulation starts at 41 and the key is F major with half notes ♩ = 52. This is one of the most beautiful sections in the symphony which Mahler marks as *sehr zart und ausdruckvoll gesungen* (very tender and expressive singing). Giulini observes these directions and achieves smoothness of phrasing, flexible tempo, and close observance of the expressive dynamics to capture all the nuances of this expressive melody. Ray Still's artistry on the oboe is evident as he plays a variation on the melody at 42 and inserts a slight breath pause at the end of his poignant interpretation of the melody which really sets off the phrase before the strings come in. At 44 at the climax of the phrase marked *f*, Giulini inserts a cymbal crash, which is not in my Dover score.

As this beautiful melody dies away (*morendo*) to nothing, the mood is abruptly changed by the viola entrance fourteen measures before 45 marked *fff* starting a fragment of a theme which prepares for the entrance of the first violins and celli in canonic imitation of motive one at ⬚45. Giulini conducts this section at a tempo of ♩ = 96–100. Dynamics for the start of this canon is *ppp* but grows in intensity as other instruments enter with melodic fragments of the theme.

The music explodes at ⬚52 with fanfares marked *fff* in the orchestra and Mahler asks for this section to be played with great power as if the sun suddenly comes out from a dark cloud.

From ⬚53 to the end the music pushes on in great triumph as Giulini unleashes the Chicago Symphony Orchestra in all its splendor. At ⬚56 Mahler asks the seven horns to stand, and it is one of the great moments of orchestral performance. The symphony ends triumphantly in D major.

This symphony, like other Mahler works, goes through many mood and tempo shifts, and some conductors consider each change as an opportunity to exhibit flamboyant indispensability of an over- active conductor. Not Giulini. In the days when classical music was often televised, an interviewer asked the maestro what went through his mind when he watched himself at work on the podium. Giulini's answer was that he never watched videos of his conduct-ing. When asked why not, Giulini replied, "Because I might see some gesture or movement I liked, and the next time a similar situation occurred I might be tempted to use it again – and that's not why I am on the podium. I am there only to faithfully bring out the sounds the composer wanted."

When Mahler died in Vienna in the spring of 1911, his last wish was that not a word be spoken nor a note of music be sung at his funeral. In accordance with his wishes he was buried with silent reverence. At the end of Giulini's marvel-ous performance of Mahler's First Symphony I reflected that music and life both begin and end with silence. Giulini's career spanned a golden age of conducting. With a gentle, voice on the podium he brought forth glowing sounds that still resonate with devoted musicians.

I feel that all will be right with the world as long as there are musicians like Giulini, who maintain the highest standards of performance and dedicate their lives to finding the heart of every work. They are the individuals who open our hearts. ✍

CHAPTER 25

Boulez on Boulez

If you have a precise idea of the score and an inner representation of the score, then the gestures will come almost automatically. —Boulez

Pierre Boulez is at the forefront of the movement that celebrates scientific, highly rational ordering of musical materials in composition. An early pioneer in magnetic tape and sound synthesizers, Boulez was also one of the first composers to use computers in composition. At the same time, like Edgard Varèse, he searches for transparent tonal images and creates rhythmic and metric patterns.

Boulez studied with composers Olivier Messiaen and René Leibowitz and emerged during the 1950s as the *enfant terrible* of contemporary music. The avant-garde championed his music as fluent and assured with surreal delicacy, and it was accepted by traditional musicians for its craftsmanship. He caustically dismissed all but the most cerebral 12-tone works and even hissed at Stravinsky's music at times. Although largely a supporter of Schönberg's music, a few weeks after Schönberg's death Boulez wrote an inflammatory article "Schönberg est mort," which he recently described as simply meaning that the early 1950s were a "time for the musical world to move on." In the 1940s and 1950s he conducted the orchestra for a progressive Paris theatre company that contributed to his international prestige. In 1954 he left France to establish himself in Baden-Baden, and in 1963 he was a visiting professor at Harvard.

His concerts and recordings of such works as Debussy's *Pélleas et Méisande* and the Stravinsky ballets with European orchestras introduced a clarity and lucidity of performance previously unknown for these works. He directed the New York Philharmonic from 19971–1975 and at the same time was music director of the BBC Symphony Orchestra. Presently he is the permanent guest conductor of the Chicago Symphony Orchestra. After a recent rehearsal with the orchestra for a performance of Schönberg's *Moses aund Aron* he discussed a range of subjects, from his musical influences to the future of music.

Your father was a mathematician and you excelled in math. Do you find a correlation between math and music?

Not exactly, although the mind works logically in both subjects. I don't like to be fuzzy about things. To understand the score I have to analyze it, not just develop an impression about the music. If the music is interesting to me, I analyze it. At first I may be in the darkness because I don't know the score and I try to find my way. After analyzing it I am in full light and understand the work. Still, as I dig further into the deep meaning of a work, I see that it cannot be fully understood. In performance I try to go beyond the point where I merely understand the rationality of the music.

How did you develop an affinity for Stravinsky's music, which you have called the birth certificate for contemporary music?

I discovered *The Rite of Spring* in a class with Messiaen in 1944 during the war, a time when sheet music was scarce. All I had was a reduction for piano four hands. In the class students performed the piece. The first real performance I heard was with Charles Munch in 1945 or 1946, but this was a very poor performance because it was not at all his cup of tea. He was not educated in the musical style, and his interpretation was like riding on ice. I was aware of the danger of performing this piece, but during this wartime when I was in Paris, nobody played *Rite of Spring*. Orchestras know how to play the rhythms precisely now, but then it was unachievable. When I began to conduct the work, I knew the style and had memorized the score. With time I went from a mechanical transmission under Messiaen to a reflection of the piece.

Messiaen loved nature and birds, and his compositions include birdcalls. Are some of the musical effects you write in compositions indicative of birdcalls?

No, not at all. The importance he gave to bird sounds puzzled me because it pervaded practically everything. When I was his student from 1943–1944, his pieces included the allusion to birdcalls, but by the 1950s he became absolutely hypnotized by birds, which I could not understand. His birdcall transcriptions were permutations of real birds; I have never heard a bird singing in the registers he chose. He had a vivid imagination and transformed the sounds of nature.

As a conductor, how do you achieve clarity in orchestral interpretations?

I approach the score from the composer's point of view because I am aware of the effort that goes into writing a score. I analyze the score carefully to see what he wants, from dynamics to exactitude in phrasing, and emphasize this clarity. Balancing the dynamics according to chord position also brings out clarity. Intonation and rhythm should not be ignored; for instance, if the violins have perfect intonation but are not rhythmically together, then it simply sounds dirty, not clear. My notion of clarity includes the sound itself, which is intonation, rhythm, exactitude, timing, and the balance between instruments. Such clarity is difficult to achieve in *The Three Pieces* by Berg or in *Variations for Orchestra*, Op. 31 by Schönberg because the main line is not obvious, but this is the conductor's job. Berg and Schönberg were not conductors, and their works were not performed much in their lifetime. A comparison of the scores of Berg and Mahler makes it obvious that Mahler was aware of the weight of the instruments, of balance; he wrote a dynamic for each instrument. When he wrote *forte* for one instrument and piano for another, he wanted this difference for the balance. In Berg a conductor has to make practical decisions about dynamic markings because these are not in the score.

When learning scores such as Berlioz's "Symphonie fantastique", composed just three years after Beethoven's death, do you approach it as a Classical or a Romantic work?

I am not keen on reconstituting the performance of the day. In Berlioz's memoirs he wrote that he was never satisfied with the conditions of this day, especially in Parisian orchestras. To reconstitute the conditions of Berlioz's day is not possible because musicians today know the piece. Berlioz included remarks about the difficulty of the music, but conditions have changed and playing levels have improved. Now all violinists play this type of scale with great facility; but it was not the case in his time. It would be nearly impossible to reconstitute the Romantic orchestra.

Why don't you conduct with a baton?

I have never used a baton because I began conducting chamber groups and it was unnecessary. I did not feel it a necessity even in front of an orchestra because I am able to do what I want with my hands. What a conductor generally does with the left hand, I can do with both hands. I can conduct with my left hand and still shape the sound as I want with the right hand, especially to indicate smoothness or very sharp rhythms after the beat. People know exactly what I want; this I cannot do with a baton.

Do you ever use an anticipatory beat?

That's a problem with some German conductors. I like to anticipate the beat from time to time, especially in a *sforzando-piano* to pull the sound; the sound is not pushed. I remember when I conducted in Bayreuth and ran into problems with beginning chords. Finally I found a trick with a slow gesture to pull the sound. Sometimes the French react too quickly, which doesn't work in 19th-century German music. The *sforzandos* in Stravinsky, for instance, are very precise in Germany.

Do you find that there's a difference in the interpretation of some of the markings, such as a tenuto, which German orchestras play very short?

I think that depends upon the schooling. Today orchestras in all countries are exposed to many conductors; one day it's Abbado, the next it's Maazel, the third it's Barenboim, all of different nationalities and with different interpretations. There is not always a confrontation, but a conductor has to make do. Generally we find a compromise. In Bayreuth I found a solution whereby I could have my say and at the same time let the orchestra keep its personality. When we recorded *Passacaglia* of Webern, the beginning pizzicato was not together no matter what gesture I used. Finally I told the violins to pinch the string. By pinching they pressed and produced more sound, and finally we adjusted. It is up to the conductor to indicate discrepancies.

How do you feel about using the piano for score study?

I once said this is like taking morphine: it kills the inner ear. When I studied solfege in the Conservatoire in Paris, we had to write down all the exercises by ear. This forced me to really listen to what I write. I don't need a representation of how a chord will sound; I just hear it. That's how the inner ear is forged.

Do you ever go back and change what you've written?

Sometimes the position of a chord, but I never have to check anything at the piano.

What would you like to see emphasized in the training of conductors today?

Score study is the main thing. If you have a precise idea of the score and an inner representation of the score, then the gestures will come almost automatically. Conducting gestures come from the music; the gestures do not make the music. There are some mechanical aspects—to get an upbeat you have to give an upbeat. I compare conducting to driving: it's basically very simple but then very complex. To drive, you learn to put the motor on, put the car in gear, and to use the brake, but this does not make you a racecar driver. All the knowledge of conducting comes from the score. If you want a soft chord you use one gesture and the music will come out softly. If you want something strong you use another gesture. Everybody has these types of gestures, they're like the voice. You cannot teach these gestures, conductors simply have to respond to what they want to hear. Also, you can detect mistakes much more easily if you have an inner representation of the score; if this representation does not coincide with what you hear, you detect the mistake automatically.

What advice do you have regarding the development of internal hearing?

Begin with listening exercises, playing chords, and finding the interval. Start with two voices, then three, four, and so on. It is very mechanical work.

Back in the 1970s, an exciting time in the development of new music, Georges Pompidou was president of France, and he wanted to bring you back to France to develop the IRCAM. Do you feel connected politically as a composer/conductor?

Not in the sense that I have a connection with the political world, but when there is an artistic project in which I am interested, not especially for me, but for musical life generally, then I'm very obstinate and try to achieve what is necessary. I was very involved in creating *cetede la Musique*, and I am again fighting for having a big hall in La Villette because it's necessary now. I do not fight for the sake of fighting, but because I find that certain projects are important. Sometimes they fail. I remember working for the Opera *Bastille*, but it was a waste of time because finally it collapsed. The opera house should have had a mobile stage especially for production of new music, but it did not happen.

Your failures have been few because you've had good connections.

For a long time I had no connections in France, and I left without regrets. As a result, I know the world better than many French people. These possibilities were not offered just because they wanted me to come back but because they knew I would be able to make important changes.

What are you most proud of among your many accomplishments?

Some of my works, first, because I am first a composer. That's how I want to be remembered. As a conductor, I disseminated the music of the 20th century in my programs because I wanted the music to be part of normal life, not an exception. My concerts and recordings represent an anthology of 20th-century music, and the institutions I have created continue for future generations.

Some of your works have been compared to Schönberg's "Pierrot Lunaire". Do you consciously acknowledge Schönberg in your writing, as in the flute and voice in "Pli selon pli"?

Yes, that's a direct homage, but it has nothing stylistically to do with Schönberg, especially the allusion in the piece for flute and voice. I recently conducted a piece written for three pianos, three harps, and three percussion. Of course, I had in mind the Bartók sonato for two pianos and percussion and the Stravinsky piece for piano and percussion and voice. I am not at all disturbed by showing an influence, but at the same time the influence should be absorbed so that one cannot be confused with the other.

You mentioned earlier that "Rite of Spring" was a cornerstone of the 20th century. Could you name other works that you feel the same about?

Yes, for instance *Pierrot Lunaire* by Schönberg, Berg's *Wozzeck*, and the works of Webern. Even somebody who has a rather small output can be very important to the 20th century like Varèsse is for me. I can enjoy a piano concerto of Prokofiev, but if I have to choose between the piano concerto of Prokofiev and the Bartók piano concerto, I choose the Bartók because for me it is much more important. Between the Variations of Schönberg Op. 31, and the *Four Temperaments of Hindemith*, I would choose the Schönberg because I find it much more important, but I don't refuse to listen to Hindemith. I simply use a kind of hierarchy of values, which for me I find important.

The Elliot Carter clarinet piece, performed last spring by John Bruce Yeh with the Chicago Symphony Orchestra, is a fantastic piece, with tone clusters of different instrument combinations across the stage moving from station to station, and the sound changes with the voicing of the instruments. It takes incredible inner hearing to know how to compose such a work.

I like my late works, especially those that mix theater and music. Not theater opera, but the music itself is theater. The musicians play simply; I don't want them to be actors. Sometimes the public is in the middle and the sound is all over, so the concert is a different experience. I frequently compose in this way to develop a different relationship between the audience and music using some element of theater within the music, not outside of it.

What drives you to develop unusual sound effects for instruments, pushing the limit to find new possibilities?

I am interested in the expansion of sound, whatever it is, with percussion instruments, electronics, and different instrumental combinations. We are in an age where there is a lot of expansion in other domains, so why not expand the sounds also?

Do you depend on instrumentalists like flutist Pierre-Yves Artaud to experiment with sounds on their particular instruments?

The relationship of the musician with the microphone and electronics cannot exist in theory alone; it has to be experienced. The composer doesn't know all the possibilities. For instance, when writing for orchestra a composer can extrapolate ideas from extant works. However, electronic music is still in its infancy, and in the last 20 years the technology has mushroomed. Each perception has to be experienced to be achieved. It is an interesting and long process. We try everything and listen to what it produced. Sometimes we think it will be something extraordinary and it is not, and sometimes we don't expect much and it is extraordinary.

Some of the multiphonics that flutists produce are barely audible to the first row of the audience without a microphone. How do such techniques serve the music?

In *Explosante fixe* I included several extended techniques and sampled them. The slap sound, for instance, can only be played at a certain speed, but once it is sampled it can be very quick. The computer helps achieve a speed that is humanly impossible. The multiphonics can be transformed completely and transposed into a very low register where the spectrum of sound is wonderful. I call this transgression because the instruments cannot do everything at the speed required or the range is too limited. Sometimes multiphonics are very tricky, but the transgression makes it perfect, either in speed, spectrum, or dynamic. My clarinet piece also includes recorded clarinet. The instrument can produce a certain *fortissimo*, but the recorded sound through a loud speaker provides a much bigger contrast than an instrumentalist can. That is transgression. Expansion and transgression of sound are the basis of music.

Incredible sounds are possible through singing, talking, or tonguing into instruments. What would the old masters say about these modern sounds?

The instruments are richer in possibilities than we think and the sounds are indefinite. We can always find new things. I am sure that Guarneri or Stradivari never thought that Schönberg's Concerto was possible on their instruments. I did a piece last year, *Violin and Electronics*, that uses a sampled sound of violin pizzicato at a great speed that would be otherwise impossible. It is pizzicato, but with greater speed and resonance. Through electronics we can play with the sound.

Why are you so intrigued by the tritone interval?

I think it is simply the most uncertain interval. The fourth is more stable but the diminished fifth or augmented fourth can resolve in many ways. Some intervals like the minor ninth are very tense; on the contrary the major ninth is very pleasant. I often use this contraction of chords according to the tension of the intervals and the relationship they have with the normal harmonic scale. For instance, in my recent *Notation* pieces I use chords that multiply by themselves on the whole scale. It sounds very nice, if I may say so, because they are in harmonic proportion.

In the 20th century many trends have come and gone, but what is the current trend and where it is going?

At the time of Schönberg few people knew 12-tone music, but after a period of time it becomes commonplace. I believe in music that is demanding, that goes into the depth of the human being, not music for entertainment. I don't find that terribly satisfying. The music that goes back to Romantic or post-modernist music is not terribly attractive to me because there is no depth to it. I am frustrated when I hear such shallow music. If a work does not pose a question mark, then it is a waste of time. At least this question is puzzling and challenging. Some works may be too splashy, and a work that was not immediately convincing might just be the work which will convince you completely ten years later. Therefore, you have an evolution.

In earlier years of composing you embraced the 12-tone music of Schönberg, but shortly after Schönberg died, you wrote the article "Shönberg est mort". What were you telling the musical world?

My title was very misunderstood at the time. I said *Schönberg est mort* because we had to cope with the end of his life: he invented all that he had to invent, and we had to go beyond that. In the Japanese *Noh* there is a wonderful image: when a person dies, he passes through a white paper screen to another form of existence. To continue to experiment with music, we had to pass through this paper screen of Schönberg. Schönberg being the paper screen. Once beyond him, we could find something that has its roots in Schönberg, but go farther. We cannot continue with 12-tone rows forever. That's nonsense.

What is the direction of music in the new millennium?

I think the visual aspect of music will be more important, but I'm not certain; however, the visual aspect explains the depth of the music.

Will there be traditional concerts?

Yes, even though we're in the age of computers, at the same time, the real concert will be important. Virtual concerts will be enjoyed at home with sophisticated sound environments. At the same time, the experience of hearing a concert with an expanded sound will draw an audience. It will be a different experience and will include new sounds. ☙

Left to right: Pierre Boulez and John Knight.

CHAPTER 26

Freedom With Discipline:
An Interview with Christoph von Dohnányi

Christoph von Dohnányi was born in Berlin and attended law school at the University of Munich. He gave this up to pursue music full time and went on to win the Richard Strauss prize for conducting. Dohnányi followed his grandfather, Ernst von Dohnányi, to America and studied with him at Florida State University. Later he studied conducting at the Tanglewood Institute, and by 1952 he coached and conducted at the Frankfurt Opera as Georg Solti's assistant. In 1968 he became artistic and music director of that company for ten years. From 1978 to 1984 he was principal guest conductor of the West German Radio Symphony Orchestra in Cologne and principal conductor of the Hamburg State Opera. Dohnányi became the conductor of London's Philharmonia Orchestra in 1997 after three years as a guest conductor. From 1982 to 2002 he was music director of The Cleveland Orchestra.

What was the process leading up to your decision to become a conductor?

While studying law in Munich I started composing and making music. Living close to the academy of music and the opera house in Munich, I attended many opera performances and learned of the work of Sir Georg Solti. After attending some of his rehearsals, I decided to become a professional conductor. Solti was a wonderful teacher and gave me many conducting opportunities and even performed one of my compositions.

Did you continue composing?

I had composed a few pieces early on but when I became Solti's assistant in Frankfurt I decided to focus on being a conductor.

What were your impressions of studying at the Tanglewood Institute?

Because I was just a beginner then, and I was not among the four or five students who studied with Bernstein, I was in Simon Lipkin's conducting class. Later I became acquainted with Bernstein in Hamburg, and he tried to convince me to conduct a show in New York.

     What is tremendously attractive about this country is the professionalism and the training of musicians, which is far superior to the training in Europe. I believe that Curtis, Juilliard, Oberlin, and other institutes are very special places. You will have hard times finding schools like those in Europe. The Musikschule in Cologne and a few schools in Germany are very good, but in Europe there are not the fine student orchestras.

That's strange because we commonly think there are many more orchestras in Europe.

There are at least two thousand orchestras in the United States, but unfortunately people only talk about the first five.

How much has training as an opera conductor helped you to conduct the orchestral repertoire?

Opera training is essential because it teaches form, discipline, and above all the flexibility to breathe and articulate freely. The operatic approach to music making is a bit more dramatic. Through opera conductors learn to relate music to theater and to develop flexibility by working with and coaching singers. All music is ultimately derived from singing.

What are the essential qualities of a young conductor?

One aspect is the ability to pull sound from an orchestra and to control that sound. A conductor has to develop enough taste to achieve a sound that fits the music. People establish this kind of taste in childhood. Sound is important, but the highest priority is to get the right sound for each composer. Many conductors can produce a tremendous sound, but it doesn't always fit the composition. The goal is to know where to place Brahms and Beethoven, and not to play Beethoven like Gershwin or Gershwin like Beethoven.

With Berlioz's "Symphony Fantastique", which was composed just three years after Beethoven died, should it have a romantic approach or should the sound be tempered with classicism?

Berlioz certainly extended the compositional style, but he had a very different approach to music making than Beethoven. Berlioz is more comparable to Ives or Sibelius in the 20th century. These composers break some of the laws of composition and bring reform, innovation, and new ideas to music; but let's face it, the last Beethoven string quartets go far beyond Berlioz.

You have said that beating time is not really related to music because the bar-lines interrupt the phrasing. To what extent should conducting gestures simply flow from the music?

By the end of the rehearsal period for any work the act of beating time should be unnecessary. Some orchestras seem to ask for a lot of time-beating, but usually this is because there is too little time to prepare. In contrast, chamber musicians do not like to watch someone beat time. The more musicians play together and listen to each other, the less they need time-beating, but with an orchestra of 100 musicians it is sometimes essential.

 If musicians feel too secure with a conductor, the sound is usually not very interesting. Musicians should feel they have to listen to each other because the beat is not a crutch they can rely on. As soon as musicians start listening, the sound becomes more musical. Conductors who beat time in a military-band style are not the ones who make music.

Would Furtwängler be a great example of not over conducting?

Yes, but he conducted four or five orchestras that knew what he wanted. This relationship between an orchestra and a conductor is like a marriage in which both parties begin to know instinctively what the other wants.

What would you like to see emphasized in the training of young conductors today?

They should read a great deal, learn to speak different languages, and study theater, ballet, chamber music, and singing. I think it is important that young conductors not listen to too many recordings because it becomes difficult to escape from someone else's interpretation.

How do you evaluate George Bernard Shaw's statement that a conductor who takes time from a metronome and gives it to the musicians is a public nuisance, while a conductor who takes time from the music and gives it to the ensemble is a good conductor?

The tempo, if you read Leopold Mozart for instance, is inherent in the music. If a conductor has the right taste, he will find the right tempo. Since Beethoven started the trend, more and more composers wrote metronome markings in their music, in part to defend against people who obviously do not know how to interpret music well. Composers in the 20th century added even more notations to music. Mahler wrote a tremendous amount of notes to conductors because he didn't trust them. I think he was partly right.

How reliable are Beethoven's metronome markings?

Beethoven said many things about his metronome markings, and sometimes conductors have trouble following these markings. Although the markings are important, conductors still have freedom to adjust these. Beethoven gives a basic pulse for each movement, but conductors have the freedom to modify the tempi within a movement. It would be boring to perform each movement from beginning to end in the same tempo.

How much have your decisions about tempi changed over the years?

I was much more rigid when I was just starting out and wanted to keep a consistent tempo. Over time I realized that certain music needs to breathe more and have more freedom. I began to adjust and shape the tempi within a movement.

How do you persuade large orchestras to play music of Schönberg, Berg, and Webern?

With some orchestras it is hard to approach music of these composers, but this music is now 60–70 years old and many professional orchestras will work on all music with a professional attitude. That doesn't mean that they necessarily like it, but even the conductor doesn't have to like a piece. What is important is to respect the music and give a high-quality performance.

Why do you think Americans have a tradition of choosing foreign-born conductors for major orchestras?

This will change. With about ten openings for orchestral conductors at the present time, I hope some of them will choose American conductors. There are wonderful American conductors, some of whom have worked in Europe and could easily come back and be fine conductors in this country. I think it is good for European conductors to come to the United States and go back to Europe, and it is good for Americans to go to Europe and come back to the United States.

How much of the Cleveland Orchestra's ensemble sound, tonal clarity, and chamber music approach can be attributed to the teachings of George Szell?

I would say that with Szell, Reiner, and even Solti there was a clear Toscanini following. Szell and Reiner tried to go back to what was printed on the page, and from this they found freedom. When these conductors started out there were other conductors who gave interesting but very weird interpretations that almost completely disregarded the text. It is a good thing that some conductors decided not to begin a crescendo earlier than it was written. Most conductors today try to combine freedom with discipline. Democracy works the same way. For freedom to exist there must be discipline instead of concluding that freedom means being able to do anything we want. There has to be discipline in freedom and a balance between these. What applies to a citizen is also what a conductor must do.

What is your philosophy of choosing music for concerts?

I don't have much of a philosophy about programming. I like music from all periods. I love jazz, and would not hesitate to program jazz together with Mozart.
Unfortunately, I am not gifted in jazz. I would not program *Die Fledermaus* with
Brahms Requiem, but I might program Alban Berg's Violin Concerto with the
Brahms Requiem. It is a mater of finding the quality and intention of the composers. If a composer wrote a funny piece, I would think twice about programming it with the Mozart Requiem. Once I have defined a composer's intentions it
becomes easy to find another piece that fits with it, but whether the pieces come
from the period does not matter to me.

Do you alone chose the programs or do you have to go through a committee?

People sometimes think that the donors dictate the programs to the conductors
of American orchestras, but that never happens. The donors are wonderful here,
and I have never had any big disagreements over programming contemporary,
classical, or romantic music. I don't think that kind of interference happens here
or in Europe. Occasionally it happens in opera because a tremendous amount
of money is raised from a different type of public. They may want to hear certain
voices and have particular stage directors.

What are you most proud of among your many accomplishments?

It will be a good feeling to have been with the Cleveland Orchestra for 20 years.
I hope that this orchestra maintains its quality and captures an even bigger
public than in earlier days. The orchestra has a terrific reputation. Our is such
a wonderful profession because we get paid for doing what we enjoy. This has
been a great time, and I think we really have achieved something with the new
concert hall.

Is the Cleveland Orchestra the most recorded of all orchestras?

No, the Philharmonia in London is the most recorded orchestra in the world.
Cleveland recorded more than any other American Orchestra during a certain
period, but now recordings are less popular. Today orchestras only record newer
pieces by composers like John Adams or perhaps a new orchestration, such as
Gustav Mahler's *Lied von der Erde* in a chamber music version. Nobody would
record a new Beethoven cycle.

What recordings are you most proud of?

We have recorded a very good set of the Mozart symphonies and almost all of
the orchestral pieces by Webern on the London (Decca) label. The reason I chose
to record Mozart with Webern is because good music fits together no matter

what. Many people do not know that Webern was one of the very few composers who was not fond of Mozart. I also recorded a terrific Wozzeck with the Vienna Philharmonic, which I think was a very true performance.

What essential qualities make up a great interpretation?

That is a hard question to answer. Sometimes extremely gifted people will not have a career because they are missing only one component. There are people who can learn pieces and perform them very quickly, but their interpretations are boring. Others such as Carlos Kleiber will take a year to study a Haydn Symphony before giving a wonderful performance. I cannot conceive performing pieces by Beethoven or Richard Wagner after one run through. Interpreting music is a process of dealing with a piece for a very long time.

Bruno Walter said, "the spirituality of the music is what I always try to achieve, and it takes just living."

Absolutely. Let a piece go and take it back again. I am working on pieces I will perform six months from now because I want to feel good about them before it is time to perform them.

Do you listen to interpretations of different conductors now?

Oh yes. I am very interested in what Reiner, Szell, Furtwängler, or Toscanini did. It is wonderful that we have the ability to go back and study their interpretations. However, I always know how I feel about a work before listening to someone else's version.

I have a videotape of Carlos Kleiber conducting Beethoven's 7th; everything is so very free, yet he is somewhat of a recluse.

Beethoven's 7th Symphony is a piece that needs a strong personality, and Carlos is a very educated, well-read man who has a tremendous and very complicated personality. He speaks many languages and has something to say. Many times an orchestra needs a conductor to give them a spiritual view of a piece. Musicians can fix many small musical problems themselves and soon become dissatisfied with conductors who only organize notes.

What do you have to say about the art of conducting?

There are two separate aspects; the art of conducting and the craftsmanship. The craft is very easy. Beating time is something musicians learn quickly; a skilled ear is a gift and requires training to develop. Intonation is something many well-trained conductors cannot correct because they lack a gifted ear, so often the orchestra members have to fix these problems by themselves. Conductors can learn about intonation by singing and by working with singers.

The art of conducting is completely different. It is the ability to influence art-ists in an orchestra to do what you want them to do and to respect the music and the composer. It's psychological. I always thought that I was rather lucky because I had one grandfather who was a famous psychiatrist and another who was a famous musician. To be a good artist a conductor also needs experience. It is dif-ficult being very young and facing a group of people who have already lived half a life. Perhaps that is why we don't have child-prodigy conductors.

A conductor can only be considered to be a real conductor somewhere in his forties. We have tremendously gifted young people, and if pieces were not so demanding there would be more twenty-year-old conductors. As we all know there are geniuses who have more to say at 20 than less gifted ones at 80, but on average I think having life experiences is essential to becoming a good conductor.

CHAPTER 27

My Real Idol was Bruno Walter:
An Interview with Kurt Masur

Since 1991 conductor Kurt Masur has developed a reputation for consistently high-quality performances and artistic spirit with the New York Philharmonic, an ensemble that has had diverse conductors this century, including Mahler, Toscanini, Bernstein, Boulez, and Mehta. In 1974 Masur made his U.S. debut with the Cleveland Orchestra and led the Gewandhaus Orchestra on its first tour of this country. As Kapellmeister of the Leipzig Gewandhaus Orchestra, Masur had to meet the standards met by Mendelssohn, Nikisch, Furtwängler, and Walter, all of whom had held that position. On his departure in 1996 the 254-year-old Gewandhaus named Masur its first conductor laureate. In 1998 Masur celebrated 50 years as a professional conductor, and in 2000 he became principal conductor of the London Philharmonic Orchestra..

Which teachers influenced and inspired you to become a conductor?

Nobody inspired me. Conducting was the only possibility for me. I started as a young pianist and wanted to be an organist. At age 16 I had a disease in my hand that caused a finger to become bent. My doctor said to forget about organ, forget about piano, and this was at a time when I already played piano very well. I had also started to play the cello. I was so involved in music that I couldn't imagine doing anything else. I had no other talents.

© *The Instrumentalist*, November 1999. Reprinted with Permission.

I grew up in a very small city with no orchestra, nothing; I did not attend my first concert until the age of 16—and I was so deeply moved by it that I told everybody I might be a conductor. Nobody believed me because I was such a shy young man and had just experienced my first concert. Then I started to discover why people didn't believe that I could do that. They said you are not so flexible, you are too weak and much too soft with everybody around you.

Near the end of 1944 at the age of seventeen I was a soldier for half a year during the last days of Hitler. Of 130 young guys in my unit there were only 27 survivors. This was a very hard school and a learning experience for me. For a lot of us this was the first time that we felt how brutal life can be. After the end of the war I could not go back to my home so I went to Leipzig and started to study there in 1946.

As a young conductor were you particularly drawn to Mahler or some other composer?

At that time knowledge of Mahler nearly disappeared because Mahler had not been allowed to be played. The same was true with Mendelssohn and Tchaikovsky during the last years of the war.

Now you are regarded as a great interpreter of Tchaikovsky.

I grew into that. At first my piano teacher gave me Bach, but later I learned how to feel Brahms, whose compositions were so close for me that I felt they really were in my blood. I grew up a little bit outside the normal way. In a big city you may go to concerts at an early age; I heard my first opera when I was 16, nothing before.

Some say that conducting techniques can be learned, but the art cannot. Is this true?

The techniques of conducting can be learned. For artistry you have to bring imagination to the piece and have the will to bring this knowledge to the orchestra. If the orchestra understands what you are doing, ultimately the audience understands.

If you measure a conductor through technique, a lot of conductors can keep an orchestra together, but this doesn't mean it is conducting. Conducting means to inspire an orchestra with such a convincing idea about the piece that all these outstanding musicians believe you. Otherwise the musicians may decide they know more about the music than the conductor. Young conductors sometimes have great difficulty winning the respect of an orchestra. Some musicians might have played with Toscanini, and now they only have Masur. The only way to become a convincing conductor is to find yourself, to believe in yourself, and to be able to transfer this to the orchestra. Developing confidence as a conductor takes experience. An orchestra is not like a piano, which plays what you want. It is group of people who don't always play what you want.

How does a young conductor develop the imagination to interpret a major work, such as Mahler's First Symphony?

In Mahler's First you have to learn the themes he used and why he used them. This symphony was composed in Leipzig, so I grew up with the music. This is the only symphony in which Mahler went the same way Beethoven did. Beethoven often starts symphonies with a kind of sadness but never ends that way. Mahler's First is his only symphony that really ends triumphantly. All the others end with a question mark, and some ask whether it is better to live or to die. A young conductor has to learn the music well, otherwise he cannot follow his imagination. In the second movement what Mahler wrote is so full of poetry and so full of love. The *Ländler* in his Ninth Symphony is just the opposite, and it conveys unhappiness and tragedy.

What talents are essential in a young conductor, without which he will never make it?

You will never see me ask students to imitate my style because I have a special body language that is different from other conductors. What I ask it that they really learn to use the baton, which some want to do without because it feels more flexible and they have more to say with hand gestures. From your hands and gestures an orchestra has to know what you want, what you feel. If a young conductor is unable to convey the beat on a difficult piece, I tell them to put their hands in their pockets, and just breathe; the orchestra will breathe together. They are always astonished how this works. I would advise young conductors to be careful how they treat an orchestra; beating them is not the right way. You have to work together.

Have you always conducted without a baton?

I conducted with a baton until my car accident in 1972. This was a very hard time: I couldn't move much, so I just used my fingers. I was scheduled to conduct a performance of Bach's B Minor Mass, which I did with only two fingers. Now I actually conduct better without a baton. If the orchestra couldn't play precisely enough, I would use a baton.

How do you teach conductors to avoid becoming so overwhelmed with emotions that their technique suffers?

The first key is to learn to beat precisely. The second is that in front of an orchestra you have to believe fully in what you do. You cannot doubt your ability. If you doubt, you are lost. Developing an imaginative musical vision matters more than beating time in a particular way. Furtwängler used an irregular beat, but he was so full of electricity that the musicians exploded with energy.

Was Furtwängler one of your early conducting heroes?

I would say he was the man I could hear the most often. I grew up in the Nazi times, so he was the conductor then. Karajan was very young and not as important. My real idol was Bruno Walter, who came back to Germany after the war. I heard him conduct the Mozart G Minor Symphony and Beethoven's *Eroica* on a radio broadcast. It was breathtaking. I remember thinking that the orchestra was so free and full of beauty. He was not a dictator but a musician who led other musicians.

That's interesting because so many young conductors today study the great interpretations, from Toscanini and Reiner back to Furtwängler.

Remember that tastes were different then, and no one can imitate Furtwängler. Toscanini was so driven and impatient. Furtwängler did not conduct any bar without meaning. If he made a ritardando, there was a reason for it. You may or may not like his interpretation. Then there is Walter and you must listen to his Mahler Ninth. This is philosophy in conducting: this is leadership among friends. He made a wonderful recording with the Columbia Symphony Orchestra of the Beethoven Fourth and the Mozart *Linz* Symphony.

How important is studying the interpretations of other conductors?

I never marked on my score what other conductors did because I very often didn't accept their interpretations. My feelings about the subito pianos in Beethoven are quite different from those of others. Beethoven had such an incredible imagination, but very often we hear this in a very sentimental way, which is why I never imitate other conductors. Find out why composers mark these changes in manuscripts. It is so incredible. Sometimes the change is just the instrument taking over without interrupting the line. You have to understand the reasons for each marking in a score. I feel we have too many conductors who are going first for success and not for the truth.

Mahler once wrote that what is best in the music is not the notes, yet Toscanini said blessed are the arts which need no interpreters. These are conflicting statements, but aren't both true?

I think we shouldn't forget that Toscanini grew up in Italy, where orchestras were not disciplined. Conductors had to shout and be horrifying to get the intended result. He was perhaps a bit too demanding and didn't trust the musicians. In a rehearsal with the Vienna Philharmonic, Toscanini became so furious with the orchestra that he threw his score to the ground. The room became silent and everybody was shocked. The first cellist picked up the part and laid it on Toscanini's stand without a word. This was the point where his approach went too far, and it wouldn't work anymore.

Fritz Reiner had a keen sense of rhythm, and this is one of the most important skills for young conductors to learn, but how do you teach rhythmic precision?

I'm simply disturbed if an orchestra plays an eighth instead of a sixteenth because the excitement is much more with a sixteenth. We just played Beethoven's Seventh, and the conductor always has to insist with everything that's in the work, that the musicians don't play straight. I often conduct in six if they play a wrong rhythm. The main rhythm must dance; it's Italian in style. The first time with this orchestra there was much trouble, but that was years ago. Now they know exactly what I want, and the subtle changes affect the character of the music so much. Toscanini's 1936 recording of the Seventh Symphony with the New York Philharmonic is a little bit too fast, but it is breathtaking. The performance is incredible because he insisted on a precise execution of the dotted eighth and sixteenth rhythms, bringing a tremendous rhythmic tension and power to the symphony.

Could you talk about the commitment you have shown to music education?

When I came to New York in 1991, I found the same problems we have in Europe because students do not learn music in elementary school. I spoke to the orchestral committee and asked to give free concerts for young people. The students would come in with a teacher in the morning and instead of having a music lesson, they would hear a brief concert. It was a stunning experience. I know Leonard Bernstein gave similar concerts back when television stations were interested in broadcasting such concerts. We should pay television stations to show performances for students. If young people grow up in New York and only hear rock and roll, they end up thinking all other types of music are boring.

When I grew up, my sisters and I sang folk songs for half an hour before we went to sleep. These songs were the basis of my musical education. The music was simple but wonderful. Rock and roll can be exciting, but it does not warm the heart. We have to give students a place where they can feel at home, where they remember that they still have a soul, a heart. Music can make them feel this.

Now the New York Philharmonic has a department of education and hired Bobby McFerrin to give school concerts for children. I conduct three conservatory orchestras each year and sometimes even elementary school orchestras. One school wanted to play Edvard Grieg's *Holberg Suite*. Some of the children were so small, but in the end they were shocked how well they could play. Inspiration made them forget how difficult the music was. This is where we should return. The young generation of conductors has to feel that even with the simplest music they can inspire. I would like to do more and find a concert hall that will sell tickets to students at very low prices. At the Royal Albert Hall, young people stand in the aisles, no chairs, nothing; they just listen to everything. I have done the War Requiem there, the Brahms Requiem, and other serious pieces. This is a fascinating audience. Before I start, they are so crazy, so loud that I think we cannot do the War Requiem here. The moment we start, they are silent. This is the way I would like to continue with the orchestra, to help the younger audience discover a musical language they too will love. They shouldn't give up rock and roll; I grew up with jazz and classical music, and my son did the same.

Among all your accomplishments, of which are you most proud?

I watch my pride very carefully, perhaps because of my first piano teacher, who taught me until I was ten. She felt I was proud and asked, "Why are you so proud? Other people play better than you. Why are you proud? You have a talent. This is not something to be proud of. God has given it to you. Use it." When I started at the Gewandhaus in 1973, this was something some people could be proud of, but I was not because I felt the burden and the responsibility. When I started with the New York Philharmonic, I couldn't be proud; I just had to prove that it could work. How this orchestra played Mahler One yesterday was just perfect. As a result of our collaboration I have the feeling that the audience understood. Regardless of whether they cheer at the end, I am happy if I feel they understood. Once in Rio de Janeiro where audiences are always loud after concerts, at the end Beethoven's Ninth Symphony, they were silent for a half a minute. I still was not proud.

As you prepare for a concert of Prokofiev and Mahler, do you think much about these composers?

I am so full of stories about composers. I always remember that Mahler changed radically during his life, from the first symphony to the ninth. I have often heard the ninth played with a sad, depressed ending. However, I feel that Mahler was thinking about life and death. This is not a tragedy because Tchaikovsky's Sixth is truly a tragedy, but Mahler is going to heaven. This has to be brought out of the orchestra so the audience can feel it. You never should think that the audience does not understand; they may not with their brains, but they do with their hearts.

Besides being a distinguished conductor, you became recognized in 1989 as a peacemaker.

I'm always a peacemaker in the sense that making music brings understanding to people. The musical language of Beethoven or Mahler is language everybody can feel. In China young people feel the same way about the music. A touching moment for me was in Taiwan two years ago when I was asked to talk to students about Beethoven. I discussed the remarkable moments of his life and how his first eight symphonies were composed in ten years. After the Eighth Symphony he was unable to compose another for ten years. In the Ninth Symphony he found such a new style. The beginning of the Ninth Symphony is new music. Mahler once said that this is not Beethoven and not classical. He must have had a breakthrough to write the Ninth Symphony and find a way to give mankind hope. This is something incredible. Like the creation of the world, it is full of explosions, lightning, thunder, whatever you want to imagine. I told these young people that Beethoven was deaf at the time he composed the Ninth. This was not a miracle because with his inner ear he could write, but he was not very healthy. Afterwards three very shy girls of 15 or 16 asked if I thought that Beethoven could overcome all these difficult circumstances because he believed in God. Yes. This is the message that I feel exactly. If you are honest as a conductor and as an artist and want to say something special about these pieces, you are understood. You shouldn't think music speaks by itself. That's nonsense. 🐟

Left to right: John Knight and Kurt Masur.

CHAPTER 28

Precision with Spontaneity:
An Interview with Herbert Blomstedt

Born in the United States and raised in Sweden, Herbert Blomstedt learned the craft of conducting from Igor Markevitch, Jean Morel, and Leonard Bernstein. He became the music director of the Staatskapelle in Dresden and later of the San Francisco Symphony, which gained prominence under his leadership and was recognized for its recordings of the works of Carl Nielsen. His concept of conducting combines the precision of Toscanini with the spontaneity of Furtwängler and Bernstein. He believes, "Musicians in the orchestra expect a conductor to be a musician who knows the orchestral sound rather than the sound coming from a piano. In chamber music you learn how music works in a group. Any orchestra will be happy to have a conductor who actually hears what they are doing and reacts by giving them a clear idea of what they are supposed to do."

What inspired you to become a conductor?

The main interest of my early years was the organ and violin, especially the organ music of Bach and the chamber music of Haydn and Mozart. By playing chamber music I became involved with the other voices but never dreamt of becoming a conductor. The wish to stand in front and command a big group of people was not my prime motive for studying music. I did go to the Göteborg Symphony each Thursday and Sunday to hear concerts, and I never could get enough. During my training at the Royal Conservatory in Stockholm I had to take a half-year of conducting, and that was the beginning of it. Obviously my teacher, Tor Mann, thought I had some talent and began asking me to rehearse and conduct area orchestras. He encouraged me to study conducting after graduation.

What was it like to study with Igor Markevitch in Salzburg, Jean Morel at Juilliard, and Leonard Bernstein at Tanglewood?

I studied with Markevitch in the early 1950s. He was a marvelous teacher, but many of my colleagues didn't like him. I don't know why. For me he was absolutely perfect. In Stockholm my teacher had been very good in the music of Sibelius, but he was not a good technician. He was a born musician who could make music with other musicians, but he was rather awkward and could give only the rudiments of conducting, and didn't know how he was making music. In contrast, Markevitch was superb technician and musician, and he was absolutely convinced that there is a technique for conducting just as there is for

---

violin, cello, or trombone. A student just had to follow his system to learn how. Markevitch was from the same school of conducting as Hermann Scherchen and Toscanini: both were very economical, effective, and didn't get in the way of the musicians. They gave only the necessary signs and nothing more. Don't fuss about on the podium and be absolutely clear. One of Markevitch's great feats as a conductor was that he recorded Stravinsky's *The Rite of Spring* after only two rehearsals. Back then *Rite of Spring* was a fiendishly difficult piece, but today any good youth orchestra can play it. Markevitch's technique was so economical and so scaled to the musicians that he knew exactly what they needed and would do nothing more. If they received the right signs, there would be no problems. He was very good for conducting students like me who loved music but were not very disciplined.

Markevitch stepped in at the last moment to teach the conducting class at Salzburg when Karajan canceled, although Karajan did come and give a lecture on conducting. Markevitch taught the course, and I thought that was a very good change. Many who had expected Karajan to teach the class left after a few days, but Daniel Barenboim also stayed. In this class Markevitch had a system to teach us to control the basic techniques. Of course, there is a lot more to conducting besides that, but this was the aim of the course. The second important thing he taught was thorough score analysis.

I took his class for four years, and he asked me to become his assistant. I called him Papa Igor and we remained emotionally close as long as he lived. The last time I saw him was right here in this room where we are sitting now when he was here with the Vienna Philharmonic but in bad health. He smoked as we talked, spilling ashes from his cigarette that he tried to clear from my tie. It was quite emotional to see him in that state. I admired him very much as a musician and there was also some common ground we had together that is difficult to define.

When I received a scholarship to study at Juilliard, I met Jean Morel, a wonderful teacher in his way. I studied with him at a time he was concentrating on solfege, which was one of my favorite subjects at the conservatory, but of course French solfege is completely different from what I had learned. Morel was a wonderful and interesting person; he even played percussion on the first performance of Stravinsky's *L'Histoire du Soldat*.

As a conducting student I auditioned for Leonard Bernstein and was accepted at Tanglewood. Bernstein was very important to my growth as a conductor, but his personality was completely different from mine. He was more instinctive and emotional, and I learned the spontaneous approach to music. Like others I had thought of him as a showman, but he was sincere in his music making.

How did winning the 1953 Koussevitzky Conducting Prize at Tanglewood and the first prize at the 1955 Salzburg Conducting Competition help your conducting career?

The Koussevitzky Conducting Prize was a scholarship of $100 a week to study at Tanglewood. This was a great experience, and Charles Munch came and rehearsed the student orchestra, but he was used to the Boston Symphony and didn't like conducting a student group. He would stop, stamp his feet, yell at the students, and lose his temper completely. He was so temperamental that he refused to conduct the concert and I was asked to replace him. The Salzburg prize gave me the opportunity to conduct the Brussels Chamber Orchestra and the Lausanne Chamber Orchestra, but led nowhere. What got me started was a debut concert with the Stockholm Philharmonic in 1954 when I was 26.

How can young conductors create opportunities that will advance their careers?

One of the most difficult aspects of a conducting career is being patient until openings occur. I had several chances when the conductor of the Stockholm Radio Orchestra became ill. I led the Berwald Symphony with one month's notice. I rented a car and drove to the conductor's summer place to ask him for advice on the score. He was very kind and helped me gain some experience, which led to conducting the Radio Chamber Orchestra in Haydn's Symphony #104 and a Mozart violin concerto. I had to wait four years before my debut with the Stockholm Philharmonic, but the answer to your question is that each young conductor has to make the best of every chance. There is always a need for good conductors who really know the repertoire. I suggest getting experience with smaller orchestras. Never be ashamed of the status of the orchestra, just do the best you can. It is like throwing a stone in the water and letting the rings attract the attention of others.

For four years after my debut I studied musicology at the university and continued to learn conducting from Markevitch. I went to Darmstadt for new music and Basel to study old music. I received a scholarship in America but I was getting frustrated because I had a girlfriend I wanted to marry but had no position. I had applied for an organist position at one of the main churches in Stockholm but didn't get it. One orchestra asked me to be its music director, and I was very interested, but there was one drawback. Because of the Sabbath, I didn't rehearse on Saturdays, and the orchestra had their main rehearsals on Saturday. I followed my convictions, didn't get the job, and waited for something better to come along. Only a month later another much better orchestra asked me the same question about not rehearsing on Saturday. I knew that if I declined I might not get another chance, but could not betray my beliefs. They finally agreed to change the Saturday rehearsal to Sunday mornings. We rehearsed on Sunday mornings and gave concerts on Sunday nights. This was quite exceptional but they had decided that I was the man they wanted for the job. I was very fortunate and these were happy years with my own orchestra.

What are some common mistakes young conductors make with a professional orchestra?

They listen too little. A conductor not only leads but also has to listen. Only if you listen can you fix anything, much as it is when playing chamber music. That is not easy for a young conductor who is full of himself because he thinks he knows the score. Unfortunately many young conductors come to rehearsals with preconceived ideas. The essence of being a conductor is to listen closely and respond to what you actually hear. Knowledge of the score allows you to hear things that are wrong but not to anticipate what will go wrong. No orchestra is perfect, not even the Berlin Philharmonic; every orchestra needs some reaction from the conductor to what they do. I would say that the most important thing is to listen to them and then respond.

Certainly you must have a clear concept of what you want to hear, but be ready to adjust to what actually comes from the orchestra. This is what constitutes artistic give and take between conductor and orchestra. An orchestra will respect a young conductor who does these things.

Eugene Ormandy once ascribed the opulent sound he got from the Philadelphia Orchestra to his being a violinist, and Toscanini was always playing the cello as he conducted. How has your background with the organ and violin influenced your concept of orchestra sound?

My string background helped to suggest bowings, but I don't use the orchestra as an instrument. An orchestra is an orchestra. One of the special pleasures of conducting is getting to know all the problems and strengths of the instruments. A conductor can learn more by meeting new musicians. I treat the orchestra as a living organism of different instruments. I become so completely involved in the music that I don't think about it anymore, but there has to be a special communication with the eyes of each player, as in playing chamber music. A conductor should understand that although he is necessary, he can also do great harm by doing a poor job. If he doesn't fuss around unnecessarily but gives the musicians clear ideas about how to play their best, the music will come out in all its beauty. This reality should make all of us humble and grateful.

You once said that the nature of music is revelation, that it should tell a truth that is human, divine, or both. Just delivering notes, even perfect notes, doesn't produce revelation, but how do you search for the truth in a musical interpretation that will make it revealing?

Of course music should be a revelation as we listen to it, but it cannot reveal what is not in the soul of the score. No conductor can just pretend to have feelings that do not exist. The music and the conductor can only reveal what is there. A good conductor has a personality and experiences that he recreates and gives to others, but so too must a composer have experienced something when he wrote the music. Mozart's music is a miracle of polyphony, but it is much more than that, with emotions that change in each bar, and the music goes into different directions and never seems to know where it will land. It is full of surprises if the musicians playing or conducting can identify and go along with that and reveal what is there.

I was fortunate to receive some good advice from my violin teacher at the Royal Conservatory who explained that I had to get a university degree in order to be a complete musician. How right he was. A broad education includes not only learning to play fast, pure 16th notes but also getting as much experience in life as possible without going to extremes. Every time we play music it reflects the experiences we have had in our lives.

What would you like to see emphasized in the training of conductors?

First of all a musician must really know the score to the extent of being able to explain why the composer wrote F# there instead of F. Some conductors are extremely gifted and can learn a score in a few days while others take months. Many conductors don't know the score. They just know the melody because it is the easiest to learn. That is not conducting. I prefer to know a few scores well instead of many scores superficially. I work through analyses of harmony, rhythm and where the piece fits in the composer's life. When I conducted Schumann's Symphony #1 for the first time I had started studying the score two years before the performance. When I was finished with the analysis I wrote in the score, "For the glory of God, and thank God I'm through!" I knew why Schumann wrote each note because I knew the harmonic structure, the periodic structure, and the motivic structure. I have to get a piece under my skin and in my heart. The next stage is to decide how to interpret this music, the tempo, how loud the *forte* and how soft the *piano* markings should be. The length of each note and the balance are specific choices to make after thoroughly analyzing the score. An interpretation is not something we get from God or from outside revelation. It comes from studying and struggling with the score, but this stage takes much less time than the analysis. The third stage is deciding how to conduct a work, to consider what kind of bowing would be best in the difficult parts. There are parts of the score the musicians may overlook that need some extra life and places to beat in two rather than four. These practical questions take a little less time, but after spending so much time on a score I am not nervous any longer and can honestly step onto the podium and be ready to make music.

When I conducted the Amsterdam Philharmonic 30 or 40 years ago, the orchestra and I were very happy to have such good rapport. The concertmaster said, "Most conductors learn the piece when we play it for them and simply follow us, but with you we feel that you know the score and know what you want. We play what you want." I commented that I had thought everybody makes music as I do. "No way," he laughed. I was very surprised at that.

How can a conductor convey a love of music during rehearsals and performances, as Furtwängler was famous for?

Markevitch and Furtwängler were exact opposites. Markevitch was cerebral and analytical, whereas Furtwängler was a great improviser, who also had a profound knowledge of the score. Markevitch admired Furtwängler enormously. It might also be that Markevitch did not have improvisation inside himself. I heard Furtwängler very often, and it was magical because he really created music in the moment. It was different every time. His magic was built on profound knowledge and rehearsal technique. He rehearsed very intensely, often without any instructions. He would simply repeat the passage and not give up until he heard exactly what he wanted. He would build enormous tension based on knowledge of the piece.

His performances were like giving a speech. My father was a great preacher and was very well prepared, but his sermons would sound improvised. You have to know exactly what you want to say and build up a framework going from point to point emphasizing different parts of speech and seeing how the audience reacts. When I talk I also like to improvise but I think through very carefully what I want to say. Improvisation should be built on knowledge and not go on too long. Music has a definite text, and notes must not be violated. It is like the Bible; only if you know the Bible very well can you really use it.

It is a happy occasion when you have an orchestra that also knows and respects the text and works hard with the conductor. The orchestra wants to know that the conductor is listening to them. If they see this, they are willing to give more.

What is your personal credo about the art of conducting?

To never pretend to know more than I do or that I am perfect. It only takes an orchestra a few seconds to see through such pretense. I try to have a clear concept of how each work should sound but to be flexible enough to react to the musicians. Otherwise it doesn't work. A conductor must remember what works and doesn't work after each performance, and after each concert. I always make notes in my score about what to do differently the next time. I believe the conductor should be an authority for the musicians but at the same time be very self-critical. Never show that you don't believe in yourself, for that is the death of all cooperation. You have to believe in what you are doing while realizing that you might do it differently tomorrow. This is a tricky balance, but musicians understand this very well.

It is important to respect the orchestra. From the first moment he is in front of an orchestra a conductor should not hide anything. The members must feel that the conductor is sincere, or they will immediately suspect his intentions.

CHAPTER 29

From Vaughan Williams to Elgar:
An Interview with Conductor Richard Hickox

O n a sunny London day I made my way over to the Phoenix recording studios where one of Britain's most celebrated conductors, Richard Hickox, was rehearsing Elgar's First Symphony and Ralph Vaughan Williams' *Fantasia on a Theme* of Thomas Tallis with the Philharmonia Orchestra. Hickox first took the ensemble all the way through each movement before going back to work on particular segments, a departure from the usual start-and-stop approach. Throughout the three-hour session his respect for the music was evident in each gesture and facial expression. There was much warmth between conductor and the orchestra.

While watching Hickox rehearse the Elgar and Vaughan Williams I was struck by the singing quality and spontaneity of the music. It sounded free and lyrical, but at the same time Hickox was molding the musical line into his preconceived idea of the score. As a result his singing approach lifted the music from the page and gave it a beautiful musical line.

Hickox explained that one of the keys to understanding British music is to follow the rise and fall of the spoken English language. "Think of the melodies of Elgar, for example. The Dutch speak in a monotone, and for the life of me I can't think of any famous melody from that country. English music is also linked to the environment, the countryside of Worcester in Elgar's music, Cheltenham with Holst, and Gloucester with Vaughan Williams."

The rehearsal of this Elgar work conveyed a high plane of musical feeling through closely observing the dynamics and extreme lyricism. The Vaughan William *Fantasia* in Hickox's interpretation evoked visions of rolling green landscapes in 16th-century England. In his hands the ethereal Thomas Tallis theme became hauntingly beautiful.

After the rehearsal as we rode through the streets of London, Hickox discussed the art of his profession. "I started conducting in front of the mirror at the age of two or three, and it was an instinct in me just as my father had the instinct to become a priest. I wanted to make the sounds I was hearing in my head, and it had nothing to do with power. I always wanted to conduct. I wanted to make sounds that I heard in my head, but this was purely a creative thing.

"My mother, who taught piano and ran a percussion studio, took me to the Royal Academy of Music to see her old professor and find out if I had any talent as a conductor. After acknowledging that I did, he warned me that the life of a conductor is much harder than that of a doctor. Now I think he is right because it

---

can be a very lonely life. I love my craft more and more, but it is a bloody hard life and full of disappointment. All of the traveling takes me away from my family, and it is hard on them too. The press often finds a conductor to be brilliant one day and knocks him the next, and very often the comments are made about the same concert. Of course, I always believe the bad reviews."

In 1964 at the age of 16 Hickox's father gave him the job of conducting a large church choir, and at age 19 he studied for a year at the Royal Academy of Music. Soon after this he won an organ scholarship to Cambridge, where he often conducted. "I was first interested in church music above all other types and couldn't help but be influenced by choirs and organs. I'm glad to be an organist because it is an orchestra in one instrument and can create so many colors. This was very good preparation for becoming a conductor."

In 1971 Hickox founded the City of London Sinfonia, and is still its music director. In describing the essential qualities of a good conductor he says, "The conducting technique will come if the musical ideas are there. It is very important for a conductor to be clear and have clear musical ideas. The technique has to come from the music instead of imposing technique on the music. A conductor must have confidence in his ability to convince the ensemble. I can't say this any better than Sir Colin Davis, who noted, 'Conducting is 80% psychology and 20% music.' I have to persuade the orchestra that the way I am interpreting a piece at any given moment is the way it should sound. It is best if they don't know how hard you are working to get them on your side. The Philharmonia works best with the team-effort as long so they know I am the team leader.

"I started the rehearsal today by stating how proud I was of their performance of Britten's *Gloriana*. You saw the overwhelming response of the members, who know that I wouldn't say this if I didn't mean it. I have to be sincere and honest, or the orchestra can see through it in ten seconds or less."

Hickox explains that another part of the psychology of conducting is in choosing guest conductors who will work well with the orchestra. "This is extraordinarily difficult, and I cannot always predict if the chemistry will be right. All conductors cannot be a wow with all orchestras because personality is such a big factor. I work well with the London orchestras, but we are all only as good as our last note. Guest conducting suits me well because I enjoy the spirit of the London groups.

"Of course, there is also the way of the martinet, but this should be rare. The Karajan days are gone, and I find that very refreshing. There are still a few conductors today who work that way, but not many."

Hickox believes that conductors today interpret music differently from the usual styles of the 1940s and 1950s. "The biggest change has been the development of the Baroque and Classical orchestras that play on period instruments or in a more authentic style. Now I find it almost impossible to listen to a large orchestra play Mozart in a uniform way."

Hickox has a soft spot in his heart for the conductors he worked with during his apprenticeship: Andrew Previn, Colin Davis, and Charles Mackerras. "Davis took me under his wing in his kind way, and he used to give up whole mornings, often weekly, to talk through scores with me. Now that I am so busy I realize what a huge amount of time he sacrificed on my behalf. He just loved to talk about music. My first project with Davis was as chorus master for *Missa Solemnis.* Mackerras was the same way and was incredibly generous with his time.

"When Claudio Abbado was appointed principal conductor of the London Symphony Orchestra, I became very close to him and learned an enormous amount. Just being able to talk to him about scores and how to hold the stick meant an awful lot to me.

"I also knew Leonard Bernstein well because I worked with him so much and prepared several recordings for him with the London Symphony Orchestra. When he wasn't feeling well, he let me conduct parts of rehearsals while he stood back and listened to the balance of the orchestra. His conducting of Mozart, Haydn, and his own music was terrific, but I couldn't take his interpretations of the *Enigma Variations.* William Walton was also an inspiring conductor of his music, but he never conducted anyone else's works. His recording of *Belshazzar's Feast* was truly outstanding, and I wore that recording out. John Barbirolli and Malcolm Sargent also influenced me."

According to Hickox, the qualities of an excellent interpretation are difficult to define "but it's unmistakable when it is there and equally obvious when it's not. The opera we played last week absolutely got through to the psyche of the orchestra.

"Sometimes everything comes together at just the right moment. This is more than technical precision, almost as if a spiritual factor takes the music to a different plane. It's possible to rehearse something to death and then wonder why it doesn't come together, but then there are nights when everything goes marvelously."

One quality Hickox finds essential to a good performance is that the conductor "must really love and believe in the music. Some very famous conductors sound to me as though they have lost their love of music. This undermines everything they do, even though they are technically right on."

Hickox advises those interested in a conducting career to "watch a lot of rehearsals, talk to conductors, and attend master classes. Once you are beyond that stage, particularly in America, try to get a position as an assistant conductor. Very few British orchestras have this post, and there was only one position in the U.K. when I started out. There are only two or three more now, but this position is incredibly useful for a student and also valuable for the conductor and the orchestra. If the assistant is good, he can help the conductor. They used the system at Bournemouth for years, and the assistant was an enormous help with sectionals or as another set of ears in the recording room. I would never dream of taking on an opera without having another conductor standing in the hall and listening for balance; to do without is nonsense."

Hickox contends that the study of voice is fundamental for conductors. "Young conductors should be made to sing all the parts, play as many instruments as possible, and be prepared to conduct anything at any time. Especially with singers, a conductor is successful only if he breathes with them. This is also true with an orchestra. Some conductors study the score at the piano and forget that breathing with the orchestra is so fundamental to a good interpretation. My background in choral conducting helped my career, and I will be the music director of Opera Australia and run the Sidney Opera House in 2005."

Hickox advises young conductors to try new pieces. "A really harmful choice would be to conduct a potboiler program that includes the Tchaikovsky Fifth Symphony, which the orchestra has played more than 100 times and knows better than the neophyte conductor. It is better to select a program that interests the orchestra and with which they are not overly familiar. This is why Simon Rattle is going around the world performing the Mahler Tenth Symphony. Everyone already knows the first nine, and this is a smart move. A conductor should be extremely well prepared and quietly authoritative but should try not to talk too much. He should show through the body what he wants."

Hickox has more than 221 recordings to his credit, most with Chandos. His recordings with the Philharmonia follow in the legacy of Claudio Abbado, John Barbirolli, Adrian Boult, Guido Cantelli, Carlo Maria Giulini, Herbert von Karajan, Otto Klemperer, Riccardo Muti, and Giuseppe Sinopoli. Hickox has received the Gramophone Award for best choral recording for Britten's *War Requiem* and for Delius's *Sea Drift* as well as Grammy awards for Vaughan Williams's London Symphony and Britten's *Peter Grimes*.

"Every recording is different," he says. "There were many rehearsal-record sessions in which we went straight in and made the CD. This is the least satisfactory way of doing it, but we have made some good recordings this way. The best method is to have an intense rehearsal period, a concert, and then go to the studio. I am able to do this with the BBC Orchestra in Wales. Concert recordings with a patch session can also yield good results, but the studio recording is often much better. I get just as much of a kick from a microphone as from an audience. Many conductors don't, but I love psyching the orchestra up to that indefinable moment when the recording comes to life. It may take two or three takes during which I rehearse, pick at it, and then say 'Here we go!' That's when I know something is special."

One of Hickox's favorite recording projects was the Vaughan Williams *London Symphony* because he was given permission by Ursula Vaughan Williams to make a recording of the original 1913 version. There are three versions of the symphony: the 1913, the 1920, and the third and final in 1934. Williams's biographer, Michael Kennedy, was able to convince Ursula that "it would make the work a far greater one, or that it would do no damage. She has now given permission for one public performance at Barbican Centre next November with the LSO, and

Kennedy thinks that the original version will probably become the norm in time. It becomes an epic experience. Leonard Slatkin once tried to record the extra bits from the 1913 recording, but Ursula was in the box and stopped him. Poor man, Slatkin, but it was worth a go. He tried to slip it underneath, and I would have done the same, I'm sure."

The music of Percy Grainger has also been an inspiration to Hickox, who recorded Grainger's music on the Chandos label. "In the 1970s Benjamin Britten made a famous recording called *A Salute to Percy Grainger.* I couldn't stop playing that record; it put Grainger on the map in the U.K. Certainly Britten was an excellent conductor of Mozart and Elgar, but the Grainger recording was one of magic.

"Grainger's music is eclectic, mad, and fun, but so hard to program in a concert. *Except for The Warriors, The Power of Rome and The Christian Heart,* most pieces are short and call for unusual instruments, such as three harmonium or two celeste, which makes them expensive to record. The only way to really program pieces is to reserve half of the concert for Grainger miniatures, which I have been successful with at the Proms."

Hickox says the recording industry is at the point where the only reason to make a new CD is to fill in gaps in the catalog. "Rattle has just made a recording of the Beethoven Ninth Symphony, but even he hasn't sold that many of them."

Our conversation ended as the driver pulled up to the next concert hall in which another orchestra was awaiting Hickox's arrival. Hickox's rehearsal with the Philharmonia will always be a moveable feast for me. The music stayed with me after the last cadence faded, as in the line in Shelly's poem: "Music when soft voices die vibrates in the memory."

Remembering Maestro Richard Hickox (1948–2008)

I was shocked and saddened to learn of conductor Richard Hickox's unexpected death on November 23, 2008. He died in his Cardiff hotel room after a recording session of Holst's Choral Symphony with the BBC National Chorus of Wales.

Only 60 years old, which is still young for a conductor, Maestro Hickox was an extraordinarily gifted musician who worked tirelessly to champion instrumental and choral works of 20th-century British composers. As one of Britain's busiest and foremost conductors, he was renowned for his lyrical and insightful interpretationsof Vaughan Williams and Elgar. His interpretations of Percy Grainger were also inspirational.

I was fortunate to meet Hickox in 2003 on a mild and sunny day in London. Our interview that day was later published in the October 2003 issue of *The Instrumentalist*:

Before the interview, I watched Hickox rehearse with the Philharmonia Orchestra on Elgar's 1st Symphony and Vaughn William's *Fantasia on a Theme of Thomas Tallis*. His music making with this great orchestra lasted three hours and was a thrilling memory I will always cherish.

The rehearsal moved quickly as Maestro Hickox was consistently engaged with the orchestra. His enthusiasm and knowledge of the music were evident in every measure with sweeping movements of the baton that conveyed the musical line. Mostly he was interested in helping musicians understand the long singing line and therefore, his conducting technique was based on the rise and fall of the phrase and not the measures. This emphasis on phrases set the music free, making it spontaneous and lyrical.

After the rehearsal Hickox was exhausted but had to go directly to another rehearsal with the London Symphony Orchestra on the other side of the city. He invited me to ride with him in his chauffeured limousine for the interview. The colorful and busy streets of London made a kaleidoscopic background for the informative ride while he shared his ideas on conducting and interpretation.

He emphasized that the key to understanding British music is to follow the rise and fall of the spoken English language. English music is also directly linked to the local countryside: the hillsides of Worcester in Elgar's music, Cheltenham with Holst, and Gloucester with Vaughan Williams. Conducting technique will come if the musical ideas are there. It is very important for a conductor to convey clear musical ideas. The technique comes from the music instead of imposing technique on the music.

© *The Instrumentalist*, March 2009. Reprinted with Permission.

Maestro Hickox acknowledged that an excellent interpretation is difficult to define but obvious when it is there. He encouraged young conductors to sing all the parts, play as many instruments as possible, and be prepared to conduct anything at any time. He believed that a conductor will be successful if he is able to breathe with the ensemble.

First and foremost for a good performance, the conductor must love and believe in the music. If the love of music is lost, even if the conducting and performance are technically perfect, the musical result is undermined and fails. As our conversation ended, I noticed the exhaustion creep back into his voice.

He concluded, "Conducting is a bloody lonely profession. You have to sacrifice a lot for your art. I don't like being away from my family for so long a time, and there are always the critical reviews to read. One critic will love a concert, and another will hate the same performance. What makes it all worthwhile is when it comes together and you capture the spirit of the composer. However good your geometry is as a conductor, unless you have the spirit of the music inside you, it's worth nothing."

Reproducing the spirit of the composer and giving it to the orchestra and to the audience are the marks of a great conductor. Throughout history, conductors come and go, the memories of some fading faster than an early morning fog. Time passes and death is inescapable. At best a conductor's fame is transitory but the interpretations by the great ones ennoble the spirit of mankind and leave an indelible mark in our hearts.

In the history of British music-making, I consider Richard Hickox, along with Barbirolli, Beecham, and Boult, to be among the great ones. With over 300 recordings on the Chandos label, Hickox's fame and reputation are secure and will continue to inspire us. I find his recordings of Vaughan Williams, Britten, Elgar, Holst and Delius to be especially evocative, lyrical, and hauntingly beautiful—a lasting tribute to his legacy and humanity.

I will always remember his smiling boyish charm and good humor. Most of all, I will remember a London day bathed in sunlight when Maestro Hickox took time away from his hectic schedule to share his passion for the conductor's art. He will be deeply missed. ✍

CHAPTER 31

Evaluating Conductors from the Orchestra: An Interview with Michel Debost

Although there are many biographies about the lives and musical interpretations of famous conductors, only a few give a performer's point of view of the art of conducting. Unfortunately this leaves young conductors starting careers on the podium without the observations of orchestra members who played the music that made past conductors famous.

From 1960 to 1990 Michel Debost played principal flute in the Orchestra de Paris and performed under the baton of Charles Munch, Herbert von Karajan, Georg Solti, and Daniel Barenboim. He was professor of flute at the Paris Conservatoire from 1982–1990, succeeding Jean Pierre Rampal, and has since been a professor of flute at Oberlin Conservatory. He is a consulting editor for *Flute Talk*.

Who most influenced your decision to become a professional musician?

My mother was a singer and she encouraged me to play the piano. My father was not musically inclined, but he was a friend with a semi-professional flutist who had a curious mind and was a very interesting person. My father's friend was a professor of electricity and started me on the flute in 1944. Later I was introduced to the professor of flute of the Paris Conservatory, but I doubted that I had the stuff to make it as a professional. When I auditioned for the conservatory and failed, I majored in pre-med, but a year later I reauditioned for the conservatory. The happiest day of my life was when I was accepted. Music became my life, and I have always been happy to be a musician.

In the days of the German occupation of France during World War II, the Sociètè des Concerts du Conservatoire de Paris was the best orchestra in Paris, but it was not affiliated with the Conservatory. I thought to myself, "My God, if I could get into an orchestra like that, I would be the happiest guy in the world."

My oldest memory of the orchestra is from December 1944, when my mother took me to an orchestra concert on a Saturday morning with Charles Munch conducting. The concert started late, but Munch, who was Alsatian born, stormed onto the stage and told the audience, "Strasbourg has just been liberated, so we will play *La Marseillaise*." As the national anthem was performed, everyone stood with tears streaming down their faces. This was a poignant moment in my life. Twenty years later when I played for Munch, I didn't dare tell him of this memory, but I should have because it was so emotional.

Frantz Strauss, a famous horn player in Munich, and the father of Richard Strauss, declared "when a new conductor faces the orchestra—from the way he walks up the steps to the podium—before he ever picks up the baton—we know whether he is the master or we." How true is this, and how long does it take orchestra members to determine whether a new conductor is a maestro or a charlatan?

I don't agree with Franz Strauss and have always been reluctant to judge people before I see them at work. Some conductors are interesting and strong at first but do not pan out later. At times conductors and musicians have power conflicts, but this often varies between different sections. I know that string players hold cohesive opinions and ideas about a conductor who doesn't cater to the needs of the strings, but it is impossible to tell anything concrete from the way a conductor walks to the podium or greets the orchestra.

My impressions have changed from what they were when I was a young man in the orchestra. At age 20, I loved every piece because I was discovering the masterpieces for the first time. I enjoyed the conductors, too, even though some didn't turn out to be the greatest. However, I have marvelous memories of playing with these people.

I thought Bernstein was great because he was a wonderful musician with a personality that inspired us. He added a dimension to everything he did. It bothers some musicians when conductors are a little off the wall, but I always thought Bernstein was fascinating.

Rafael Kubelik was wonderful with Mahler, Buckner, and of course, Dvořák . He was basically a classical conductor. Istvan Kertesz was a terrific, young Hungarian conductor who drowned while swimming in the Mediterranean Sea. I liked Bernard Haitink very much. He was a deep but extremely vulnerable person and subject to depression; but he was touching. The best Beethoven I ever played was with Joseph Kripps, and his conducting of the *Leonore Overture #3* was just breathtaking.

I loved Munch and thought he was so great that I named my son Charles after him. Munch had an almost mystical approach to conducting. He had a long stick of a baton and made these windmill gestures, but he was not very precise; yet he brought something to the music that had a certain humanity and mysticism to it. I always looked for this in other conductors but rarely found it.

Then there was Andre Cluytens, a Belgian conductor who was highly regarded as a fine interpreter of French music. I liked Carlo Maria Giulini, also a mystical conductor, and we thought he was always praying because his face became almost transfigured when he conducted. When we were both young I played *The Barber of Seville* with him; his conducting style was completely different and very Italian. As he got older he became very reserved, intense, and introspective.

Among the younger conductors I liked at that time were Zubin Mehta, Seiji Ozawa, and Daniel Barenboim. I also respected Pierre Boulez, but with reservations; he has terrific knowledge of the score and the way the score is built. I played with him for a very long time before he became famous, but his conducting never had tension; I missed that. Munch and Bernstein had plenty of tension; it was awesome. Boulez's performances are clear and good, but too clinical for me.

I didn't like Herbert von Karajan as a person, not only because of his Nazi past, but because he was such a prima-donna conductor. The phenomenon of Karajan was very strong and he was a magician with the sound of the orchestra. He understood how the players related to him, and he got the maximum from the music.

When Karajan was our musical director in 1975, he was scheduled to conduct the Ring Cycle at the Metropolitan Opera, but they went on strike; and he couldn't stand having a month with nothing to do. He called Paris, said he was free, and the orchestra was assembled to record some music they had never played with him before. We gathered on a Tuesday morning and started recording as soon as the red light came on. As we listened to the playback, I asked him, "Maestro, why do you so carefully rehearse for a concert but not for a recording?" I remember once spending an hour rehearsing the first 16 measures of a Beethoven symphony with Karajan for an upcoming concert. His reply in fluent French was, "It is very simple. The only thing that you will never do again is a concert, but if you are not happy with a recording session, you can do it again tomorrow." I have always thought that was such an intelligent statement.

Among the things I do not like about conductors are arrogance and musical snobbery. Some conductors try to stage a master class on the podium; others are severe taskmasters and are only interested in precision. These conductors tend to lack depth, and their interpretations are often superficial. Others are best at pleasing the ladies at cocktail parties, but not as good at pleasing the members of the orchestra with a clean beat.

Were the interpretations of conductors 25 or 50 years ago as well as today guided by rhythmic precision, subjective flexibility, or other discernable traits?

I don't think that it is possible to make a general comment concerning precision because this leads to the question of what precision is. For some precision means simultaneously occurring sounds as in clockwork, but precision also refers to how the sound is sustained, which is contrary to metronomic rigidity. Solti had great precision in the sense that he was very exact, and perhaps Barenboim needs more of this. Markevitch was a stickler for precision and had great ideas about conducting, but nothing ever came of them.

Maazel subdivides everything precisely, but that does not always lead to exactness. I think the most important thing for a conductor to know is how an orchestra lives on a chord. The fact that an orchestra responds wham on the beat or that the sound starts later from the double basses and finally reaches the piccolo are entirely different concepts of precision.

A conductor is there to bring an orchestra to life. If he is a windmill conductor or goes after only precision, there cannot be much humanity in the concert performance. What must be there is flexibility. For a convincing performance there must be flexibility in the rubato and the dynamic changes.

Solti once stated that he could judge the talent of a young conductor by his ability to pull sound from an orchestra, but is this your view?

When a young conductor comes to lead a great orchestra, the best thing he can do is to shut up and run through an entire piece. Just start the machine going, and let them play. They will love you because the rehearsal will end early. I think the greatest conductors should work with the not-so-great orchestras and that young conductors should work with the greatest orchestras.

As to Solti's statement about pulling sound from an orchestra, I would disagree. A conductor should not pull sound but should give his sound to the orchestra. Despite all the reservations I had about Karajan as a person, he did bring his sound to the orchestra, and it was always as beautiful as silk.

I was never impressed by the gestures of the stick. I think if a person knows the music, feels the music, and can convey what is in the music for him, the baton technique and gestures will take care of themselves.

I also played with Leopold Stokowski, who didn't use a baton on his last tour of Europe, but he was sick then and not himself. Klemperer didn't use a baton because he had a stroke. He conducted only with his outstretched hands, and it was fantastic. Klemperer brought the depth of what he felt about the music and could only convey that depth with the little gestures he had left; yet he could make it come out. However, I prefer that conductors use a baton because this was the way I was trained, although Boulez is very clear even though he doesn't use a stick.

What would you like to see emphasized more in the training of conductors today?

I believe more emphasis should be placed on in-depth score study so conductors know what sound to aim for.

Why do American orchestras follow the tradition of choosing foreign-born conductors to lead the major orchestras?

For the true answer you should ask the boards of trustees who appoint each conductor, but my guess is that the choice is partly reputation, partly snobbism, and partly an attempt to please the ladies at the parties in the cocktail circuit. I think there should be more American conductors conducting here, but this is not only an American problem. The same thing is true in Europe. Eschenbach, a German, conducts in Paris and Ricardo Chailly, an Italian, conducts the Concertgebouw Orchestra, and so forth.

What are some of the things conductors do in rehearsals that irritate the musicians and detract from the rehearsal?

Any conductor who gives the impression that he doesn't know the score and rehearses for himself by repeating a section ten times until he learns it will irritate everyone. I dislike a conductor who talks too much; if he is clear enough with his conducting, he doesn't have to speak.

My advice to a young conductor would be to listen to the orchestra for at least the first half of a rehearsal. The orchestra wants to do it right, yet too many conductors stop the orchestra before they have a chance to play. Boulez is like that because he starts breaking the score down after playing only three measures. When he does this, the orchestra starts losing concentration. In spite of what conductors may say, professional musicians want to do the job well.

Some conductors are not very good at rehearsing, but they do a terrific job at the concert. Munch was like this. Barenboim rehearses the music inside and out and knows exactly what he wants, but I always thought his rehearsals were better than his concerts. In the orchestra we used to say, "The world is not well made. We should have rehearsals with Danny and concerts with Abbado." Abbado never knew what he wanted in rehearsals, but the music always came to life in the concert. A conductor should let the orchestra play through complete movements during rehearsals to see and hear how the musicians react before he starts taking things apart.

How much have tempos changed in the past 25 years?

I believe that tempos were much faster in the past, especially on the music of Brahms and Beethoven, which probably was because the influence of Toscanini.

William Steinberg once said that the trouble with many present-day conductors is that they are short of breath, that they get caught up in trifling details but are unable to plan a long, intense musical line. How true is this with the conductors with whom you rehearsed?

Steinberg is absolutely right. Actually, someone who knows what he is doing with the stick and truly knows the score can transmit the tension of a phrase and sustain a long musical line.

How important is it to a conductor's credibility with the orchestra to have thorough knowledge of each instrument?

I don't want a conductor to tell me how to play my instrument because that is my job. How I get there is none of his business. He should only state if he wants a passage to be louder, shorter, and so forth. I don't think a conductor should cater to the psyches of the musicians because that's an analyst's job. Some conductors learn scores at the piano and forget that wind players need to breathe. It is not what a conductor knows about the instruments that matters, only what they bring to the music. This is the most important quality, and it is difficult to define.

Richard Strauss once said, "Conducting is, after all, a difficult business—one has to be 70 years of age to realize this fully." How much does age matter, and do older conductors elicit more profound interpretations from an orchestra than the young ones?

I don't think that age matters, I really don't. I think some young conductors today bring a lot to the music, and some old fuddy-duddies are just a bore. 🖎

CHAPTER 32

Evaluating Conductors from the Trombone Section: An Interview with James DeSano

James DeSano joined the Cleveland Orchestra in 1970 and has been its principal trombonist since 1989. He retired form the orchestra in 2003. He has taught trombone at the Oberlin Conservatory since 1999.

What prompted your decision to become a performing musician?

My grandfather played baritone in several Italian bands in upstate New York, and I went to the rehearsals with him on many occasions. He gave me an old baritone and taught me to solfege with stationary *Do*. I didn't learn how to read music for several years. Later I switched to trombone and played it all through high school. My band director once took me to hear a Philadelphia Orchestra concert that included *Der Rosenkavalier* by Richard Strauss. It was then that I set my sights on playing in a professional orchestra and started to practice six hours a day. At that age I didn't realize that the embouchure needs to rest to rebuild itself, and the extra effort did more harm than good.

When it came time to choose a college, my high school band director persuaded my parents that I should get an education degree for job security. This was a blessing in disguise because I have always loved to teach. I attended Ithaca College and studied trombone with Walter Beeler. During junior year I auditioned and made it into the Syracuse Symphony, where I learned a great deal of the symphonic repertoire. I remained in school and was a practice teacher with Frank Battisti at Ithaca High School. This was a great experience, and I learned the value of discipline and hard work. After graduation I continued to play part time with the Syracuse Symphony.

I applied for a teaching job in the Syracuse City schools and became a band director at three elementary schools and a junior high for the next four years. I even had a junior high marching band. Many students could not afford private lessons, but I gave them free lessons and the band started to grow.

I also started a master's degree at Eastman and studied trombone with Emory Remington, an outstanding gentleman who took an interest in me as he did with all his students. His vocal approach to trombone playing was perfect for me; I am perpetuating his legacy here at Oberlin. After three and a half years with Remington he encouraged me to audition for the assistant trombone position with the Cleveland Orchestra. During the final round of auditions I was asked to play an excerpt from Alban Berg's *Three Pieces for Orchestra*. I got through it without mistakes but when I had finished, assistant conductor Louis Lane asked me to play the excerpt again. As I repeated the passage, I hoped for a miracle and once again there were no mistakes. I got the job with the Cleveland Orchestra and started to believe in miracles.

Franz Strauss, father of Richard, and famous horn player of Munich, once said that "when a new conductor faces the orchestra—from the way he walks up the steps to the podium and before he ever picks up the baton—we know whether he is the master or we." What criteria do orchestra musicians use to determine whether a conductor is a maestro or a charlatan?

I cannot judge the worth of a conductor by the way he walks and I have seen many great conductors limp or hobble to the podium. Usually after 30 minutes I can judge the depth of his musicianship. Most are somewhere between a maestro and a charlatan. I look for the preparatory beat he gives to establish a relationship with the music and the orchestra. My standard is whether the prep beat prepares us for a musical journey by shaping the phrase and taking us across the barline. I watch for rhythmic integrity and if he knows the inner workings of the score.

Who has impressed you among the great conductors?

Claudio Abbado, Colin Davis, Pierre Boulez, Bernard Haitink, and Rafael Kubelik all give beats that have a certain rhythmic tension, and ask for the desired sound. This is a mystical process, but those conductors communicate the spiritual essence of the work and show what they want yet still give the ensemble the freedom to breathe and share in the creation of the music. Some conductors are so controlling that the music lacks spontaneity. They get in the way of the music, and it suffers from a kind of paralysis by analysis. The best conductors stay out of the way and collaborate musically with the orchestra.

Were the interpretations of conductors 25 or 50 years ago guided by rhythmic precision, subjective flexibility, or other variables?

Past conductors realized that tradition is very important to a musical interpretation as the basic foundation to build on. Conductors today seem not to understand these traditions, and some break the music down so much that they lose the rhythmic integrity of the ensemble. George Szell always stressed subdivisions during rehearsal, and the Cleveland Orchestra had certain cohesion of sound and rhythmic drive. Many conductors have forgotten about instrumental colors with the subtle adjustments to match each other and create a cohesive sound. On a passage with the clarinets, I will produce a smaller sound than on a passage with French horns.

Sir Georg Solti once stated that you can judge the talent of a young conductor by his ability to pull sounds from an orchestra. Do you agree with that?

I believe that a conductor can be judged by his ability to lead the orchestra without getting in the way. Not many conductors can do that. Orchestral musicians should have a sense of freedom within the overall interpretation the conductor wants. I really do not have a preference whether a conductor uses a baton. Pierre Boulez is one of the finest conductors in the world and does not use a baton. Lately I find it distracting if a conductor uses a baton but also moves his elbows and shoulders too much.

In the training of conductors there should be more emphasis on score study and understanding musical traditions. Students should learn that a clean entrance depends on the upbeat yet too many conductors use a stab and grab technique on the prep beat. This results in sloppy playing even at the professional level.

Why do American orchestras continue to seek foreign-born conductors?

In the past conductors who came from Europe had extensive experience with opera conducting and were better trained as a result. This is no longer the case. American conductors are on the same level as their European counterparts. A conductor who has opera experience will usually bring a singing quality to a performance and a flexibility that is lacking in those who do not. The Vienna Philharmonic is a good example of an opera orchestra that is noted for its singing quality in orchestral performances. The Cleveland Orchestra is often compared to the Vienna Philharmonic, and I believe this is an apt comparison.

What are some of the things conductors do in rehearsals that irritate the orchestra and distract from the rehearsal?

A conductor who breaks down the score after the first few measures and does not allow the orchestra to play is a problem. The first rehearsal should be a discovery time for the orchestra, but the phrasing can never be established with the breakdown technique. By the time the concert takes place, the composer's intentions are lost. This is difficult for the orchestra because it tires the players and they lose concentration.

Another irritating trait is the conductor who cannot make an exact transition, especially for the music of Bruckner. Transitions are a lost art to many conductors, but Bernard Haitink is a master at it.

Some conductors have no knowledge of this and forget that wind players need to breathe or don't know how loud or soft an instrument can be played in each register. A conductor should know what is difficult or if repetitive rehearsals will hurt the chops of the brass player. Conductors also need to know how to follow the instrument playing a solo passage or performing a concerto. Lorin Maazel is wonderful at working with a soloist. He is always precise and follows the soloist with uncanny skill.

We recently performed the *Firebird Suite* at a tempo that one could not dance to. The conductor undoubtedly forgot that *Firebird* is a ballet and lacked any understanding of traditions. A cellist friend once described a conductor's choice of tempo as "if he doesn't have it, it's forever."

Richard Strauss once said, "Conducting is, after all, a difficult business—one has to be 70 years of age to realize this fully." How much does the age of a conductor reflect in the interpretation he seeks from the orchestra?

I find that age does matter. A great many young conductors have shown potential at the start but they stop growing after about six years. Perhaps they start to believe their press clippings. The great conductors continue to grow and improve with the experiences they go through and with in-depth study of each new score.

After playing in the Cleveland Orchestra for 33 years I have found that conductors can create great music if they sincerely respect the orchestra members and meet them halfway. A good interpretation is a two-way street. Musicians are serious about every performance and will resent a conductor who tries to control every detail. Robert Shaw, Kubelik, Abbado, Haitink, and other great conductors understood that a great performance is collaboration between the conductor and the orchestra.

With each passing decade I hear fewer great performances. I believe that young conductors should follow the advice of Richard Strauss and never look encouragingly at the brass. If it seems that the brass are not blowing hard enough, then tone it down another shade or two.

Coda

The Poet Kahlil Gibran once wrote "work is love made visible." This is true to me because writing *The Golden Age of Conductors* has been a work of love and now made visible through Meredith Music Publications.

For many years I have dedicated myself to studying and writing about the musical interpretations of the great conductors. Studying the interpretations of Arturo Toscanini, Fritz Reiner, Bruno Walter and the other greats included in this book has been a fascinating musical journey leading me to many profound and aesthetic learning experiences. The legendary performances of these conductors have opened a world of beauty, honesty and humility, related to the disciplined creativity needed for the art of conducting.

Above all, I am thankful for the sharing of their deep insights into the art of musical interpretations—Interpretations which have left an indelible mark on the soul of humanity. According to Bruno Walter "Musicianship will spread and grow in proportion as he sinks his roots firmly and broadly into the soul of universal humanity."

To Walter, this means that the value of a conductor's artistic achievements and communication with both the orchestra and the audience is dependent upon his human qualities, his moral convictions, the richness of his emotional life, and the breadth of his musical horizon.

Although few may reach the creative and mystical mountains tops of the conductors encountered in this book, it is my sincere hope that reading *The Golden Age of Conductors* will be a source of inspiration as you climb upward on your musical journey.

John Knight
Oberlin Conservatory

Resources

Bibliography

Antek, Samuel. *This Was Toscanini*. New York: Vanguard Press, 1963

Baker's Biographical Dictionary of Musicians. Seventh Edition, New York: Schirmer, 1984

"Bernstein on Bernstein." http://www.leonardbernstein.com

Blum, Ronald. "Sir Georg Solti: The Last Superconductor". www.cron.com

Boult, Sir. Adrian. *A Handbook on the Technique of Conducting*. London: Paterson's Publications, 1l68.

Brochure. "Leonard Bernstein's Young People's Concerts with the New York Philharmonic."

Burton, Humphrey. *Leonard Bernstein*. New York: Faber & Faber, 1994.

Burton, William. *Conversations About Bernstein*. New York: Oxford University Press, 1995.

Chapin, Schuyler. *Leonard Bernstein: Notes from a Friend*. New York: Walker,1992.

Chase, Gilbert. *America's Music*. New York: McGraw Hill, 1955

Chasins, Abram. *Leopold Stokowski, A Profile*. New York: Hawthorn Books, 1979

Daniel, Oliver. *Stokowski, A Counterpoint of View*. New York: Dodd, Mead, 1982

Esselstrom, Michael. *A Conductor's Guide to Symphonies 1, 2 and 3 of Gustav Mahler*. New York: The Edwin Mellen Press, 1998.

Ewen, David. *The Man With the Baton*. New York: Thomas Crowell, 1936.

Ewen, David. *The World of Twentieth Century Music*, Englewood Cliffs, N.J.: Prentice-Hall, 1968.

Floros, Constantin. *Gustav Mahler: The Symphonies*. Portland: Amadeus Press, 1985.

Furlong, William. *Season with Solti: A Year in the Life of the Chicago Symphony*. New York: MacMillan, 1974

Galkin, Eliott W. *The History of Orchestral Conducting in Theory and Practice*. New York: Pendragon Press, 1988

Haggin, B. H. *The Toscanini Musicians Knew*. New York: Horizon Press, 1967

Heyworth, Peter. *Conversations With Klemperer*. Camelot Press, 1973

Hite, Eric Walter. *Stravinsky*. Berkeley and Los Angeles: University of California Press, 1969.

Hughes, Spike. *The Toscanini Legacy*. New York: Dover Publications, 1969

Jacob,Heinrich Eduard. *Felix Mendelssohn and His Times*. Englewood Cliffs, N.J.: Prentice-Hall, 1963.

Kalmus. "Tchaikovsky on Musical Creation," *Tchaikovsky Symphonies 4, 5, 6*. New York: Kalmus Scores.

Kaufmann, Helen. *History's 100 Greatest Composers*. New York: Grosset and Dunlap, 1957.

Kennedy, Michael. *Adrian Boult*. London: Hamish Hamilton Publications, 1987.

Klaus, Kenneth B. *The Romantic Period in Music*. Boston: Allyn and Bacon, 1970.

Kupferberg, Herbert. *The Mendelssohns: Three Generations of Genius*. New York: Scribner's. 1972.

Lebrecht, Norman. *The Maestro Myth*. London: Simon and Schuster, 1991

Lewis, Laurence. *Guido Cantelli*. San Diego: A.S.Barnes & Co., 1981

Mahler, Alma. *Gustav Mahler: Memories and Letters*. Donald Mitchell, ed. New York: Viking Press, 1969

Monteux, Doris. *It's All in the Music*. New York: Farrar, Straus and Giroux, 1965.

Northrop Moore, Jerrold, ed. *Music and Friends: Letters to Adrian Boult*. London: Hamish Hamilton Publications, 1979.

Opperby, Prehen. *Leopold Stokowski*. New York: Hippocrene Books, 1982

Osborne, Richard. *Conversations with Karajan*. Oxford: Oxford University Press, 1989.

Painter, Karen, ed. *Mahler and His World*. Princeton, N.J.: Princeton University Press, 2002.

Papp, David. "The Great Leveller-Reiner in Chicago," *Gramophone Magazine*, October 1993, Vol 71, p. 21.

Perényi, Eleanor. *Liszt, the Artist as Romantic Hero*. Boston: Little Brown, 1974.

Peyser, Joan. *Bernstein: A Biography*. New York: Billboard books, 1998.

Rodzinski, Halina. *Our Two Lives*. New York: Scribner, 1976.

Rosenberg, Daniel. *George Szell: Portrait of a Perfectionist*. Quoted by John Mack, *Symphony Magazine*, Dec. 1980, p. 18.

Rudolf, Max. *The Grammar of Conducting*. New York: Schirmer, 1994

Russcol, Herbert. *Guide to Low-Priced Classical Records*. New York: Holt Publishing, 1969.

Sachs, Harvey. *Toscanini*. J.B. Philadelphia: Libbincot Company. 1978.

Schmidt-Gorg, Joseph. *The Life of Ludwig Van Beethoven*. Hamburg, Germany:Polydor International Press, 1974.

Schonberg, Harold C. *The Great Conductors*. New York: Simon and Schuster,1967

Siegmeister, Eli, "Modeste Musorgsky", *The Music Lover's Handbook*. New York: W. Morrow, 1943.

Sitwell, Sacheverel. *Liszt*. Boston: Houghton Mifflin, 1934.

Smith, William Ander. *The Mystery of Leopold Stokowski*. London: Associated University Presses, 1990

Solti, Sir Georg. *Memoirs*. New York: Alfred A. Knoph, 1997.

Stewart, Dee. *Philip Farkas, The Legacy of a Master*. The Instrumentalist, Chicago, 1990.

Stoddard, Hope. *Symphony Conductors of the U.S.A.* New York: Thomas Crowell, 1957

Stoessel, Albert. *The Technic of the Baton*. New York: C. Fisher, 1928.

Stravinsky, Igor. *An Autobiography*. New York: Norton, 1936

Trotter, William, "Dimitri Mitropoulos: The Forgotten Giant," *Journal of the Conductors' Guild*, Vol 15, Winter/Spring 1994, p. 6.

Trotter, William. *Priest of Music: The Life of Dimitri Mitropoulos*, Portland, Oregon: Amadeus Press, 1995.

Untermeyer, Louis, ed. *Modern American Poetry*. New York: Harcout, Brace and Company, 1950.

Van Doren, Mark, ed. *An Anthology to World Poetry*. New York: A&C Boni, 1928.

Walsh, Michael. "Bernstein". *Time* Magazine. October 29, 1990.

Weingartner, Felix, Weingartner. *On Music and Conducting*. New York: Dover Publications, 1969

World of Music Encyclopedia. New York: Aberadale Press, 1963.

White, Eric W. *Stravinsky*. Los Angles: University of California Press, 1969.

Recordings, CDs, and Videos

Angel S 35835. Klemperer conducts *Beethoven Symphony # 3, Eroica*. Recorded 1961.

Angel S 36420, *Holst: The Planets*, Adrian Boult conducts Philharmonic Orchestra. "Program Notes"

BMG Music CD. *Pierre Monteux Edition*. Stravinsky: Le Sacre du Printemps. with Boston Symphony, 1951.

CBS 37763 *Great Performances: Szell, Dvořák's New World Symphony*

Columbia DSL 224. *Bruno Walter conducting the Columbia Symphony Orchestra. The Birth of a Performance*. Mozart Symphony No. 36 in C Major "Linz", Rehearsal.

Columbia Odyssey 32160298. *Mitropoulos conducts Schönberg: Transfigured Night*

EMI Classics 7243. *Carlo Maria Giulini: The Chicago Recordings. "Program Notes."*

EMI Classic 65614 CD. *Stokowski. Debussy Afternoon of a Faun.* original on Capitol record SP8399

London CS 7083. *Richard Strauss Ein Heldenleben*, The Vienna Philharmonia with Sir Georg Solti. (Quote by VirginThomson, Program Notes.)

Mercury Living Presence CD. *Rafel Kubelik conducting the Chicago Symphony Orchestra: Moussorgsky Pictures at an Exhibition.*

Pearl CD GEM0008. *Mengleberg Conducts Strauss*. Sussex, England. "Program Notes."

Phillips VHS 070200 -3. Carlos Kleiber. *Beethoven Symphonies Nos. 6 & 7* on VHS with Concertgebow Orchestra in Amsterdam, 1983.

Radio Years CD. *Artur Rodzinski Conducts Tchaikovsky:* Italy. The 1946 New York Philharmonic recording reissued on CD in 1998.

RCA GD 60307 CD. *Arturo Toscnini Collection. Barber: Adagio for Strings*

RCA 1510, *Immortal Performances: Koussevitsky/Boston Symphony. Sibelius: Symphony No. 2.* Recorded Nov. 29, 1950. "Program Notes."

RCA 09026 CD. *Legendary Performers: Serge Koussevitsky.* "Program Notes."

RCA VICS 1110. *Reiner conducts Bartók: Concerto for Orchestra*, 1955. "Program Notes".

Sony Classical Video SHV 48311. *Symphony # 6, Pathétique* by Peter Tchaikovsky, Vienna Philharmonic conducted by Herbert Von Karajan.

Sony Classical CD SBK 48279. *Ormandy conducts Philadelphia Orchestra, Rachmaninoff Symphonic Dances for Orchestra.* Recorded 1960.

Sony Classical Video SHV 48311. *Karajan conducts Tchaikovsky: Pathetique*, with Vienna Philharmonic, 1984.

Sony Video SHV 46377. *Solti conducts Mahler's Fifth* with Chicago Symphony in Tokyo, 1986.

Turnabout VOX 4408. *Wilhelm Furtwängler conducts the Vienna Philharmonia Orchestra.* Beethoven's Symphony No. 6 in F Major, Op. 68, "Pastoral." "Program Notes."

About the Author

DR. JOHN KNIGHT is Professor of Conducting and Ensembles and Music Education at Oberlin Conservatory, Oberlin, Ohio. He has been a member of the Oberlin Conservatory faculty since 1978 and served as chairman of the Conducting Division for many years. He received his baccalaureate degree from the University of Central Arkansas and the master's and doctoral degrees from Louisiana State University. He is a guest conductor of professional orchestras and bands, all state and honor ensembles throughout the nation, Europe and Asia.

At the Oberlin Conservatory he was awarded numerous teaching grants to study wind pedagogy with members of the Chicago Symphony and has been the recipient of the H.H. Powers travel grant to visit the major music conservatories of West Germany, Italy, Holland, England, Japan and China where he presented lectures and workshops concerning the teaching of conducting and music education in the United States. At the Parma Conservatory in Italy, Dr. Knight did extensive research on the conducting techniques of Arturo Toscanini. In England, he researched the wind music of Percy Grainger, Gustav Holst, and Ralph Vaughan Williams. Three times he has been visiting professor of conducting at Salford University and the Birmingham Conservatory, England where he was guest conductor of wind bands, brass bands, and guest conductor of the Birmingham Conservatory Orchestra.

Dr. Knight is consulting editor to *The Instrumentalist Magazine* where he has had over 100 published articles on conducting. For his articles he received the Citation of Excellence for creative writing from the Educational Press Association of America. Dr. Knight is the author of *The Interpretive Wind Band Conductor* published by Meredith Music Publications in 2007, which is devoted to the conducting pedagogy needed for the interpretation of major concert band repertoire. He is also co-author of the popular textbook *Prelude to Music Education*, published by Prentice Hall, which is used in college classrooms throughout the nation.